Consultation:
A Book of Readings

Consultation:
A Book of Readings

Don Dinkmeyer
Communication Motivation Training Institute
Coral Springs, Florida
and
Adjunct Professor, Florida
International University
Miami, Florida

Jon Carlson
Nova University
Fort Lauderdale, Florida

1975

John Wiley & Sons, Inc.
New York • London • Sydney • Toronto

Copyright © 1975 by John Wiley & Sons, Inc.

All rights reserved. Published simultaneously in Canada.

No part of this book may be reproduced by any means, nor
transmitted, nor translated into a machine language without the written permission of the publisher.

Library of Congress Cataloging in Publication Data:

Dinkmeyer, Don C   comp.
   Consultation : a book of readings.

Includes index.
1.   Personnel service in elementary education—Ad-
dresses, essays, lectures. I. Carlson, Jon, joint comp.
II. Title.
LB1027.5.D467   372.1'4   74-34048
ISBN 0-471-21562-7

Printed in the United States of America

10 9 8 7 6 5 4 3 2 1

Contributors

Richard Abidin, Department of Foundations of Education, University of Virginia, Charlottesville, Virginia 22901

Roger Aubrey, Director of Guidance, Public Schools, Brookline, Massachusetts 02146

Beth Sulzer-Azaroff, Training Consultant, Mansfield Training School, Mansfield Depot, Connecticut

Donald Blocher, Professor, Department of Educational Psychology, University of Minnesota, Minneapolis, Minnesota 55400

Norman Bowers, Overseas Dependent Schools, Kaiserslautern, Germany

Jon Carlson, Director of Guidance, The University School and Associate Professor of Psychology, Nova University, Fort Lauderdale, Florida 33314

Oscar Christensen, Professor, Department of Counseling and Guidance, University of Arizona, Tucson, Arizona 85730

John J. Cody, Chairman, Department of Guidance and Educational Psychology, Southern Illinois University, Carbondale, Illinois 62901

Don Dinkmeyer, President, Communication and Motivation Training Institute, 11061 Northwest 23 Court, Coral Springs, Florida 33065

Marvin Fine, Chairman, School of Psychology Training Program, School of Education, University of Kansas, Lawrence, Kansas 66044

Daniel W. Fullmer, Professor, Department of Counseling, University of Hawaii, Honolulu, Hawaii 96800

Thomas Gordon, President, Effectiveness Training Associates, Pasadena, California

Marie Grubbe, Counselor, 27398 Fairview Avenue, Hayward, California 94552

Theodore Grubbe, Psychologist, 27398 Fairview Avenue, Hayward, California 94542

Loyce Mc Hagens, Director, Guidance Services, University of Corpus Christi, Corpus Christi, Texas 78400

Ray Hosford, Dean, College of Education, University of California, Santa Barbara, California 93100

Dan Kennedy, Associate Professor, School of Education, Division of Special Education and Pupil Services, Florida International University, Tamiami Trail, Miami, Florida 33144

John Krumboltz, Professor of Education and Psychology, Stanford University, Stanford, California 94305

Ronald Lippitt, Professor of Psychology and Sociology, Center for Research on Utilization of Scientific Knowledge, University of Michigan, Ann Arbor, Michigan 48103

Roy G. Mayer, Associate Professor, Department of Guidance, California State University, Los Angeles, California

Donald Murray, Research Assistant, Center for Advanced Study of Educational Administration, University of Oregon, Eugene Oregon 97401

Barbara Peterson, Counselor, Terman Junior High School, Palo Alto, California 94300

Rita Rapoza, Graduate Student, Department of Educational Psychology, University of Minnesota, Minneapolis, Minnesota 55400

Alexandra Robbin, Classroom Teacher, Stone Mountain, Georgia 30083

Seymour Sarason, Professor, Psychology Department, Yale University, New Haven, Connecticut 06500

Virginia Satir, Consultant and Family Therapist, San Francisco, California

Richard Sauber, Director, Preventive Services and Training, Newport County Community Mental Health Center, Newport, Rhode Island 02840

Richard Schmuck, Professor of Educational Psychology, Center for Advanced Study of Educational Administration, University of Oregon, Eugene, Oregon 97401

Milton M. Tyler, Professor, University of the Pacific, Stockton, California 95207

Drage "Bud" Watson, Professor, University of Redlands, College of Education, Redlands, California 92373

To Our Children
Don, Jim
Kirstin, Matthew
And Their Happiness

Preface

Pupil personnel specialists, psychologists, counselors, and social workers are being challenged to give evidence of their relevance for the educational process. The medical model featuring diagnosis and treatment has not provided a solution to the problems of the schools. Despite the increasing number of specialists, reading problems, rebellion, underachievement, and apathy continue to plague the schools. It is apparent that a service beyond identification and individual or group counseling must be developed.

In 1966 an ACES-ASCA committee identified consulting as one of the three major areas of service for elementary school counselors. An extensive study indicated that consulting, counseling and coordinating were the essential functions for the elementary school pupil personnel worker. However, nine years later there is little evidence that training programs for these specialists are currently training graduates with skills in consulting. While University programs may be recognizing the importance of the concept, it is only recently that one can observe that instructional time is definitely being assigned for consultation. Thus, we have the dilemma that both national policy-making groups and educators are aware of the need for new priorities. But training programs have failed to meet this need.

It is interesting to note that practitioners in the field have noted the need for consultation. Teachers increasingly are skeptical that referring students for evaluation or counseling is solving their problems. It should be apparent that often the teacher who refers a student is the real client— the person with a concern and desiring change. Unfortunately, too often the medical model has involved the specialist in extensive evaluation and therapeutic work with the wrong client. Teachers are becoming more aware that they need help in working with these students.

At the same time, parents are experiencing difficulty in relating with and disciplining their children. They are seeking assistance in a variety of ways and are a logical clientele for the pupil personnel specialist.

Professionals in pupil personnel work are increasingly seeking workshops and advanced training opportunities to acquire skills in consultation. It has been the authors' experience that the demand for workshops on consultation has increased dramatically in recent years.

Secondary school pupil personnel specialists have been influenced by the changing role of the elementary school specialist. Parents are beginning to expect programs which involve their concerns. Teachers of high school youth are also concerned with how the pupil personnel specialist relates to their task—the educational process.

This book is intended for basic courses in pupil personnel work offered to administrators, counselors, psychologists, and social workers. It is designed to acquaint the reader with the significant literature on consultation. The articles have been selected to give a rich selection of the best thinking available on consultation.

The text begins wtih a consideration of varied theoretical positions on consultation. This acquaints the reader with a thorough consideration of role and mission and suggests definite steps involved in program development.

It is recognized that the system may be the significant client and this section suggests specific approaches to consultation with the system. From these considerations the text moves to presenting actual consulting processes. The reader is introduced to Adlerian, learning theory and behavior modification approaches. Specific articles dealing with individual and group consulting with teachers and parent consultation are included.

The motivation for compiling this book came from our personal experiences in consulting with school districts locally and in 44 states of the nation. The need for a new conceptualization of the most effective way to consult is essential if pupil personnel work is to make a dynamic contribution. Failure to consider innovations may result in school boards and administrators reevaluating the value of these services. It is our hope that this text in some way may contribute to improving the lives and learning experiences of students, teachers, parents, and administrators as well as specialists.

We want to acknowledge the detailed and helpful critique of Howard Splete of Wayne State University. It provided excellent guidance in finalizing the manuscript. We would also like to recognize the contributions of the many practitioners who took time from busy schedules to share their experiences in consulting with the readers. The critiques of the experts on consultation are valued because they add the wisdom and dimension of their varied orientations and years of practical experience.

Don Dinkmeyer

Jon Carlson

Contents

Introduction

Educators have been forced to consider the question of accountability. The public and the educational profession have asked for data which indicates that the educational experience makes a difference in dealing with the major challenges of life. This has been difficult to demonstrate, and administrators have turned to pupil personnel specialists for data to support the effectiveness of the educational process.

The traditional roles of the pupil personnel specialists do not lend themselves readily to accountability models. The psychologist primarily concerned with diagnostic evaluation can identify the number of students assessed, but this does not correlate with behavior or attitude change. The social worker can identify the number of homes visited or individuals referred, but that data does not relate directly to the major concerns of educators. The traditional counselor can report on students now attending college or those with poor grades or disciplinary problems who have been counseled, but usually has little information about rate of counseling success in these endeavors. Unfortunately our pupil personnel data has indicated the number of persons contacted but has given little evidence of change produced.

It is obvious that the profession is desperately looking for new and comprehensive models which can deal with human needs and the demand for accountability. The psychological theories which are currently of greatest interest all have elements of accountability. The behavior modification approach necessitates gathering data and supplying specific results; Glasser's Reality Therapy is characterized by involvement and specific commitment; and the Adlerian approaches have focused on involvement of the total community and procedures which involve parents, teachers and classrooms.

These psychological approaches share a common bias—the belief that the specialist too often is involved with the wrong client. When the administrator is concerned with a teacher's behavior we should look at the communication between administration and this teacher and determine what can be done to make this communication more effective. Instead, we may treat the teacher as an isolated factor and fail to see her as the product of a system. When the teacher or the parent approaches the specialist regarding a relationship problem with a student, how often do we attempt to deal directly with the student instead of working with the person who posed the request—the parent or the teacher?

Behavior Modification, Reality Therapy, and Adlerian Psychology have all traditionally advocated the consultant role. They have suggested that we must deal with specifics and focus on bringing about change which involves the client in specific change of his behavior, attitudes, and values. While the emphasis is different, the focus is on pragmatic procedures which assist the consultee (the one asking for help) and client (person of concern to committee) to make choices which improve the situation. The end product of consultation is a responsible individual who makes decisions which enable him to function more effectively while demonstrating his concern for the welfare of the community.

Consultation, as we view it, is a process in which the consultant is available to the consultee in order to produce change in the system, growth for the consultee, or an improved relationship with the consultee's client. The consultant relationship is based upon the necessary and sufficient conditions for a helping relationship: empathy, genuineness, concreteness, respect, and confrontation. Beyond the relationship, the consultant must understand a pragmatic theory of human behavior which can be applied in the consultation process. The consultant is capable of working with the consultee individually or in a group. He has an orientation that is concerned with perceptual meanings, beliefs, and creating an atmosphere for change. The consultant is able to develop a collaborative, clarifying, confrontative relationship in which the consultee looks at specific behaviors of the client, his own responses, and the consequences of the interaction. Together, consultant and consultee consider alternatives and the consultee decides, plans, and makes commitments.

This book presents the best thinking of a number of leaders in the area of consultation. The reader has an opportunity to consider the theoretical orientations of the behavior modification, developmental, change agent, and Adlerian points of view and to see how these orientations are applied in actual practice.

Consulting is considered first as an approach to the total system (section II). The reader has an opportunity to consider a number of tried and tested procedures for working with the system.

The specifics of the consultation process (section III) are set forth in articles detailing Adlerian, Learning Theory, Behavior Modification, and Ecclectic procedures. These processes are then set forth in their application to individual consultation, (section IV) teacher groups, (section V) and parent and family groups (section VI).

Consultation:
A Book of Readings

Rationale and Theory of Consultation

Consulting is a process by which administrators, teachers, parents, pupil personnel specialists, and other significant adults in the life of a client communicate about him. Although pupil personnel services originated to provide direct diagnostic and therapeutic services to students, it has become apparent that direct services cannot effectively cope with referral needs. Furthermore, as the articles that follow will show, increasing pupil personnel staffs appear only to increase the number of referrals.

A humanistic and efficacious approach to pupil services necessitates that we use our resources more effectively. Indirect services whereby the specialist works as a consultant with the consultee has the potential for initiating meaningful staff in-service programs, educating parents, and increasing the skills and self-understanding of all concerned. For example, the teacher "C" group can influence the experiences of 125 to 750 students, dependent on the educational environment of self-contained classrooms, departmentalized grouping, or team-teaching. The five teachers in a "C" group represent 5000 pupil contact hours each year, and that number can be multiplied by the number of years these teachers remain in the profession. Parent groups not only enable the consultant to work productively with more parents but also make pupil personnel services visible to parents as well as staff. Thus, aside from educational and time benefits, consulting has inherent public relations values and presents opportunities to develop public support.

Equally important is the growing awareness that specialists have often assumed that the referral of a student indicated that the student was the problem. But it may be equally valid to consider that the real client, based on motivation readiness and lack of effective procedures, is the referring source.

In the first selection Carlson analyzes the present status of guidance, counseling, and pupil personnel work as well as outlines some of the future trends in the helping professions. From this evaluation the relevance of the following selections become clear. It is important to have a clear understanding of the larger situation to comprehend the related nature of the component parts.

Abidin encourages us to look beyond the "problem child" and to consider the implications of the internal assumptions and expectancies of the teacher with regard to the child, and the contingencies that apply to the teacher's behavior in terms of the social system of which he or she is a part.

Abidin indicates that consultants should not naively assume that the child must be changed but, instead, should decide whose behavior it is most effective to change. He emphasizes that the acceptance or rejection of an idea or method is often not a function of its technical adequacy but, rather, of its acceptability to the social system. This article is significant because it makes us aware that consulting involves more than the application of behavioral technology.

Dinkmeyer bases his model for consulting on certain psychological premises that are socio-teleological and phenomenological. The developmental program's guidelines are concerned with delivery of services to all children. A specific hierarchy and priority of consulting roles is established.

Kennedy believes that the traditional clinical approach of school psychology as practiced in most systems is not practical. He clearly indicates why the clinical model can never meet the challenge and suggests models that are developmental, with clinical or remedial functions becoming a smaller part of the total program. He believes more time should be devoted to helping teachers develop contingency management programs in their classrooms, and to working with parent education groups. He advocates keeping more children involved in the regular class environment through the consultation process.

Sarason discusses the complexity of the processes of change and calls attention to how little there has been in psychological theory and practice to serve as guidelines. His observations, which are derived from consulting with schools, indicate that the more things change on the surface, the more conditions remain basically the same. This occurs because of the tendency for change proposals to emanate from the top without involving the feelings and opinions of those who must implement the change.

Sarason points to the naivete of psychological theories (e.g., learning and psychoanalytic) which do not face the fact that individual behavior always takes place in the context of social systems. He goes so far as to indicate that any theory that claims to explain behavior and does not account for man-system relationships is not only naive but incomplete and mischief producing. He encourages us to avoid the tendency to restrict ourselves to developing molecular theories about molecular-sized problems and to seek a psychology of change.

Eckerson, as a result of her involvement in the 1970 White House Conference on Children, presents the imperative nature of the counselor-consultant acting as a change agent. She delineates the areas in which consultants need to become involved. This conference provides further support for the consultant function.

Lippitt provides an excellent description of what a consultant **is**. He discusses the role of the consultant in working with groups and organizations as clients, adding a new dimension to the consultant's role of working with individuals, or individuals in groups.

As these articles are read, consider the following:

● What are some psychological premises for establishing a theory of consultation? Consider how contrasting theories would view the consultation process.
● What are the problems involved in moving the focus of consultation from the child to the teacher and the system?

Given a school system with 3000 students and four pupil personnel specialists, develop your hierarchy and priority of functions. Indicate your objectives, processes, and how you would achieve these objectives.

● What are the problems involved in working with the internal assumptions and beliefs of the teachers?
● What are some of the internal assumptions and beliefs of pupil personnel specialists that may keep them in clinical instead of consulting roles?
● What social system theories might now be available to deal with the problems posed by Sarason?

1. THE FUTURE OF SCHOOL COUNSELING

Jon Carlson

Until recently, everybody talked about the future, but no one did anything about it. We still are doing a lot of talking (perhaps more now than ever) but now we also are experiencing a lot of *doing*. The doing has become necessary in order to cope with the results of a past history of apathy and poor planning. These results generally can be seen in our problem-ridden cities, schools, government, in our congested rivers, air, highways and, specifically, in the widespread failure of large numbers of children to read, the alarming increase of suicide and hard drug use among children and youth, the sizeable rate of absenteeism in city schools, the increase in violence and crime, the busing dilemma, the large number of college and university graduates who are unemployed—need we continue? The need to *invent* or to *plan* a future or not to have one at all has become a reality. The concern has shifted from "this is the way things will be in 'x years'" to "this is the way things will be unless we do 'so and so.'" The shift seems to be from describing future crises to preventing them.

The question for those of us in counseling is whether we are going to be a part of this process and facilitate change or continue to resist and "defend the status quo." In this article, we shall assume that counselors want to have a future and will begin to plan change. The purpose, then, is to examine where the counseling profession is *now* and to sketch what future counselors will be *doing* to make the world a better place in "x years."

CURRENT STATUS OF SCHOOL COUNSELING
WHERE WE ARE TODAY

The age of accountability is here, and our existence is being questioned. As Gelatt (1971) recently speculated,

Jon Carlson, "The Future of School Counseling" *Focus on Guidance*, 1973, Vol. 5–7, March, 1–10. Copyright © 1973 by Love Publishing Co.

". . . guidance is in danger of becoming like Charlie Brown's baseball team: 'They don't win many games, but they have a lot of interesting discussions.' The customer is now asking us to keep score. We have to win some games and we have to show the box score." [p. 3]

Counselors and psychologists persist in dealing with the microcosm rather than the macrocosm in which the individual lives. Sinick (1967) feels that

". . . many a counselor deals with his client as though the two of them are hermetically sealed from society. A counselor should abhor a vacuum just as much as nature does, for no client exists in a vacuum. Every client is inevitably involved in interaction with environmental variables." [p. 1]

Counselors do not seem to understand the *real* situation. According to Hays (1972b),

". . . school counselors seem to be eternal optimists about the improvement of their situation. All we need is to reduce the counselor-student ratio and we can do our job. 'Give us an adequate share of the finances, and we can provide programs to solve the problems of counselors.' 'Take away the "administrivia" and we can counsel.' Unfortunately, it just isn't so!" [p. 93]

Since the end of the 1960s disenchantment with counselors has been steadily increasing to the extent that their value and success in the public schools has been seriously questioned (American Personnel and Guidance Association, 1972; Arbuckle, 1972; Berdie, 1972; Eckerson, 1971; Gazda, 1972; Gelatt, 1971; Lewis, 1972; National Advisory Council on Vocational Education, 1972; National School Public Relations Association, 1971). Recent epitaphs by Arbuckle (1972), Berdie (1972) and Eckerson (1971) have identified the ineffectiveness of counselors. This criticism is spreading to people outside of the guidance profession as students, teachers, administrators, federal agencies (for example, the guidance section of the U. S. Office of Education recently was eliminated) and the general public are viewing counseling skeptically. Counselors are losing their jobs in today's economic pinch. Although several warnings have been issued (Arbuckle, 1970; Eckerson, 1971; Island, 1972; Lawton, 1971; Riccio, 1970; Zerface & Cox, 1971), it seems as though the counselor may join ranks with the barrel-maker, blacksmith, farmer, trapper, viking and druid.

There appear to be several persuasive reasons as to how and why we arrived at our current destination (be it plight or crisis). Articles by Arbuckle (1970, 1972), Brammer & Springer (1971). Carey & Garris

(1971), Island (1972) and Lewis & Lewis (1971) point out the inadequate nature of counselor training. Programs have only recently required practicums and other forms of training that involve actual supervised experience, group work, elementary school guidance and counseling, and nonwhite concerns. Few programs include such courses as consulting with teachers, parents and administrators, a practicum in group counseling, behavior modification procedures, family and marriage counseling, social problem solving, accountability, change process or psychological educational procedures. Yet, these activities either are being advocated by counselor educators and/or implemented by counselors.

Others have shed light on our current dilemma by leveling blame or accusations at counselor apathy (Arbuckle, 1970; Berdie, 1972; DeFeo & Cohn, 1972; Dworkin & Dworkin, 1971; Hays, 1972a; Nelson, Erickson & Milliren, 1972), the unresponsiveness of professional organizations (Hoyt, 1971; Ivey, 1970; Lewis & Lewis, 1971; Stiller, 1972; Whiteley & Sprandel, 1972) and the nebulous role/identity statements and identity of the counselor (Arbuckle, 1970, 1972; Baker & Cramer, 1972; Baker & Hansen, 1972; Boy, 1972; Carlson & Pietrofesa, 1971; Dworkin & Dworkin, 1971; Eckerson, 1972; Pancrazio, 1971; Shertzer & Stone, 1972; Sprinthall, 1972). Others have postulated that the trouble lies with the myriad, uncontrollable external forces such as the authoritarian school systems, apathetic teachers and parents, family breakdown, the new morality, the noncompassionate electorate or unsupportive government.

Eckerson (1972) after the 1970 White House Conference on Children viewed the situation as follows:

"A diagnosis of the disease that is infecting guidance in general reveals many contributing factors: faith in the objectivity of test results and grades; limitation of the one-to-one relationship in counseling; preoccupation with techniques; observance of out-moded certification requirements; disregard of non-academic talents; overinvolvement with college-bound students; and inability to comprehend and deal with the dynamics of the social revolution that is shaping the country." [p. 167]

Neglecting the educative function with relation to adults as well as children is perhaps another major problem area. The avoidance of education is partly due to a profession that until recently trained and endorsed a therapeutic/model rather than an educational approach. According to Lipsman (1969), this led to a problem-centered or remedial thrust rather than to a developmental, preventive focus which would have emphasized growth enhancement.

Counselors' mere acceptance of administrative power or rule rather than becoming power figures themselves certainly played a major role in our current status (Aubrey, 1972 and 1973). Counselors have been agents of their institutions and have helped others "adjust to" or "cope with" the structure rather than attempting to change it. Counselors have functioned as loyal members of the "silent majority." Counselors located in the institutions have been controlled by people not even in the same profession. Thus, counselors are unable to be autonomous—yet autonomy is crucial if counseling is to survive.

Counselors also have been guilty of ignoring the total living environment of people. Since counselors have not been trained in these areas, they have not dealt with rampant social problems such as ineffective child rearing, financial mismanagement, marriage disharmony, sexual dysfunction, drug abuse, family breakdown and other community and larger imposing societal problems.

In this confusion, however, a few things do seem clear. The first is that each of the above reasons probably is at least partially correct. Secondly, the chances are slight that criticism from within and without will stop in the near future. The purpose of this article, however, is not to get bogged down in the search for the genesis of our popular concerns, but rather to investigate the future.

There can be no doubt that many counselors are actively engaged in improving the helping professions and attempting to save this valued service in an attempt to help our clientele—mankind. Some counselors, counselor educators, philosophers, government agencies and professional organizations are carrying out enlightened work. Yet, the evidence for the continuation of school counseling is slight—the data does not seem sufficient to warrant the continuation of the counseling profession.

This dilemma is sadly complex, but the task does seem clear. We need to let go of our present roles and grow or change! We need to find new approaches to meeting the needs of people—approaches which will "sell." The general public is confused (socially, economically, emotionally and educationally), and school counselors seem to be adding to rather than alleviating this state of affairs. The results could eliminate the counselor along with the confusion. Good news is available, however—the fact that the ways to rebuild or get out of this mess are already available and the fact that we still have time to begin since counselors are still present in the majority of schools and since elementary school counselors even appear to be growing in number (Carlson & Van Hoose, 1971; Van Hoose & Carlson, 1972). Consider the following priorities and activities for the school counselor (or his replacement) of the future. It is not what we say but rather what we accomplish that will sell counseling.

FUTURE OF SCHOOL COUNSELING
WHERE WE CAN BE

Ecological Systems Will Be Emphasized

No matter what the work setting, the counselor will find it necessary to deal with individuals who live in and constitute the nation of strangers— people whose functioning is based on feelings of alienation in regard to family, school, work, career and possibly themselves (Packard, 1972). The counseling profession will become directly involved with humanizing the environments where people live, work, play and learn and with making this setting a place where people want to be. As Eckerson (1971) stated.

". . . today's students and many persons over 30 have deep anxieties about living comfortably in a galloping, materialistic, technological society; handling controversy and conflict; resolving personal values; filling leisure time constructively; becoming adept in peer relationships; effecting change in institutions; and preparing to build a world in which people come first." [p. 167]

The focus for the future will be on the community or the total living environment. The counselor will use an ecological systems approach and establish priorities based upon the maximum effect that the service has upon the total system. The counselor will focus on what needs to be accomplished before selecting the means.

Consider the following rationale for entering into this type of service:

"Current counseling practice depends heavily on the concepts and procedures of various models of psychotherapy. Such models, be they Freudian, Adlerian, Rogerian, or Skinnerian, share at least three crucial features. First, each one involves the notion of an 'ill' or 'disturbed' person who needs help. Second, by locating the problem within the individual, each model usually depends on the individual's cooperation in a more or less long-term effort to solve the problem either by restructuring his personality, strengthening his self-concept, or getting rid of his symptoms. Third, each model implicitly assumes a 'normal' environment to which the 'abnormal' individual must be adjusted." [Kuriloff, 1973, p. 321]

Traditionally, the counselor has tried to help people adjust to our current environment. Even if this were possible, it is probably not desirable (Glasser, 1969; Herndon, 1965; Holt, 1969; Illich, 1971; Jackson, 1968; Kozol, 1967; Reich, 1970; Silberman, 1970; Toffler, 1970). Changes in any one element or person of an ecological system usually affect all other elements. Emotional disturbance and other problems are seen in this model as an ecological phenomenon that exists in the transactions among people. The counselor works to alleviate these faulty transactions, and he must know the system and understand where minimum input can produce equilibrium within the system. Further work in this area may be found in Bateson, Jackson, Haley & Weakland (1956), Carroll, Bell, Breecher & Minor (1971), Cook (1971), Henry (1963), Kuriloff (1973), Laing (1969), Rhodes (1967), and Satir (1972).

The Counselor Will Work Directly with Administrators

As just indicated, it makes little sense to help students change if their environment remains the same; therefore, the future counselor will focus on modifying the psychological environment of the school by facilitating the development of school administrators who will inspire, lead, understand and utilize group dynamics in order to administrate effectively.

There are a number of organizational factors in the school which really work to impede human development (i.e., lack of communication, the importance of failure, rigid time constraints). The counselor will meet with central school administration and the local principals to consider school policy insofar as it affects both human potential within the system and the impact on teachers and students. Because he is concerned about the learning climate, he often may be a process observer at faculty meetings or may meet with curriculum specialists to process feedback about the effect of certain curriculum programs upon staff and students. The counselor will bring to the administration his expertise in human relations, group dynamics and the affective domain. He will function to help the administration implement effective educational procedures. He will serve as a consultant to the principal by dialoguing and consulting on concerns which originate as an outgrowth of his role with staff, parents and children. He will do this on both an individual and a group basis.

It must be recognized that it is the administrator who provides the school counselor with leadership and personnel support, who schedules the counselor's time and who provides the physical facilities, supplies, clerical assistance, etc. The administrator has *power*. The counselor will not merely react to this force but will become a force for change himself. He will direct input and serve as a catalyst in the school environment with a focus on stimulating new ideas and humanizing the curriculum. He will collaborate with the administrator to insure that they work *together* toward the same goal. When disparity exists, the counselor will use appropriate stratagems to insure that a humane course is followed. This administrator effectiveness training may require the use of learning principles in order to teach the administrator to respond in a more appropriate fashion or the utilization of systematic procedures which allow the administrator to experience the consequences of his actions. (See Postman & Weingartener's, 1971, *The Soft Revolution* for examples.)

Teachers Will Be Assisted Both Individually and in Groups

Since teachers are key figures in the learning system, the counselor will work directly with teachers on a regular basis. The purposes of these consulting contacts (Carlson, 1972) are primarily threefold:

1. Acquiring an understanding of self and developing awareness on the part of teachers of their role in the teacher-child conflict.
2. Developing an understanding of the practical application of the dynamics of human behavior.
3. Developing acquaintance with new concepts and procedures while integrating them with one's own value system. [p. 85]

The counselor will be working primarily with groups of teachers. By working with teachers in groups, he recognizes that most problems basically are interpersonal and social. The C-group approach of Dinkmeyer & Carlson (1973) will be used to clarify teachers' thinking about specific children and the relationships between teachers' beliefs and attitudes. Through this approach, the counselor will develop better relationships among staff members and facilitate commitment to change.

The counselor will realize that direct help for even a few teachers provides indirect services for many children. By dealing with teachers' needs, the counselor will help create a more mentally healthy environment for students.

Psychological Education Will Be A Major Focus of All Curriculums

The counselor will encourage the acceptance of innovative ways to reach *all* students. The counselor will be directly involved in creating and maintaining a humane, growth-producing environment. The goal will be to develop *whole* persons rather than dwelling on separate aspects (i.e., physical, psychological, social, emotional, intellectual). Elements are singled out only in laboratories and schools—not in life. In order to accomplish this goal, the counselor will deal directly with the classroom or learning system.

The counselor of the future realizes his unique position to help teachers acquire techniques which promote psychological growth in the classroom. The counselor will facilitate and encourage individuals to learn and will assist them in effectively applying their learning to life. His concern will be with the total learning environment which promotes or interferes with learning and with the learner's ability to make maximum use of this newly acquired skill or knowledge. Gelatt (1971) further indicated that,

". . . to begin with, guidance will need to modernize its services. This means that it needs to *demonstrate,* to *model,* to be *active!* One of the main characteristics of our profession is *talk.* Our two major functions, counseling and consultation, are highly verbal. But students today, and teachers, may be helped more by *showing* than *telling.*

"I'm pleading for the development of *other* skills: role-playing, simulation, modeling, demonstrating, active participation with students and teachers, and the creative use of multi-media." [p. 4]

The following list contains a variety of specific techniques, procedures and approaches to psychological education which will help the counselor to *demonstrate, model* and be *active.*

> *Program Work Awareness Kit* (Frost & Ratliff, 1973)
> Simulation games (Boocock & Schild, 1968)
> *First Things: Values* (Selman & Kohlberg, 1972)
> The encouragement process (Dinkmeyer & Dreikurs, 1963)
> Values classification (Simon, Howe, & Kirschenbaum, 1972; Raths, Harmin, & Simon, 1965)
> Encounter group principles (Roark, 1971)
> Psychological education (Stanford, 1972; Mosher & Sprinthall, 1971)
> Confluent education (Brown, 1971)
> Human development training (Bessel & Palomares, 1967)
> *Developing Understanding in Self and Others* (Dinkmeyer, 1970, 1973)
> *Self-Enhancing Education* (Randolph & Howe, 1966)
> Large group discussion (Glasser, 1969; Dreikurs, Grunwald & Pepper, 1971)
> Natural and logical consequences (Dreikurs & Grey, 1968)
> *Dimensions of Personality* (Limbacher, 1969)

The counselor advocates that the learner is a human being. He will seek to reach this goal of humaneness through the dual roles of *facilitator* of communication and *coordinator* among those involved in contributing to learning and development. He will be totally involved in the learning process and school environment.

Parents and Families Will Be Integral Areas of Emphasis

An individual's initial and most basic learnings come from parents and the family setting. Hence, we take for granted that people "innately" know how to function in these settings. Life doe not bear this out, however. As Carkhuff (1971) suggests, "where parents have not been sources of nourishment for their children, they must be equipped to do so." Therefore, the counselor of the future will be involved with family education programs (Carlson & Falbe, 1973), parent education training (Dinkmeyer & McKay,

1973; Gordon, 1970; Harris, 1967) and family counseling programs (Christensen, 1972; Fullmer, 1972; Satir, 1972). These programs will go beyond the teaching and counseling of child management procedures to the creation of improved human systems within the community.

The future will provide certain benefits for citizens who take part in programs of this nature, much like individuals who have completed drivers training courses receive insurance breaks. These benefits may include tax deductions or other incentives to facilitate participation in these programs.

The counselor will use a C-group format to deal with parents (Carlson, 1969; Dinkmeyer & Carlson, 1973). The concern will be to reach a large number of parents in order to help them understand their children and to develop more effective ways to relate with and motivate them. The overall purpose lies in establishing a sound communication network and a psychologically positive system for each individual's "primary group." When the counselor is not free to conduct C-groups, others (teachers, parents) will be trained to establish and conduct parent education and study groups.

The Use of Paraprofessionals, Volunteers, Parents, Community Resources, Peer Counselors, and Senior Citizens Will Be Commonplace

The counselor will demonstrate his enlightenment through the utilization of the available "human talent pool." Recent research (Carkhuff & Griffin, 1970; Gluckstern, 1972) suggests that minimally trained or even lay counselors obtain results that are essentially no different from professional counselors. They have the added asset of being members of the neighborhood, and their involvement helps to facilitate the development of "community."

Major attempts to involve the available talent are already documented in the guidance area (Carlson, Cavins & Dinkmeyer, 1969; Carlson & Pietrofesa, 1971; Muro, 1970; Fredrickson, 1969). Recently, the American Personnel and Guidance Association published a monograph on support personnel (Zimpfer, Fredrickson, Salim, & Sanford, 1971).

The use of volunteers for within school activities will not be the only thrust. National efforts at peer counseling, such as the re-evaluation counseling paradigm of Harvey Jackins and the microcounseling model of Allen Ivey will be continued. The recent popularity and seriousness of this movement was documented in song—"lean on me if you need a friend."

The counselor of the future will be involved in the teaching of counseling and human relations skills. He will be doing what Miller (1969) called "giving psychology to the public." He will begin to teach the developmental skills of living to elementary, junior and senior high school-aged children as well as adults.

Community Mental Health and the Area of Human Services Will Occupy a Major Slot in the Counselor's Work Role

The total living system or community in which a school is located will not be ignored by the counselors. The counselor will realize that a system which does not meet or nourish human needs creates dysfunctional members of society. An entirely new role similar to that of "community service worker" postulated by Gazda (1972) will be present.

"These 'human services' workers will work in such areas as child development and day care centers, probation and the whole area of corrections, welfare, vocational and adult education, law enforcement, religion, and in the increasing variety of mental health treatment centers, including speciality areas of drug, sex, and alcohol." [p. 2]

The counselor with his knowledge and expertise in the area of human relations will spearhead work in the aforementioned areas. The counselor will not do all the work of creating a mentally healthy community since religious organizations, government agencies, service organizations, etc. all have this function as part of their goals. The counselor will organize these groups, coordinate their services and insure that collaboration among the various thrusts occurs and that overlap is minimized.

Community Leaders Will Be Identified and Trained in Effective Human Relations Skills

In order to insure the success of his plan, the counselor will identify the community leaders and involve them in his program. This will involve mutual planning sessions as well as human relations training for these key adults in order to establish models of effective communication as well as effective people. By working directly with the leaders of the community, the counselor indirectly will reach their representatives or constituents.

The counselor will probably spend as much time in the community as in school. The counselor, as a social activist, will prevent problems arising from racial and ethnic prejudice, poverty, ecology, etc. He will train others to help themselves. This role will be similar to his role with school administrators in that the counselor becomes a source of power rather than being controlled by power.

Power Bases Will Be a Necessity

The counselor of the future will be a change agent who has power as a prerequisite. As Aubrey (1972) puts it, "without power, a viable means of influencing the school policy makers, counselors have little or no chance of effecting changes for children." Through work with parents, teachers, the community and other environmental influences on children, counselors will build these sources of power.

Computerization and Other Rapidly Developing Technologies (Systems Analysis, Media Therapy, Retrieval Systems Multimedia Technologies) Will Be Assets in the Counselor's Repertoire

The fear, threat and resistance to technological innovation in the helping professions will be conquered. The counselor will understand technology and use it as a tool. Recently entire issues of the *Personnel and Guidance Journal* (November, 1970) and *Educational Technology* (March, 1969) have been devoted to this important area.

The Role of Learning Specialist Will Be Important

"Learning *how* to *learn* cannot just be a catch phrase we all give lip service to. It has profound meaning. It means you must learn a *process*, a *method* as well as a set of skills and content. It means that *how* you learn may be more important than *what* you learn. It means that how you *feel* about your learning is important." [Gelatt, 1971, p. 2]

The counselor will help people learn *how* to learn—not *what* to learn. The process of learning will take precedence over the product. Learning how to learn[1] will apply to social, emotional, physical and intellectual learnings. A learning system will flourish in which each individual will learn the process of learning, not the facts but how one learns, and how to use this learning in life.

The tremendous power of the computer will make it clear that intellectual knowledge is not data but is the process of handling data. A new kind of curriculum, therefore, will be developed—one that does not concentrate on any particular subject, content or basic concept, but instead defies and teaches the *process* of an educated mind, the ways of gathering, evaluating and acting upon information. These processes (methods, skills, purposive behaviors) cut across subject disciplines and are of such fundamental applicability that once a student learns them he can apply them constantly for the rest of his life (Borton, 1970). The educated mind will no longer be left to chance.

Real Problems Must Be Dealt With

Historically, the counselor has ignored or rationalized the real world issues of people. He continues to function helping kids find jobs, colleges,

---

[1] This is a concept that received considerable support at the 1970 White House Conference on Children and the U.S. Office of Education's 1971 National Conference of Pupil Personnel Services.

friends; yet problems of sex, color, religion, environment abound in an insane proportion. World peace has become a joke. We need a social revolution! Will counselors lead it or even be a part of it? In order to survive, the answer must be *Yes*.

Stress, for example, will not be ignored or rationalized away. Stress is here and is normal (Toffler, 1970; Fabun, 1971), and counselors will help people accept this fact and train them to deal with it. The counselor knows that a smooth sea never made a skillful mariner. The counselor will get involved with problems such as racial and sexual stress and "future shock."

The Majority of Students Will Receive Service

The school counselor will move into a developmentalist role and view the world in terms of strengths and normality. In this preventive posture, the school counselor will strive toward meeting the developmental needs of *all* children. The program emphasizes work with school-aged children but also realizes that life develops before the formal-schooling experience and continues after its termination. The counselor's role will be seen as one that focuses on the human organism from birth to death. The counselor will of course get involved with pathology and remediation, but these take a back seat to his primary function.

The Counselor Will Be Certified on the Basis of Performance

The future will provide us with qualitative standards for the profession of counseling—standards that are not based on credits, degrees, course titles, experiences but on competency level or performance. The state of Washington has already begun to move in this direction (Allen, Cady, & Drummond, 1969; Brammer & Springer, 1971). In establishing new criteria we will not be restricted to our current skills level, since the future need not be an extension of the past. The problems of tomorrow will require new and different skills. Counselors will be involved in a self-renewing process in order to maintain their skills at criterion level. Also, systematic upgrading of the counseling profession will be accomplished by mandating all practicing counselors to meet the norms.

Systematic Training Will Be Commonplace

In order to meet the demands of required change, a system which insures the best training for each counselor will be needed. Through job analysis, specification of objectives and utilization of learning principles, such a system will be developed. Material which has already been developed by Carkhuff (1971), Ivey (1973), and Blocher & Rapoza (1972) is of this type. Blocher (1969) feels that counselors will need to master at least three technologies:

"1. They must be human relations experts who are able to initiate and manage growth-producing interpersonal relationships and facilitate others in doing the same.

"2. They will need to be able to analyze and diagnose the communication components within social systems and help to create broad-band channels to two-way communication within the client system and between it and its linking supra- or sub-systems.

"3. Finally, counselors will need to understand the area of data processing and learn to generate, code, store, retrieve, and communicate appropriate information to client systems." [p. 18]

The Ability To Be Held Accountable Will
Determine Who Will Survive

It is reasonable for a school system to hold each counselor in its employ accountable for his work. As Hays (1972b) stated,

". . . the school counselor must prove himself. He cannot expect society to accept him just because he is a counselor. He must earn his position and with it his freedom—if he is to have freedom and not be a servant to the expectations of a demanding and critical school system and community. What it means for the school counselor is total commitment." [p. 101]

Accountability will involve planning and specifying clear overriding objectives and priorities.

"Too often counselors fail to identify and define what it is they are trying to do (what is required) and how it differs from what they are doing (what is). What they currently are doing may have no significant justification other than 'We've always done it this way!' " [p. 101]

Practical research and statistical tools will be used to constantly monitor the counselor's position.

Counselor Educators Will Be Preparing Counselors
To Function in the Aforementioned Fashion

Members of the helping professions (i.e., psychology, social work) will work cooperatively. The counselor will be more involved in the area of career education as lifestyles continue to change. Professional organizations will continue to gain support from counselors in an era of increased stress. Risk-taking will become more commonplace as counselors begin to realize that all great things in life (birth, suffering, friendship) imply risk.

Priorities Will Be Necessary

Through *total* involvement, counselors will be effective. In order to do and be all of the aforementioned, however, the counselor will have established a clear-cut system of priorities and hierarchies. Aspects of the consultant's role (Carlson, 1972) will be applicable to the counselor of the future:

"The consultant's focus is on serving all children. However, the consultant must learn to avoid the trap which has often encapsulated other specialists in pupil personnel. The consultant cannot be all things to all people. It is necessary to establish some priorities as to how to utilize his time and resources in the most efficacious manner. The consultant needs to identify where he can make his greatest contribution in terms of his time and ability. He uses strategies and establishes priorities. He needs to look at his total potential impact upon the *whole system* and how he can best serve the total school population." [p. 87]

The counselor will have developed a comprehensive plan which details where *his* services will yield the greatest results and meet the most basic needs.

PROGNOSIS AND CONCLUSION

The years must bring a counselor who is action-oriented, risk-taking and, in general, a creative dreamer. The person with counseling-consulting skills will be perceived accurately as an architect of change. The counselor will move into new roles including human relations trainer, learning development consultant, coordinator of remedial services, psychological educator, family counselor, community services worker and more. He will be a generalist in function and an activist in attitude and commitment.

Whether or not all counselors will move into this new role will depend upon their ability to adopt the new ideas now being advanced in the literature of school counseling and guidance as well as in the other social and behavioral sciences. More than any other element, the future of school counseling depends upon each counselor and his commitment. How we fare with today's challenges will determine not only what our future will be—but whether we deserve a future at all.

References

Allen, W. C., Cady, L. V. & Drummond, W. H. "Performance Criteria for Educational Personnel Development: A State Approach to Standards." *Journal of Teacher Education, 20,* 1969 (133–135).

American Personnel and Guidance Association. "A Question of Survival." *Guidepost,* March, 1972 (1–2).

Arbuckle, A. S. "The Counselor: Who? What?" *Personnel and Guidance Journal, 50,* 1972 (785–790).

Arbuckle, A. S. "Does the School Really Need Counselors?" *School Counselor, 17,* 1970 (325–330).

Aubrey, R. F. "Organizational Victimization of School Counselors." *The School Counselor,* 20, 5, 1973, (346–352).

Aubrey, R. F. "Power Bases: The Consultant's Vehicle for Change." Elementary School Guidance and Counseling, 7, 2, 1972 (90–97).

Baker, S. B. & Cramer, S. H. "Counselor or Change Agent: Support from the Profession." *Personnel and Guidance Journal, 50,* 1972 (661–665).

Baker, S. B. & Hansen, J. C. "School Counselor Attitudes on a Status Quo-Change Agent Measurement Scale." *School Counselor, 19,* 1972 (243–248).

Bateson, G., Jackson, D., Haley, J. & Weakland, J. "Toward a Theory of Schizophrenia." *Behavioral Science, 1,* 1956 (251–264).

Berdie, R. F. "The 1980 Counselor: Applied Behavioral Scientist." *Personnel and Guidance Journal, 50,* 6, 1972 (451–456).

Bessell, H. & Palomares, U. *Methods in Human Development.* San Diego: Human Development Training Institute, 1967.

Blocher, D. H. "Counseling as a Technology for Facilitating and Guiding Change in Human Systems." *Educational Technology, 60,* 1969 (15–18).

Blocher, D. H. & Rapoza, R. S. "A Systematic Eclectic Model for Counseling—Consulting." *Elementary School Guidance and Counseling, 7,* 1972 (106–112).

Boocock, S. S. & Schild, E. O. (Eds.). *Simulation Games in Learning.* Beverly Hills, California: Sage Publications, 1968.

Borton, T. *Reach, Touch and Teach.* New York: McGraw-Hill, 1970.

Boy, A. "The Elementary School Counselor's Role Dilemma." *School Counselor, 19,* 1972 (167–172).

Brammer, L. M. & Springer, H. C. "A Radical Change in Counselor Education and Certification." *Personnel and Guidance Journal, 49,* 1971 (803–808).

Brown, G. *Human Teaching for Human Learning: An Introduction to Confluent Education.* New York: Viking, 1971.

Carey, A. R. & Garris, A. L. "Accountability for School Counselors." *School Counselor, 18,* 1971 (321–326).

Carkhuff, R. R. *The Development of Human Resources.* New York: Holt, Rinehart & Winston, 1971.

✳Carkhuff, R. R. & Griffin, A. H. "The Selection and Training of Human Relations Specialists." *Journal of Counseling Psychology, 17,* 1970 (443–450).

Carlson, J. "Case Analysis: Parent Group Consultation." *Elementary School Guidance and Counseling, 4,* 1969 (136–141).

Carlson, J. "Consulting: Facilitating School Change." *Elementary School Guidance and Counseling, 7,* 2, 1972 (83–88).

Carlson, J., Cavins, D. & Dinkmeyer, D. "Guidance for All through Support Personnel." *School Guidance, 16,* 1969 (360–366).

Carlson, J. & Falbe, R. "Facilitating Human Potential: A Birth to Death Model." Mimeographed. Governors State University, Park Forest South, Illinois, 1973.

Carlson, J. & Pietrofesa, J. J. "A Tri-level Guidance Structure: An Approach to Our Apparent Ineffectiveness." *Elementary School Guidance and Counseling, 5,* 1971, (190–195).

Carlson, J. & Van Hoose, W. H. "Status of Elementary School Guidance in Large Cities." *Elementary School Guidance and Counseling, 6*, 1, 1971 (43–45).

Carroll, J. F. X., Bell, A. A., Breecher, H. & Minor, M. "Psycho-educational Services for Elementary Schools: A Preventative Systems Approach." *Journal of the National Medical Association, 63*, 6 (November), 1971 (450–454).

Christensen, O. "Family Education: A Model for Consultation." *Elementary School Guidance and Counseling, 7*, 2, 1972 (121–129).

Cook, D. (Ed.). *Guidance for Education in Revolution.* Boston: Allyn & Bacon, 1971.

DeFeo, R. A. & Cohn, B. "Budget Cut: Two Guidance Counselors." *School Counselor, 19*, 1972 (319–322).

Dinkmeyer, D. *DUSO* (Developing Understanding of Self and Others). *Manual.* Circle Pines, Minnesota: American Guidance Service, 1970, 1973.

Dinkmeyer, D. & Carlson, J. *Consulting: Facilitating Humaneness and Change Processes.* Columbus, Ohio: Charles E. Merrill Co., 1973.

Dinkmeyer, D. & Dreikurs, R. *Encouraging Children to Learn: The Encouragement Process.* Englewood Cliffs, New Jersey: Prentice-Hall, 1963.

Dinkmeyer, D. & McKay, G. *Raising a Responsible Child.* New York: Simon & Schuster, 1973.

Dreikurs, R. & Grey, L. *Logical Consequences: A New Approach to Discipline.* New York: Meredith, 1968.

Dreikurs, R., Grunwald, B. B. & Pepper, F. C. *Maintaining Sanity in the Classroom.* New York: Harper & Row, 1971.

Dworkin, E. P. & Dworkin, A. L. "The Activist Counselor." *Personnel and Guidance Journal, 49*, 1971 (748–753).

Eckerson, L. O. "White House Conference on Children: Implications for Counselors as Change Agents." *Elementary School Guidance and Counseling, 6*, 1972 (239–244).

Eckerson, L. O. "The White House Conference: Tips or Taps for Counselors?" *Personnel and Guidance Journal, 50*, 1971 (167–174)

Fabun, D. *Dimensions of Change.* Beverly Hills, California: Glencoe Press, 1971.

Fredrickson, R. H. "Support Personnel for School Counselors: Role Analysis by Tasks and Levels of Responsibility." Unpublished Mimeo. University of Massachusetts, 1969.

Frost, J. & Ratliff, L. *Program Work Awareness Kit.* Morava, N. Y.: Chronicle, 1973.

Fullmer, D. W. "Family Group Consultation." *Elementary School Guidance and Counseling, 7*, 2, 1972 (130–136).

Gazda, G. M. "Message to the Association." *Counselor Education and Supervision, 12*, 1, 1972 (1–2).

Gelatt, H. B. "Confronting the Status Quo." *Focus on Guidance, 4*, 2, 1971 (1–8).

Glasser, W. *Schools without Failure.* New York: Harper & Row, 1969.

Gluckstern, N. "Development of a Community Training Program for Parent-Consultants on Drug Abuse." Paper presented at the meeting of the American Personnel and Guidance Association, Chicago, April 1972.

Gordon, T. *Parent Effectiveness Training.* New York: Peter H. Wyden, 1970.

Harris, T. A. *I'm O.K.—You're O.K.: A Practical Guide to Transactional Analysis.* New York: Harper & Row, 1967.

Hays, D. G. "Counselor—What are You Worth?" *School Counselor, 19*, 1972a (309–312).

Hays, D. G. "Responsible Freedom for the School Counselor." *The School Counselor,* 20, 1972b (93–102).
Henry, J. *Culture against Man.* New York: Vintage Books, 1963.
Herndon, J. *The Way It's Spozed to Be.* New York: Simon & Schuster, 1965.
Holt, J. *The Underachieving School.* New York: Pitman Publishing Co., 1969.
Hoyt, D. P. "APGA: Cherish or Perish?" *Personnel and Guidance Journal, 49,* 1971 (431–438).
Illich, I. *Deschooling Society.* New York: Harper & Row, 1971.
Island, D. "An Alternative for Counselor Education." *Personnel and Guidance Journal, 50, 9,* 1972 (762–766).
Ivey, A. E. "The Association for Human Development: A Revitalization of APGA." *Personnel and Guidance Journal, 48,* 1970 (527–532).
Ivey, A. E. "Microcounseling: The Counselor as Trainer." *Personnel and Guidance Journal, 51, 5,* 1973 (311–316).
Jackson, P. W. *Life in Classrooms.* New York: Holt, Rinehart & Winston, 1968.
Kozol, J. *Death at an Early Age.* New York: Bantam, 1967.
Kuriloff, P. J. "The Counselor as Psychoecologist." *Personnel and Guidance Journal, 51, 5,* 1973 (321–327).
Laing, R. D. *The Politics of the Family and Other Essays.* New York: Pantheon, 1969.
Lawton, R. "Counselors Need a Green Light Organization." *Personnel and Guidance Journal, 49,* 1971 (759–763).
Lewis, F. C. "Some of My Best Friends are Counselors." *Phi Delta Kappan, 53,* 1972 (372–373).
Lewis, M. D. & Lewis, J. A. "Counselor Education: Training for a New Alternative." *Personnel and Guidance Journal, 49,* 1971 (754–758).
Limbacher, W. *Dimensions of Personality.* Dayton: George Pflaum, 1969.
Lipsman, C. K. "Revolution and Prophecy: Community Involvement for Counselors." *Personnel and Guidance Journal, 48,* 1969 (97–100).
Miller, G. "Psychology as a Means of Promoting Human Welfare." *American Psychologist, 24,* 1969 (1063–1075).
Mosher, R. L. & Sprinthall, N. A. "Psychological Education: A Means to Promote Personal Development during Adolescence." *The Counseling Psychologist, 2,* 1971 (3–84).
Muro, J. "Community Volunteers: A New Thrust for Guidance." *Personnel and Guidance Journal, 49,* 1970 (137–141).
National Advisory Council on Vocational Education. "Counseling and Guidance: A Call for Change." *6th Report,* June 1, 1972.
National School Public Relations Association. "Role of Counselor: A Misdirected Effort?" *Newsletter,* May 24, 1971 (211).
Nelson, R. C., Erickson, M. R. & Millirin, A. P. "Challenging the Counselor." *Elementary School Guidance and Counseling, 6,* 1972 (269–272).
Packard, V. *A Nation of Strangers.* New York: McKay, 1972.
Pancrazio, J. J. "The School Counselor as a Human Relations Consultant." *School Counselor, 19,* 1971 (81–87).
Postman, N. & Weingartner, C. *The Soft Revolution.* New York: Delta, 1971.
Randolph, Norma & Howe, W. *Self-enhancing Education: A Program to Motivate Learners.* Palo Alto, California: Sanford Press, 1966.
Raths, L. E., Harmin, M., & Simon, S. B. *Values and Teaching.* Columbus, Ohio: Charles E. Merrill, 1965.

Reich, C. A. *The Greening of America: How the Youth Revolution Is Trying to Make America Livable.* New York: Random House, 1970.

Rhodes, W. C. "The Disturbing Child: A Problem of Ecological Management." *Exceptional Children, 33,* 1967 (449–455).

Riccio, A. "The President's Message." *Counselor Education and Supervision, 9,* 1970 (145–147).

Roark, A. E. "Using Encounter Group Principles in Teaching." Mimeo. University of Colorado, 1971.

Satir, V. *Peoplemaking.* Palo Alto, California: Science and Behavior Books, 1972.

Selman, R. & Kohlberg, L. *First Things: Values.* Pleasantville, New York: Guidance Associates, 1972.

Shertzer, B. & Stone, S. C. "Myths, Counselor Beliefs and Practices." *School Counselor, 19,* 1972 (320–327).

Silberman, C . E. *Crisis in the Classroom.* New York: Random House, 1970.

Simon, S. B. Howe, L. W. & Kirschenbaum, H. *Values Classification.* New York: Hart, 1972.

Sinick, D. "Sociodynamics in Counseling." *Counselor's Information Service, 22,* 1967 (4).

Sprinthall, N. A. "Humanism: A New Bag of Virtues for Guidance?" *Personnel and Guidance Journal, 50,* 1972 (349–356).

Stanford, G. "Psychological Education in the Classroom." *Personnel and Guidance Journal, 50,* 1972 (585–592).

Stiller, A. "Three R's for APGA: Responsive, Responsible, Restructured." *Personnel and Guidance Journal, 50,* 1972 (486–490).

Toffler, A. *Future Shock.* New York: Random House, 1970.

Van Hoose, W. H. & Carlson, J. "Counselors in the Elementary School: 1970–71." *Personnel and Guidance Journal, 50,* 8, 1972 (679–682).

Whiteley, J. M. & Sprandel, H. M. "APGA as a Political Organization." *Personnel and Guidance Journal, 50,* 1972 (475–481).

Zerface, J. P. & Cox, W. H. "School Counselors, Leave Home." *Personnel and Guidance Journal, 49,* 1971 (371–375).

Zimpfer, A., Fredrickson, R., Salim, M. & Sanford, A. *Support Personnel in School Guidance Programs.* Washington, D. C.: APGA Monograph Series, 1971.

2.   A PSYCHOSOCIAL LOOK AT CONSULTATION AND BEHAVIOR MODIFICATION

•=•—•=•

Richard R. Abidin

During the past 5 years behavior modification, *i.e.*, the application of operant principles, has become a topic of increasing interest to school

Richard R. Abidin, "A Psychosocial Look at Consultation and Behavior Modification" *Psychology in the Schools,* 1972, Vol. 9–4, October, 358–364.

psychologists and other consulting professionals. To many consulting psychologists behavior modification programming has become synonymous with consultation, and to a degree this overlap between method and function is understandable. The purpose of this paper is to question whether adequate consultation can take place when issues and problems are considered only at the level of the overt behavior of the "problem child." Attention will be drawn to the implications of the internal assumptions and expectancies of the teacher with regard to the child and to the contingencies that apply to the teacher's own behavior in terms of the assumptions and expectations of the social system of which she is a part.

The literature is replete with reports that demonstrate that through various behavior modification strategies a wide range of behaviors of "problem children" can be altered. (Barrish, Saunders, & Wolf, 1969; Bijou, 1966; O'Leary, Drabman, Reynolds & Risley, 1968; Siegel, Lenskf, & Broen, 1969; Wolf, Risley, & Nees, 1964.) It appears reasonable to assume that the adequacy of the technology has been demonstrated. More recently, psychologists have begun to address themselves to specific effects of various types of teaching as they represent contingencies that elicit specific response patterns from children (Breyer, 1971; Buckley & Walker, 1971; Hall, Lund, & Jackson, 1968; Madsen, Becker, & Thomas, 1968). This shift in emphasis to the contingent behaviors of teachers and other caretakers of children has taken place as a logical progression of the applications of operant principles and on the basis of the collected clinical experience of psychologists. It appears that a consensus is developing that it is necessary to intervene at the level of those individuals who control the contingencies in a child's environment.

Some interesting documentation on this issue is provided by a study by Patterson, Cobb, and Ray (1970), who dealt with the results of followups of children whose behaviors had been changed successfully by the application of operant principles. Upon investigation of the social situations involved in each case, it was found that the changes in the children's behavior did not lead to changes in many of the important contingencies provided by the child's social environment to support the changes achieved. They concluded: "This experience convinced us that we should train parents, siblings, teachers, and peers rather than directly train the deviant child . . ." [p. 2]. Since teachers and parents are the major controllers of the contingencies in the child's psychosocial world, it is logical to conclude that enduring changes in the teacher's or parent's behavior will be reflected by enduring changes in the child.

One of the major weaknesses of behavior modification programs has been the fact that long-term effects rarely are reported, and, when found, they usually are less dramatic than those reported in the multitude of short-term studies in the literature. When the child ceases to get the tokens or points that lead to the artificial contingencies his behavior quickly reverts to baseline. To the classroom teacher this means that behavior modification is a gimmick that works for a short period of time. It might be argued that the teachers just don't understand the principles of behavior modification or that the consultant who tried to help was inadequate. Possibly! However, the principles of behavior modification are not that complex and difficult to understand. In the same vein, it might be argued that any teacher who has read two or three major references on behavior modification application has a good understanding of its principles. Further, most behavioral consultants generally have a reasonable grasp of the principles of behavior modification, as well as the capacity to develop excellent programs. What may be lacking to obtain stable long-term effects is the consultant's awareness and responsiveness to the teacher's assumptions and expectancies with regard to children's behavior and the contingencies of the social systems related to the teacher's behavior.

Two major issues that must be considered in relation to consultation that employs behavioral technology are:

1. *The adequacy of the theoretical base.* The concepts and principles of a rat-based psychology may not be adequate for work with humans. Illustrative of some of the problems with such a theoretical base is the fact that research in the area of social learning theory (Rotter, 1966) has pointed out that long-held beliefs that concern the nature and operation of fundamental principles of learning developed from subhuman experimentation may not apply to humans. For example, most school psychologists who are practicing today learned that the rate of extinction was a function of the reinforcement schedule, such that continuously reinforced responses displayed the most rapid rate of extinction and that variable partial reinforcement schedules produced the greatest resistance to extinction. Rotter's work clearly indicates the importance of beliefs and expectations. It appears that extinction in humans is dependent on their beliefs about whether the contingencies are under their control. When the individual believes that he can control the contingencies he will not show rapid extinction after continuous reinforcement; on the other hand, if he believes that he doesn't control the contingencies, he will show rapid extinction despite the fact that he was on a variable partial reinforcement schedule.

2. *The fact that a child is referred should not convey to the psychologist the assumption that the child is "the" problem and must be changed.* It is this issue that frequently separates the professional consulting psychologist from the behavioral technician. There should be absolutely no doubt in the mind of any psychologist of the power and effectiveness of behavior modi-

fication technology. The child's behavior can be altered one way or another, but the issue that always must be considered is the extent to which the child's "problem behavior" is truly deviant and the extent to which it is elicited or reinforced by other elements of the social system including the complaintant.

If it is assumed that the consulting psychologist is aware of the implication of the two major issues just raised and that enduring changes in the child's behaviors are justified, then the consulting psychologist must address himself to how to accomplish the necessary behavioral changes. Since teachers are both controllers and an integral part of the contingency system, it will be necessary to change the teacher or parent. The question now must be raised as to whether operant principles alone should be applied to teachers and parents. Should we begin to develop methods of "training" teachers and parents in "new" behaviors? Is it really necessary to get teachers to bar press or to use successive approximations? Do we need tokens and points to shape their behavior? I think not. All too often the behavioral technician faced with the desire or need to alter a teacher's behavior in order to affect the child probably would begin with the familiar pattern of obtaining a baseline and then applying some strategy of response-contingent reinforcers or punishers to the teacher's behavior. Can we not assume that teachers already have in their behavioral repertoires the ability to engage in almost any behavior they desire to display? Further, isn't it true that the behaviors humans display are related to the contingencies that apply to them? Therefore, to change the behavior of teachers would it not be more efficient to change the general contingency system under which they operate and to attempt to change their assumptions and expectancies with regard to children's behavior than to pursue some complicated and expensive training program? The research of Buckley and Walker (1971), who conducted a study designed to change teachers' behaviors through various training programs, produced some interesting negative results. Specifically, they found little differential effect among the various training programs used. Could it be, as was suggested above, that the critical variables in the classroom are the contingency systems that apply to the teacher and her assumptions and expectancies for the children's behavior?

CHANGING CHILDREN'S BEHAVIORS
BY CHANGING TEACHERS' BEHAVIORS

The following sections will deal with some of the important issues involved in changing teachers' behaviors, which are response contingent to children's behaviors. It is recognized that many points could be made, but the focus will remain on the cognitive aspects (assumptions and expectancies) of the teacher and on the system of contingencies applicable to the teacher.

Psychologists and other consultants have recognized for years that if behavior change is to occur in an enduring fashion the client must make certain cognitive changes as well as develop "new" behaviors (Caplan, 1970). When cognitive changes do occur, the human often is able to alter his behavior by working not only on changes through direct training, but also through mediational phenomena such as mental rehearsal. (Lazarus, 1971). For years Rogers (1951) has seen maximal therapeutic benefit and behavioral change from therapeutic situations in which the locus of control resides in the client and direct training is held to a minimum. More recently, Lovitt and Curtiss (1969) reported that even within the framework of a behavior modification paradigm, a pupil's academic response rate is maximized when he manages the contingencies and the magnitude of the reinforcement. It appears, therefore, that certain internal events, such as assumptions and expectancies, are important variables in the production of overt behavioral change.

If the importance of the above point is accepted, then it must be conceded that at least part of the attention of the consulting psychologist who deals with behavior change in children must be directed toward the development of the "cognitive" changes necessary in teachers to allow for changes in their behavior and consequently in the behavior of the children with whom they deal.

The author recently encountered two teachers who assumed that they must control the behavior of each child in their classroom and held the assumption that learning takes place only when the child is seated and on task 95% of the time. These assumptions and expectancies produced pressures and frustrations, which in turn produced behaviors such as nagging and threats that impeded the learning process. Once freed of these assumptions, the teachers were able to relax and reap the benefits of the fact that all of their children were on task about 80% of the time, which in itself is phenomenal. The frequency of tense nagging and threatening behaviors of these teachers dropped to near zero.

A more detailed account of the importance of teacher attitudes and assumptions has been presented by Grieger (1971). It appears that the consulting psychologist must not accept a referral on a child and quickly design a behavior modification program for that child, despite the fact that the program would work *if* carried out. The sensitive consulting psychologist first must determine what attitudes and beliefs the teacher holds about the child and her expectancies for both his behavior and her behavior.

Bersoff and Greiger (1971) have suggested an interview strategy that can be of considerable help to collect information with regard to teacher attitudes, expectancies, and beliefs.

THE SOCIAL SYSTEM VARIABLES

The consulting psychologist must keep in mind at all times that the teacher with whom he is working is a member of a specific social system. Further, in every social system more or less unique explicit and implicit contingencies are attached to different behaviors. To a large extent the hierarchial nature of the public school system limits the degree of freedom teachers have and hence their ability to engage in different behaviors. The zenith of stupidity and naiveté in consultation is found in the simple-minded approach of the "behavioral technician" who recommends a behavior modification program to a teacher or school that is firmly committed to a more existential approach to teaching, such as may be found in the "open classroom" concept. Failure to consider the attitudes, values and expected behavior patterns in a given social system is a fatal mistake in the consultation process often committed by the strict behaviorist.

Effective programming for change in most instances must begin with the building of a consulting relationship with the institution, with the "gate keepers," and with those individuals who are responsible for the child's general social environment. Strategies to build this relationship have been specified in detail elsewhere (Caplan, 1970), and all will not be considered at this time. One issue within the consultation process that I would like to stress is a recognition on the part of the consultant that within the context of a consulting relationship, the consultee should always be free to reject the consultant's ideas and methods. Given that the consultee must be free to reject the ideas and recommendations of the consultant, the consultant nevertheless should seek to obtain a reasonable consideration of his ideas, particularly when he believes that they will benefit the children in the school system or institution.

It is unfortunate that all too often the "behavior technician," convinced of the effectiveness of his technology, will press for the implementation of a particular program. He fails to recognize that in a social world the acceptance or rejection of ideas or method is a function not only of their technical adequacy, but also of their acceptability to the social system and its values and expectations. Social psychological research has demonstrated that when high-status individuals endorse an idea it increases in acceptability to others lower in status. It is possible, therefore, that a given psychologist may achieve greater behavioral changes in larger numbers of teachers and children by adequate attention to the psychosocial system, its values and behavioral expectancies than by the demonstration of effectiveness of a particular behavioral approach.

It is recognized that each time a consulting psychologist works on a particular case he may not be able to evaluate and effect changes in the entire social system that impinges on his consultee and her children. However, attention to the immediate social system, such as a given school building, frequently is possible and necessary. Given the hierarchial nature of school systems, what is the likelihood that a teacher will be able to carry out a behavioral program if the principal sees her actions as: bribing children, ignoring problem behaviors, and playing favorites by giving one child something the others don't get? This concern about the psychosocial system of the schools can be formulated into two hypotheses:

1. A teacher will feel free and is more likely to change her behavior if her social system supports the behavioral change in question and the philosophy it represents.
2. It is likely that dramatic behavioral changes will occur with minimal need for training of specific behaviors if the conditions in Hypothesis 1 are met.

AN EXAMPLE

As suggested earlier, it is assumed that each teacher already has the capacity to engage in a wide range of behaviors, including those that rarely are used. During the spring of 1971 an opportunity arose to test this assumption and the above two hypotheses, at least, in a case study format. The author and Mrs. Wendy Golladay were invited to participate in the evaluation of an Open Classroom Project in one of the public school divisions in Virginia. Unlike many instigated in the public schools for in-service training of teachers, the project involved the personal endorsement, support, and assistance of the teachers, parents, principals, superintendents, and local newspaper. The project involved three teacher volunteers who had been observed for baseline purposes during the end of the spring semester prior to the summer project.

The teachers in the project were informed that they were not expected to direct the learning of children, but were to function more in the role of resource people. The children were not expected to be seated at their desks, and the teachers were not expected to limit the children's movement or to enforce a tranquil environment. The conditions specified in hypothesis 1 above were met not through the efforts of the author, but through those of the teachers, the assistant superintendent of schools, a group of parents, and some other university personnel who worked on the project. Examination of the data collected revealed that the teachers did in fact display dramatic changes in their teaching behaviors during the project; however, examination of the frequency counts and graphs constructed demonstrated that the changes in behavior were present during the first week of the summer program with no evidence of continued improvement throughout the remaining 6 weeks. This finding appears to support the idea expressed in hypothesis 2, namely that teachers already possess in their behavioral repertoires the ability to engage in "new behaviors" without extensive training if they believe that the social system supports those "new behaviors." Some of the important teaching behaviors considered were: (a) direction of interaction—whether the child or the teacher initiated the interaction; (b) frequency of response-contingent teacher approval; (c) frequency of response-contingent disapproval.

Briefly, some of the findings were: (a) Teacher-initiated interaction in relation to child-initiated interaction dropped from a ratio of 2:1 to 1:1.1; (b) Teacher-approval frequency more than doubled for two teachers; the third teacher slightly increased her already high approval rate; (c) Teacher expression of disapproval essentially disappeared with a mean of .6 disapprovals per 20-minute observation period as compared to a mean of 9.0 during baseline. These data suggest that dramatic changes in behavior are possible without direct training when the social system is supportive of change.

It is recognized that this case study is only supportive of the hypotheses made earlier. The outcomes noted are not the results of a methodologically sound study, but they certainly are suggestive of the impact on behavior that can be achieved by dealing with covert variables such as values and expectancies. The issues raised in this article were selected to focus attention on the fact that consulting is a professional activity that involves more than the application of behavioral technology to overt behaviors. Successful consulting psychology demands that the consultant be sensitive to the values and behavioral expectancies of the consultee and be cognizant of the limitations placed on the consultee by the values and behavioral contingencies of the social system in which he works.

References

Barrish, H. H., Saunders, M., & Wolf, M. M. Good behavior game: effects of individual contingencies for group consequences on disruptive behavior in a classroom. *Journal of Applied Behavior Analysis*, 1969, 2, 119–124.

Bersoff, D. N., & Grieger, R. M. An Interview Model for the psychosituational assessment of children's behavior. *American Journal of Orthopsychiatry*, 1971, 41, 483–493.

Bijou, S. W. Experimental studies of child behavior, normal and deviant. In L. Krasner and L. P. Ullman (Eds.), *Research in behavior modification*. New York: Holt, Rinehart & Winston, 1966.

Buckley, N. K., & Walker, H. N. Free operant teacher attention to deviant behavior after treatment in a special class. *Psychology in the Schools,* 1971, *8,* 275–284.

Caplan, G. *The theory and practice of mental health consultation.* New York: Basic Books, 1970.

Grieger, R. M. Teacher attitudes as a variable in behavior modification consultation. *Journal of School Psychology,* in press.

Hall, R. V., Lund, D., & Jackson, D. Effects of teacher attention on study behavior. *Journal of Applied Behavior Analysis,* 1968, *1,* 1–12.

Lazarus, A. A. *Behavior therapy and beyond.* New York: McGraw-Hill, 1971.

Lovitt, T. C., & Curtiss, K. Academic response rate as a function of teacher and self-imposed contingencies. *Journal of Applied Behavior Analysis,* 1969, *2,* 49–53.

Madsen, C., Jr., Becker, W., & Thomas, D. Rules, praise, and ignoring; elements of elementary classroom control. *Journal of Applied Behavior Analysis,* 1968, *1,* 139–150.

O'Leary, K. P., & Drabman, R. Token reinforcement programs in the classroom: a review. *Psychological Bulletin,* 1971.

Patterson, G. R., Cobb, J. A., & Ray, R. S. A social engineering technology for retraining aggressive boys. In H. Adams & L. Unikel, Eds., *Georgia Symposium in experimental clinical psychology.* New York: Pergamon Press, 1970.

Reynolds, N. J., & Risley, T. R. The role of social and material reinforcers in increasing talking of a disadvantaged preschool child. *Journal of Applied Behavior Analysis,* 1968, *1,* 253–262.

Rotter, J. B. Generalized expectancies for internal vs. external control of reinforcement. *Psychological Monographs,* 1966, *80* (1, Whole No. 609).

Siegel, G. M., Lenske, J., & Broen, P. Suppression of normal speech disfluencies through response cost. *Journal of Applied Behavior Analysis,* 1969, *2,* 265–276.

Wolf, M., Risley, T., & Mies, H. Application of operant conditioning procedures to the behavior problems of an autistic child. *Behavior Research and Therapy,* 1964. *1,* 305–312.

3. A DEVELOPMENTAL MODEL FOR COUNSELING-CONSULTING

•●•

Don Dinkmeyer

The current milieu with its social and financial pressures demands relevance, involvement, and commitment from educators. The challenge to live as equals in a democratic society has emerged in the schools. Too often the

Don Dinkmeyer, "A Developmental Model for Counseling-consulting *Elementary School Guidance & Counseling Jl.,* 1971, Vol. 6–2, December, 81–85. Copyright 1971 by the American Personnel and Guidance Association and Reproduced by permission.

schools operate on autocratic and authoritarian principles; the democratic process is talked about, not lived. A commitment to persons instead of crises necessitates reconsideration and rearrangement of priorities for pupil personnel specialists.

The goals of the guidance program must be central to the task of the school. The guidance program is not a special service but is part of the mainstream of the educational effort. Man can no longer be educated as a cognitive being alone, but must be educated in terms of the interrelationship of the affective and cognitive domain (Pellegreno, 1970). He is a holistic self who acts, feels, and thinks. The child can be helped directly through contact in counseling and indirectly through the significant adults in his life, the professional staff, and the family.

Developmental guidance is the organized effort of the school to personalize and humanize the educational process for all students (Dinkmeyer & Caldwell, 1970). The focus is on assisting the child to understand himself and others in relation to his opportunities and responsibilities, to the end that he might become purposeful in his approach to the educational experience and the developmental tasks of life.

Guidance is concerned with the relationship between societal expectations and one's unique self-development as an individual. The educational program and process must both utilize and foster uniqueness. Our job is to assist each child, without force or pressure, to grow in relationship to his uniqueness through a process that takes into account his uniqueness and enables him to become a courageous and responsible contributor to society. The purposes of guidance include affective, cognitive, and behavioral objectives. The guidance program must involve the total staff.

PSYCHOLOGICAL PREMISES

A model for counseling and consulting must be based upon certain psychological premises regarding the nature of man. The developmental point of view sees man holistically as a biosocial, decision-making being whose psychological transactions and behavior are purposive. Consulting with the system requires a sociopsychological theory that accounts for and predicts the total system, adults and children. The following premises provide guidelines for the program:

1. Personality is best understood in terms of its unity. One understands behavior in terms of its unifying principles, as revealed in a characteristic pattern termed the life style.
2. Behavior is goal-directed and purposive. It is more than caused; that is, it cannot be explained simply in mechanical terms. Behavior is basically

the goal-directed attempt of an organism to satisfy its perceived needs (Dinkmeyer & Dreikurs, 1963; Rogers, 1951). Goal-striving is the essence of personality, and goals and purposes are more readily modified than causes (Allport, 1950). The goals of misbehavior—attention-getting, power, revenge, and the display of inadequacy clarify and explain behavior (Dreikurs, 1968). Understanding the purposive nature of behavior enables one to see the meaning in psychological transactions and to predict behavior based on the life style and pattern of an individual.

3. Motivation is best understood by comprehending how the individual seeks to be known, how he strives for significance. It is important to comprehend the self-concept and the self-ideal and how the child tries to enhance his self-esteem.

4. All behavior has social meaning and is best understood in terms of its social context. Behavior has meaning in terms of specific social contingencies and makes sense when the behavior's perception of the situation is understood.

5. The individual has the creative capacity to make decisions. Behavior is more than the result of a stimulus. Each response is the result of the organism's interpretation of the stimulus (S-I-R). Man is more than a reactive being—he is an active being who is motivated from within to think, feel, and act.

6. Behavior is a function of the individual's field of perception at the instant of action (Combs & Snygg, 1959). Behavior change is the result of an active being evaluating his self-percepts and relationships with others. As he changes his convictions, thoughts, feelings, and values, his behavior is modified.

7. In understanding behavior, it is more important to be concerned with idiographic laws, those that apply to the individual's style of life, than in the development of laws that apply generally, nomothetic laws. We must know the idiographic laws that govern the individual and not merely attempt to fit general principles to a specific situation.

8. It is more important to understand how the individual uses his ability than to understand what he possesses. At any given moment the child does whatever is more useful or best accomplishes his purposes, as he sees it.

9. The effective person accepts self and others and has the courage to be imperfect. He is sensitive to human relationships, aware of how others feel, but is open and congruent with himself, i.e., able to "tell it like it is" (Dinkmeyer & Caldwell, 1970). He has social interest and is responsible and concerned about cooperating for the good of society.

PRINCIPLES OF DEVELOPMENTAL GUIDANCE

The school counselor with a developmental approach finds that the following principles are guidelines for his program:

1. Developmental guidance is an integral part of the educational process.
2. Developmental guidance is for all students, not merely for the deviate.
3. Developmental guidance is an organized effort in which the teacher is expected to integrate the curriculum, the instruction, and the guidance process. Guidance is a collaborative effort among child, teacher, counselor, and parent.
4. Developmental guidance emphasizes purposeful, meaningful learning experiences.
5. Developmental guidance discovers and encourages a child's assets, shows faith in him, and recognizes his strengths and efforts (Dinkmeyer, 1968b).

The developmental program recognizes the following pupil needs: (a) to develop social relationships and to belong; (b) to develop independence through making choices and accepting responsibility for one's choices; (c) to appraise aptitudes and interests realistically and to learn to plan for purposeful participation in educational and life tasks; (d) to be loved, accepted, secure, and relatively free of threat.

The developmental counselor-consultant recognizes that the school and home environment should be modified to meet these needs. Too frequently conditions in the school and home work in direct opposition to the meeting of these needs.

CRUCIAL ELEMENTS

A developmental counseling and guidance program has several vital elements:

1. The counselor who consults, counsels, and collaborates stimulates the entire staff through his professional leadership. He is accessible and available to clientele who include children, professional staff, parents, and community.
2. The teacher is a central figure in the developmental guidance program and is involved in identifying needs and facilitating change and growth. He is concerned with developing purposeful and meaningful learning experiences through mutual goal alignment between teacher and child. The teacher also provides planned classroom guidance experiences (Bessell & Palomares, 1967; Dinkmeyer, 1970).
3. The school administrator is essential for the developmental approach insofar as he provides the leadership and personal support that bring about the necessary physical facilities and supplies. He sets the tone for human relationships in the building. Even more important, he establishes the opportunity for contact between the teacher and the counselor. He arranges for and supports formal and informal group and individual consultation. The administrator is essential to support the basic concept of developmental guidance, and, without his involvement, support, and commitment, the philosophy and program will be meaningless.

THE HIERARCHY OF COUNSELING-CONSULTING ROLES

The counselor must establish some hierarchy in connection with the services he provides. The consultant recognizes that in many instances he can service more children through teacher, parent, administrator, and community contacts than through direct work with the child.

The priorities have been developed in line with the stated psychological premises. The unit of major concern is the total system, the focus is on the significant adults who either facilitate or destroy a growth-producing climate.

Group dynamics, human relations, and group procedures are the essential competencies of the consultant. Emphasis on these areas is consistent with beliefs about the nature of behavior. The consultant focuses on comprehending patterns and styles of life as they are revealed in the social context. The group is concerned with understanding purposes, perceptions, and choices while facilitating social interest and the capacity to cooperate. The consultant's professional preparation would provide him with special competencies in understanding learning processes and the motivation of human behavior as they can be operationalized in the classroom.

A priority must be established between direct and indirect services. The hierarchy of services will certainly vary with the skills of the counselor and the particular setting in which he works. At this time, however, it is suggested that some of the following priorities might be established:

Collaboration and Consultation with Administration

The consultant meets with central school administration and the local principals to evaluate school policy insofar as it affects human potential within the system. He looks at this both in terms of the impact upon teachers and children. He is concerned about the learning environment and the learning climate. In some instances this concern will necessitate his meeting with specialists in curriculum to process feedback about the effect of certain curricular programs upon the staff and students. He is involved with staff in promoting planned programs in affective education concerned with developing understanding of self and others. The personalization and humanization of the educational process is the first priority.

Collaborating and Consulting with Groups of Teachers

It is suggested that collaboration implies the concept of working together in contrast to a superior-inferior relationship. This consulting may focus on a specific child or group of children. The model used is the *C Group* that helps the teachers to clarify their thinking about specific children and the relationship between teacher's beliefs and attitudes and the ensuing student beliefs and attitudes (Dinkmeyer & Muro, 1971). This approach is concerned with developing better relationships between staff members and facilitating commitment to change.

If the consultant is to work with groups of teachers, schedules must be developed that allow time for group meetings. While the members of the group must come out of their own willingness to participate, administration as a minimum should develop schedules that permit regular contacts.

Counseling with Groups of Children

This type of counseling is used with either developmental groups concerned with typical kinds of problems, or may become involved in crisis-oriented groups where students have particular difficulties that require more intensive assistance. The consultant becomes accessible to groups of children, and in this way he maintains a close contact with pupil needs so that he may process them into the general feedback that he relays to administration, curriculum, and the instructional staff.

Consultation with Parents in Groups

This type of consultation focuses on parent education, child study, and parent groups. The concern here is with reaching a large number of parents to help them understand more effective ways to relate with and motivate their children.

Counseling with Individuals

Counseling is either developmental or crisis-oriented (Blocher, 1968; Dinkmeyer, 1968a). The counselor makes himself accessible to the children as a resource for learning about self and interpersonal relations. He helps with crisis situations, but he is careful not to be identified by staff and students as crisis- and maladjustment-centered. The counselor develops contacts regarding normal developmental problems. Children perceive him as a "listening person" who helps them understand themselves and others.

The developmental counselor focuses on all children, the learning atmosphere, and the significant adults who provide indirect service to the child. The goal is a purposeful approach to the educational experience of life in a socially meaningful manner. The objectives of developmental guidance and counseling will be implemented only by establishing priorities and developing a systematic strategy for their implementation.

References

Allport, G. *The nature of personality*. Reading, Mass.: Addison-Wesley, 1950.

Blocher, D. Developmental counseling: A rationale for counseling in the elementary school. *Elementary School Guidance and Counseling*, 1968, 2(3), 163–172.

Bessell, H., & Palomares, U. *Methods in human development theory.* San Diego, Calif.: Human Development Training Institute, 1967.

Combs, A., & Snygg, D. *Individual behavior.* New York: Harper, 1959.

Dinkmeyer, D. Contributions of teleoanalytic theory and techniques to school counseling. *Personnel and Guidance Journal,* 1968, *46*(9), 898–902. (a)

Dinkmeyer, D. *Developing understanding of self and others (DUSO).* Circle Pines, Minn.: American Guidance Service, 1970.

Dinkmeyer, D. *Guidance and counseling in the elementary school: Readings in theory and practice.* New York: Holt, Rinehart & Winston, 1968. (b)

Dinkmeyer, D., & Caldwell, E. *Developmental counseling and guidance: A comprehensive school approach.* New York: McGraw-Hill, 1970.

Dinkmeyer, D., & Dreikurs, R. *Encouraging children to learn: The encouragement process.* Englewood Cliffs, N.J.: Prentice-Hall, 1963.

Dinkmeyer, D., & Muro, J. *Group counseling: Theory and practice.* Itasca, Ill.: F. E. Peacock, 1971.

Dreikurs, R. *Psychology in the classroom.* (2nd ed.) New York: Harper, 1968.

Pellegreno, D. The elementary school counselor and the affective domain. *Elementary School Guidance and Counseling,* 1970, *4*(4), 253–258.

Rogers, C. *Client-Centered therapy.* Boston: Houghton Mifflin, 1951.

4. A PRACTICAL APPROACH TO SCHOOL PSYCHOLOGY

•═•••═•

Daniel A. Kennedy

School psychology as practiced today in most school systems is not practical. The traditional clinical approach continues to be the most prevalent model for school psychology (Bardon, 1968; Starkman, 1966). This means that the psychologist attempts to cope individually with an overwhelming caseload of problems. He typically "works through" the staggering backlog of referrals by way of much individual testing and report writing, with rather meager attempts to implement treatment programs. The widespread disappointment of school personnel with psychological services is not surprising (Bardon, 1968). Teachers often justifiably complain that the end product of a psychological referral is a written report which tells them in detail what they already knew but offers very little in the way of helpful recommendations.

An unfortunate side effect of this situation is that many school people

Source. Daniel A. Kennedy, "A Practical Approach to School Psychology." *Journal of School Psychology,* 1971, Vol. 9–4, 484–489.

have come to view the psychological service as a source for relieving them of responsibility for the education of problem children by placing them in a special education class. If this is not possible, then at least it can be reasonably expected that a psychologist will call the child brain damaged, emotionally disturbed, etc., which the school people may interpret to mean that they cannot legitimately be expected to cope with the problem.

It used to be believed that an increased psychological staff would be the answer to the overwhelming referral backlog. We now know that this only leads to a proportionate (or greater) increase in referrals when the clinical model continues to be used. When the probable percentages of school adjustment problems are examined, it becomes glaringly evident that we can never realistically expect to handle the potential referrals effectively.

Estimates of the incidence of serious childhood emotion disturbance tend to range from about 4–10% of the child population (Bower, 1958; National Association for Mental Health, 1966; White & Harris, 1961; Woody, 1969). White & Harris (1961) made a careful survey of the research literature and concluded that a working estimate of the incidence of serious maladjustment in school children is 4–7%. Other research has indicated that the typical classroom contains two or three emotionally disturbed children (Bower, 1958). When attempting to get an estimate of the potential referrals in the school population, it is also necessary to consider the mentally retarded (2–2½%) and the slow learner (15–20%). In addition, we have an unknown number of academic underachievers who do not fit into any of the above categories.

Attention should also be given to the problem of teacher maladjustment. Research indicates that approximately three million children are daily exposed to teachers who are seriously maladjusted, and that the odds are seven to one that every school child who completes twelfth grade will encounter at least two of these teachers (Kaplan, 1959; Ringness, 1968).

When a very conservative estimate of the potential referrals is taken (4% seriously emotionally disturbed, 2% mentally retarded, 10% slow learners), we are talking about 16% of the school population.[1] These figures do not take into account many underachieving children, any attempt to help disturbed teachers, or the desirable goal of fostering positive mental health (or optimal development) in all children. When psychologist-student ratio is examined, it is clear that the great majority of school systems in this country can never sensibly expect to meet the challenge of school adjustment problems while primarily using the clinical model, a model which means trying to individually remediate the great number of currently

[1] In the school system where the writer is presently employed this would amount to over 17,600 children.

existing problems. While some of this sort of work will no doubt always be necessary in schools and in other community mental health facilities, it is futile to accept this as a model for most of the work to be performed by school psychologists. We clearly need to employ models that encourage developmental and preventive (or positive mental health) programs.

ASSUMPTIONS UNDERLYING SUGGESTED ALTERNATIVE APPROACHES

What is felt to be more practical alternative approaches to school psychology are based on certain assumptions:

1. School psychology staffs will never be able to give adequate direct, individual attention to all children who need help.
2. Most school adjustment problems can be adequately handled, and many prevented, through consultation with school personnel, modification of classroom social climates, modification of teacher attitudes, development of parent education programs, and the like.
3. In most school adjustment problems learning is a major component. For example, many adjustment problems are essentially displays of undesirable behavior that has been learned and which needs to be replaced through the learning of desirable behavior. Other examples of the importance of learning may be seen in the problems presented by slow learners and academic underachievers.
4. A learning oriented or psycho-educational approach will be most efficacious for handling the great majority of school adjustment problems. Explaining the academically inhibiting effects of perfectionistic behavior in terms of an anal retentive character, for example, will be of little value as compared with the modification of levels of aspiration. Likewise, the direct modification of classroom attending behavior by providing a child with feelings of success is preferable to reducing physical activity level (and sometimes mental alertness as well) through medication.
5. A major objective in mental health is adequate adjustment to the "normal" environment. For most children, this environment includes attending a regular school while living at home. Years of research on the problem of transfer of training tells us that the closer the treatment for problem children is to be the normal environment, the more likely that eventual adjustment to that environment will be effected. The greater the similarity in stimulus situations, the greater the chances that positive transfer from one to the other will occur.

ALTERNATIVE APPROACHES IN SCHOOL PSYCHOLOGY

It is submitted that a truly practical approach to school psychology would be to concentrate efforts on developmental and preventive programs while permitting clinical or remedial functions to be a relatively smaller part of the overall program. Developmental programs are those aimed at fostering the optimum cognitive, affective, and physical development of all children; preventive programs aim to prevent the future occurrence of adjustment problems. To the extent that developmental and preventive programs are successful, the need for remediation will be reduced. Since developmental and preventive programs overlap considerably, they will be discussed together for the purpose of providing some examples.

A common concern of teachers is that many children are not optimally motivated for academic work. Through consultation the school psychologist can help teachers secure greater motivation by developing contingency management programs in their classes (Homme, Csanyi, Gonzales, & Rechs, 1969). Such programs can be limited to specific problem areas, such as settling down to work quickly or developing appropriate lunchroom behavior, or can be applied in a generalized manner, as in Hewitt's (1968) model for the "engineered classroom." The point is that children who are well motivated for academic achievement and for showing acceptable behavior are less likely to develop adjustment problems and are more likely to realize their potentials.

I have observed that a number of initially well adjusted elementary school children develop social-emotional adjustment difficulties as a result of not performing well academically. What often seems to happen is that the poor achiever is not accepted by his teacher as well as his classmates are. Then the classmates, imitating the teacher, tend to reject the low achiever socially, causing him to develop feelings of guilt and to doubt his self-worth. Thus a problem of social-emotional adjustment has developed unnecessarily. School psychologists should help modify classroom social climates so that slow learners and underachievers are accepted by teachers and peers as worthy members of the class. This can be approached through direct consultation with teachers and/or through helping counselors learn to do the job. Unfortunately, in many classrooms where this problem exists, the necessary job of changing attitudes and feelings is not being accomplished.

Parent education offers tremendous potentiality for initiating developmental and preventive programs. It has been my experience that many counselors would like to get involved in activities such as parent study groups on child development, but that they feel unprepared for this. Often the school counselor and school psychologist working together as co-group leaders can be most effective. The counselor has information about the day-to-day functioning of the children and knows the general school environment well, while the psychologist is usually well versed in group process, child development, and behavior management techniques. In this arrangement, not only can the psychologist reach many parents, but over a period of time he can help train counselors to conduct such groups on their own.

These are a few of the activities that school psychologists can engage in for the purposes of promoting optimum development in children and preventing future adjustment problems. Other possibilities are: conducting workshops for school personnel on individualizing instruction, classroom management techniques, etc.; developing programs to integrate exceptional children into regular classrooms; establishing early identification procedures; and helping with programs on sex education and drug abuse.

There is also a need to consider some alternative approaches to the remedial aspects of school psychological services.

A "NEW LOOK" FOR REMEDIATION OF ADJUSTMENT PROBLEMS

A major trend in mental health today is that of attempting to treat adjustment problems in an environment as close as possible to the environment to which the individual is eventually expected to adjust (Brown & Long, 1968; Ringness, 1968). Thus, if at all possible, psychotherapy is conducted on an outpatient basis in the local community. If this is not possible, the treatment is conducted in a local hospital. Only as a last resort is the individual placed in an institutional facility removed from the local community. While not always explicitly stated, this approach is based on the principle of transfer of training referred to above. One result to be expected from this trend is greater involvement of the public school system in the treatment of children's adjustment problems. This involvement will include increased activity in psycho-educational treatment in the regular school setting, the reshaping of teacher behavior, and parent counseling.

For the same reasons that we try to keep mental health intervention within the local community as much as possible, we will try to keep the psycho-educational treatment of children with adjustment problems within the regular school setting, since it is part of the "normal" environment to which we want them to eventually adjust. The closer the treatment is to this environment, the greater the chances that the eventual adjustment will be attained. Using this rationale, the educational placement of exceptional children (including the socially-emotionally disturbed, severe learning disabilities, and the mentally retarded) will be mapped out in terms of steps which are increasingly removed from the regular class. The following model is based on this rationale:

Regular class
•
•
Special class in the regular
school on a part time basis
•
•
Special class in the regular
school on a full time basis
•
•
Special school in the regular
school system on a day care basis
•
•
Special residential school in
or near the local community

A child would be placed outside of the regular class only when absolutely necessary; he would be kept as close to the regular class environment as possible (Ringness, 1968).

This model has important implications for the practice of school psychology. The implementation of this approach would require much consultation with school personnel. For example, it would mean that most mentally retarded children would be integrated into regular classes. This would certainly require much modification of teacher attitudes and behavior.

Another major advantage of handling as many adjustment problems as possible within the context of the regular school is that of securing maximum coordination of efforts of the significant people in the child's life. Being able to influence a child's parents, siblings, teachers, and peers provides an extremely potent treatment strategy. Models for group work with a troubled child and the significant people in his life have been developed in recent years (Dreikurs, Corsini, Lowe, & Sonstegard, 1959; Fullmer & Bernard, 1968). Fullmer's approach has been to work with the entire family unit and sometimes with multiple family units. This can be done with the school counselor and the psychologist working together as co-counselors. The Adlerian family counseling approach of Dreikurs and his followers involves group work with varying combinations of parents, children, counselors, and teachers. These models allow for considerable manipulation of a child's environment for the purpose of facilitating adjustment. The use of this approach would obviously be most easily accomplished within the regular school setting, as compared with an outside agency. A widespread use of this approach would probably mean, in the long run, the employment of relatively fewer mental health workers in agencies outside of the schools, and the use of more of them in the public schools.

SUMMARY

The clinical or remedial model for school psychology currently prevalent is outdated and impractical as the primary means of using school psychology manpower. Developmental and preventive programs should constitute the primary model, with the remediation of adjustment problems taking a relatively smaller part of the overall school psychology program.

The remedial aspect of school psychological services also requires new approaches. In general, the treatment of school adjustment problems should be kept within or as close as possible to the regular class environment. This would mean that more exceptional children would be integrated into the mainstream of school life, and that more of the treatment of maladjusted children would be conducted within the framework of the public schools.

References

Bardon, J. I. School psychology and school psychologists: An approach to an old problem. *American Psychologist,* 1968, *23,* 187–194.

Bower, E. M. A process for early identification of emotionally disturbed children. *Bulletin of California State Department of Education,* 1958, *27*(6).

Brown, B. S., & Long, S. E. Psychology and community mental health: The medical muddle. *American Psychologist,* 1968, *23,* 335–341.

Dreikurs, R., Corsini, R., Lowe, R., & Sonstegard, M. *Adlerian family counseling.* Eugene: University of Oregon Press, 1959.

Fullmer, D., & Bernard, H. W. *Family consultation.* Boston: Houghton Mifflin, 1968.

Gray, Susan W. *The psychologist in the schools.* New York: Holt, Rinehart, and Winston, 1963.

Hewitt, F. M. *The emotionally disturbed child in the classroom.* Boston: Allyn and Bacon, 1968.

Homme, L., Csanyi, A., Gonzales, M. A., & Rechs, J. *How to use contingency contracting in the classroom.* Champaign, Ill.: Research Press, 1969.

Hurst, F. M., & Ralph, M. A. J. A survey of some of the literature dealing with the role or function of the elementary school counselor and the school psychologist. *The School Psychologist: Newsletter of the Division of School Psychologists,* APA, 1967–68, *22,* 53–61.

Kaplan, L. *Mental health and human relations in education.* New York: Harper, 1959.

National Association for Mental Health, Inc. *Facts about mental illness.* New York: National Association for Mental Health, 1966.

Ringness, F. A. *Mental health in the schools.* New York: Random House, 1968.
Starkman, S. The professional model: Paradox in school psychology. *American Psychologist*, 1966, *21*, 807–808.
White, M. A., & Harris, M. W. *The school psychologist.* New York: Harper and Brothers, 1961.
Woody, R. H. *Behavioral problem children in the schools.* New York: Appleton-Century-Crofts, 1969.

5.   DIMENSIONS OF THE CONSULTANT'S JOB[1]

Ronald Lippitt

Consultation, like supervision, or love, is a general label for many variations of relationship. The general definition of consultation used in this paper assumes that

1.   The consultation relationship is a voluntary relationship between
2.   a professional helper (consultant) and help-needing system (client)
3.   in which the consultant is attempting to give help to the client in the solving of some current or potential problem,
4.   and the relationship is perceived as temporary by both parties.
5.   Also, the consultant is an "outsider," i.e., is not a part of any hierarchical power system in which the client is located.

Some additional clarification of this condensed definition is needed. The client is conceived to be any functioning social unit, such as a family, industrial organization, individual, committee, staff, membership association, governmental department, delinquent gang, or hospital staff. The consultant is usually a professional helper, such as a marriage counselor, management consultant, community organizer, minister, social worker, human relations trainer, psychiatrist, applied anthropologist, group therapist, or social psychologist. The role of psychological "outsider" may sometimes be taken by a consultant located within the client system, such as a member of the personnel department.

Source. Ronald Lippitt "Dimensions of the Consultant's Job" *The Journal of Social Issues.* 1959, Vol. XV, 5–12. This article was the introductory article for a special issue of the *Journal*.
[1] Many of the ideas summarized in this paper are derived from my collaborations with Jeanne Watson and Bruce Westley as formulated in our joint publication *The Dynamics of Planned Change.*

This issue of the *Journal* does not consider consultation with the single individual as client. This relationship has been explored extensively in the literature on counseling and psychotherapy. The focus in this issue is on the group or larger social system as client.

One way of examining the role of the consultant is in terms of the series of questions or problems the consultant must pose for himself and work on during the course of a consulting relationship. Each of these questions can be viewed as a professional problem on which information is needed, about which theorizing must be done, action must be taken, and feedback must be sought by the consultant in order to get data about the consequences of the helping actions. The sequence of the questions formulated below does not represent any assumption that this is the orderly flow of questions and problems in the carrying through of a consultation relationship. Many of the questions are being worked on simultaneously at any one time, and the questions keep recurring as the process of consultation unfolds. But in order to formulate them as dimensions of a consultant's role we need to examine them one by one, rather than try to reproduce the multi-dimensional complexity of the consultant's job as he experiences it at any moment in time.

Question I: What seems to be the difficulty? Where does it come from? What's maintaining it?

Every consultant has a cluster of ideas, or a set of concepts, which guide his perception of "what exists" and "what is going on" when he comes in contact with a particular group or organization or other social unit. This cluster of ideas is his theory about the nature of groups and persons in groups and what makes them behave the way they do. For some consultants the theory may be largely inarticulate, and the concepts may not have much systematic refinement, or relationship to each other. Nevertheless the consultant must have some kind of theory in terms of which to select "what to see" and "how to understand it" when he views the complexities of group or organizational life. Other consultants approach their task with a relatively systematic framework of concepts such as psychoanalytic theory, structure-function theory, learning theory, social conflict theory, or role theory. Those without much theory have a harder time organizing and comprehending what they see. Those with a more systematic theory have a harder time noticing and interpreting important events which are not taken into account by the concepts of their theory.

In addition to having a systematic *descriptive-analytic theory*, the consultant must have a *diagnostic theory* which guides him in focusing on symptoms of pain or disruption in the system, on evidences that things are different from "normal" or "healthy." Usually a diagnostic theory includes both ideas about symptoms or clues that something is wrong, and conceptions about the basic causes of certain patterns of symptoms. In our study of a wide variety of consultants (Lippitt, Watson, and Westley, 1958) it seemed possible to delineate several typical diagnostic orientations such as:

1. An inappropriate distribution of power, too diffuse or too centralized.
2. Blockage and immobilization of productive energy.
3. Lack of communication between the subparts of the system.
4. A lack of correspondence between external reality and the situation as perceived by the client.
5. A lack of clarity or commitment to goals for action.
6. A lack of decision-making and action-taking skills.

These and other theories about "the source of trouble" provide the basis for selective probing to secure information from the client which will be used to interpret the nature of the difficulty and to make decisions about what type of helping should be tried. Also such a diagnostic theory helps to define the directions along which improvement is desired and expected, and therefore defines the symptoms of improvement which will be watched for in order to know whether there are desired consequences of the helping efforts.

Because these two frameworks of theory, systematic and diagnostic, play such a central role in the nature and quality of the performance of the consultant, it would seem particularly important for research to explore the use in practice of systematic theory, and the development of improved diagnostic theory. One of the most unexplored areas is that of the exact nature of the relationship between general systematic theory about groups and organizations and diagnostic theory about pathology of social systems.

Question II: What are my motives as a consultant for becoming involved in this helping relationship? What are the bases of my desire to promote change?

Being a *professional* helper implies responsibility for a high level of self-awareness about one's own values and needs as they may influence the helping relationship. Some critical observers of the American scene think we demonstrate the value that "any change is better than no change." Such a value would relieve both consultants and clients of a great deal of serious responsibility for goal setting, and would make it easy to label all resistance to change as bad. Clearly such a position is untenable. Another extreme position is sometimes taken which maintains that any planful efforts to stimulate change in others is *manipulative* and *undemocratic*. Very little significant work would get done in the world if this unrealistic conception prevailed. The observation of any meaningful social process indicates a picture of continuous efforts of people and groups to influence each other in the interest of various types of goals. The consultant must clarify for himself his own particular goals and motivations for influencing others. These questions of values are explored in Benne's contribution to this issue.

Even in the field of individual psychotherapy a large proportion of the individuals in need of help do not, for various reasons, take the initiative to seek help. Much attention is being given currently to ways of stimulating self-referral and other ways of getting help-needing individuals into contact with consultant resources. It is even harder for groups or organizations as total systems to clarify a need for help and to take initiative to seek help. And if one individual, or subgroup, from the potential client approaches a consultant asking for help, can this be considered as a request for help from the total system?

This initiative problem means that consultants who work with groups must be prepared to take active initiative to stimulate and develop helping relationships. This requires a thoughtful job of clarifying values involved in such "intervention" into the ongoing life of a group. Various consultants have formulated different bases for "the right to intervene" with attempts to give help.

1. Some consultants feel that a group situation is "calling for help" when there is evidence that the social processes of the group are causing individual suffering, such as rejection, isolation, scapegoating. Individual discomfort and frustration of group members is taken as a valid basis for the value judgment that "something needs to be done."
2. Other consultants tend to take a "group welfare" orientation and perceive a basis for intervention when there are symptoms that the group is suffering because of inefficiencies and inadequacies of its efforts to move toward its goals, such as low productivity, or failure of group efforts.
3. Other consultants may take an "institutional welfare" orientation and evaluate a group situation as warranting intervention if efforts of a group are causing disruption or "pain" for the larger organization or for neighboring groups, such as breakdown in one department of an organization, or disruption of the neighborhood life by a delinquent gang.

Many consultants whose reports have been reviewed do not present any explicit rationale for making active influence attempts.

In addition to the "justification for intervention" there is the question of "what goals for change." On the basis of his diagnostic observations does the consultant formulate goals for change in the client, or does he work only in terms of goals formulated by the client?

Some consultants feel they are justified in acting only in terms of goals which have been collaboratively formulated and accepted by both the client and the consultant. Other consultants feel they have a right to certain methodological goals, such as using good procedures for problem solving, but have no right to take positions on the answers to the problems (see the Benne discussion).

This aspect of the job of the group consultant has received very little critical exploration in the literature. There would seem to be need for active discussion and clarification of the various professional orientations.

Question III: What seem to be the present, or potential, motivations of the client toward change and against change?

The analysis of change forces and resistance forces is an important part of the initial assessment job for the consultant, and also a continuing challenge during all stages of the consulting relationship. A conceptual framework for analyzing these forces has been presented by Lewin (1947), by Coch and French (1948), and by Lippitt, Watson, and Westley (1958). Our comments here are limited to a few special aspects of the motivational situation in working with groups as clients.

In work with individuals feelings of pain and dissatisfaction with the present situation are most frequently the dominant driving forces for change, but in work with groups very often one of the most important motivations, or potential motivations, is a desire to improve group efficiency, to achieve some higher level of functioning, even though there may be no critical problems in the present situation. Therefore one of the consultant's jobs with groups is very frequently to help clarify "images of potentiality," rather than to focus on ways of alleviating present pain. Perhaps the most crucial aspect of motivational analysis in working with groups is the study of the nature and effects of the interdependence between the subparts (e.g., subgroups or departments) in the client system. An eagerness by one subgroup to change may not be a clue to readiness for change of other subgroups or of the total group or organization. Learning about the supporting and conflicting relationships between subgroups is a crucial task, and success in getting these facts will determine to a great degree whether the consultant is able to develop the necessary and appropriate relationship to the total group and to its various subparts. One of the most frequent forms of resistance to change in group clients is the perception by certain subgroups that the consultant is more closely related to other subgroups and is "on their side" in any conflict of interests.

Question IV: What are my resources, as a consultant, for giving the kind of help that seems to be needed now, or that may develop?

The requirements of time and skill needed to carry through a psychotherapeutic relationship with an individual have become fairly clear. Usually the situation is not so clear in working out a consultative relationship with a group or organization. Quite frequently a consultant relationship with a group is begun which will require much more time and a greater variety of helping skills than are available from the consultant. Two unfortunate things seem to happen more frequently in the consultation with social units than with individuals. Often the consultant offers diagnostic help and arrives at certain recommendations for improvement or change, but offers no continuity in the actual working through of the meaning of the diagnostic findings for changing procedures, practices, and interaction patterns. This dropping of the relationship with the client system at such an early stage in the process of changing often results in disruption and demoralization because of the inadequacy of the client-group to cope with the implications for change without further technical help from a consultant. As in the field of medicine, very frequently in the area of group consultation the consultant who has the analytic skills for diagnosis does not have the training and therapeutic skills required for a working through of the implications of the diagnosis. A consultant team would seem to be the creative solution in many cases.

Question V: What preliminary steps of action are needed to explore and establish a consulting relationship?

The paper by Glidewell in this issue explores in some detail the dynamics of forming a consultant attachment to a group. We would like to add three comments here about this dimension of the consultant's job.

As pointed out previously, groups as groups are much slower to develop and clarify an awareness of the need for help than are individuals. Therefore group consultants have a greater responsibility for developing techniques of helping the social system develop this awareness through appropriate communication procedures. This often requires taking an active initiative of a kind frowned on in the field of individual consultation. Examples of useful techniques are presented by Lippitt, Watson, and Westley (1958).

The defining of a "trial period" or pilot project as a basis for exploring a possible consulting relationship should also be emphasized. This provides an opportunity to establish relationships to all the different subgroups and to clarify expectations about a readiness to change and about the nature of the consultant's role.

The third problem which is typical at this stage is "getting trapped" into a special relationship with one of the subgroups which makes it difficult to move into a relationship with other subgroups and with the total client system. In initial contacts it is very difficult to know whether an administrator, for example, is speaking as a representative of the organization, as a representative of a small subgroup, or only for himself. The techniques of dual entry and multiple entry have been developed to meet this situation. Getting into contact with the whole client is one of the most challenging skill problems for the group consultant. In an organization or community this often means working closely with a group of representatives from all units to keep channels of communication open to all parts of the system.

Question VI: How do I as consultant guide, and adapt to, the different phases of the process of changing?

The consultant who works through the problems of changing with a group finds that there are several phases or stages to the process of working through, and that those phases require different levels of relationship and different kinds of helping skills. Starting from Lewin's (1947) three phase analysis, Lippitt, Watson, and Westley (1958) discovered in their comparative study of a population of consultants that seven phases could be identified with some degree of consistency. These were:

1. The development of a need for change.
2. The establishment of a consulting relationship.
3. The clarification of the client problem.
4. The examination of alternative solutions and goals.
5. The transformation of intentions into actual change efforts.
6. The generalization and stabilization of a new level of functioning or group structure.
7. Achieving a terminal relationship with the consultant and a continuity of change-ability.

These are very general labels for a great variety of activities, but do seem to help clarify some of the shifts of goal and changes of consulting activity that take place during the total cycle of a consulting relationship.

As the consultant works with a group on phase 4, the examination of alternative possibilities for improvement, it usually becomes clear that various types of special skill training will be needed to support the group's change efforts. This emphasizes the importance of Glidewell's distinction (in this issue) between the consultant and the consultant-trainer. It is our belief that most consulting relationships with groups require a consultant-trainer role to carry through an adequate job of problem solving. It is important for the consultant to clarify for himself the nature and the timing of this shift from the more non-directive role of helping a group develop and clarify its own goals for change to the more active directive role of helping the group learn the procedures and skills needed for them to move with efficiency and success toward the goals they have established.

It is an unhappy picture to see a group floundering and unsuccessful in their change efforts because the consultant has not been able to shift from the consultant role appropriate to the earlier phases of consultation to the more active training role which is usually necessary for the successful carrying through of the later phases of consultation.

Question VII: How do I help promote a continuity of creative change-ability?

A successful process of consultation with an organization or a group ends with at least three kinds of learnings:

1. The organization has learned to cope more adequately with the problem or problems which initiated the consulting process.
2. The organization has learned how to function more adequately in clarifying future problems as they emerge and to make appropriate decisions about seeking for outside help when needed.
3. The organization has learned new procedures and new types of organization to help it maintain a healthy state of changeability in adapting to changing conditions and in utilizing potentialities for creative improvement in group functioning and productivity. Perhaps the most challenging task for the consultant in this regard is to discover ways of training the group to use procedures of data collection and analysis on a continuing basis which will permit the identification of new problems and possibilities. In small face to face groups this may mean helping the group to develop functions of group observation and feedback as a continuing part of the group practice, without continuing dependency on the consultant. In larger organizations it may mean helping in the setting up of new staff functions of data collection, feedback, and skill training which will keep the organization tooled up to a continuous process of creative adaptation and social invention.

This is a very incomplete itemization of the dimensions of the consultant's job as explored in the several papers of this issue. We have tried to emphasize some of the dimensions which seem to represent a special challenge and need for exploration on the part of consultants working with organizations or groups as contrasted to those working with individuals as clients. Perhaps the greatest challenge is that of continuously exploring the relevance of systematic theory from the behavioral sciences, and finding opportunities for contributing to the body of theory through efforts to achieve a conceptual grasp of "what's going on" as we work at the job of giving help to groups in solving their problems of development and productivity. A basic integration of scientific theory and professional skills will be the continuing need as this field of social engineering develops.

References

Coch, Lester, & French, John R. P., Jr. Overcoming resistance to change. *Human Relations*, 1948, *1*, 512–532.

Lewin, Kurt. Frontiers in group dynamics. *Human Relations*, 1947, *1*, 5–41.

Lippitt, Ronald, Watson, Jeanne, & Westley, Bruce. *The Dynamics of Planned Change.* New York: Harcourt, Brace, 1958.

6. TOWARD A PSYCHOLOGY OF CHANGE AND INNOVATION [1]

·•·

Seymour B. Sarason

There is an increasing number of psychologists who are interested in how organizations or social systems work and change. One of the factors in this development is the realization that all psychologists, like the rest of humanity, are affected by the different social systems of which they may be a part. This realization is frequently not due to considerations of theory or training but an awareness forced on one by virtue of day-to-day living. I suppose it is possible for a psychologist to live his days unaware that his thinking, teaching, practices, and relationships (personal or professional) bear in some way the stamp of his past and present immersion in what may be termed organizations or social systems. It is possible, and it may even be that such a person is involved as a psychologist with problems upon which this unawareness has no particular effect. Such a psychologist would likely be a researcher who at the same time that he views his research as unaffected by the workings of social systems—such as the particular department or university of which he is a member—can usually talk loud and long about how the conduct of his research has in some measure been affected by grant-giving agencies which are, after all, organizations or social systems. There are probably no important facets of a psychologist's existence which do not reflect the influence of his relationship to one or another type of organization.

I have not made the above comments because I happen to think that

Source. Seymour Sarason, "Toward a Psychology of Change and Innovation," *American Psychologist*, Vol. 22–3, 1967, 227–233. Copyright 1967 by the American Psychological Association, and reproduced by permission.

[1] Psi Chi (National Honor Society in Psychology) invited address at American Psychological Association, New York, September 1966.

psychologists should have a keen sensitivity to the world in which they live. That would be as presumptuous as it would be ineffective. My comments were by saying that as psychological theorists move in the direction of stating comprehensive formulations about the determinants of human behavior they will become increasingly concerned with the nature of social organizations, the ways in which they change, and the consequences of these changes. This development will not be a matter of choice but rather of necessity in that in reality the relationship between the individual and "organized settings" is not a matter of choice. The problem for theory is how to go beyond token gestures to these relationships, how to study and understand the extent of variations in these relationships, and how to begin to formulate generalizations which do justice to the complexities involved.[2]

Several years ago a number of colleagues and myself became interested in the processes of change in a certain social system. In the course of studying this system we became aware, as might have been predicted, how complex the processes of change were to understand and how little there was in psychological theory and practice to guide us. The complexity of the problem would have been more tolerable were it not for the fact that we had no conceptual framework which could serve, however tentatively, as a basis for thinking, planning, and action. It has been said that there is

---

[2] It is important to note that the problem which I am stating generally is one quite familiar to the industrial psychologist, as Stagner (1966) has made clear. "Industrial psychology has since its inception dealt with problems of man in an organization, but in its early stages gave consideration only to part of the man, and took the organization for granted. . . . Decided changes began to appear after 1950. . . . Only within the past ten years, however, has this transformation of industrial psychology been completed. People like Haire and Simon began to write about the total organization as a network of human interactions; Likert and McGregor applied new ideas of psychodynamics to the managerial role. The Survey Research Center and other research institutes began to pile up empirical evidence for the reciprocal effects of organizations and individuals.

"A look at a clutch of recent books dealing with the behavior of human beings in industrial organizations confirms my feeling that industrial psychology is no longer the step-child of theoretical and research efforts. Instead there is a good deal of sophisticated work in both theory and data-gathering. Undoubtedly some industrial psychologists of what we may call 'the old school' will protest that this new baby is no legitimate offspring of their specialty. Certainly its parentage is in doubt. Social psychology, sociology, and anthropology have made important genetic contributions; even a few psychoanalytic genes seem to have been incorporated. I would hold, nevertheless, that this new growth is truly industrial psychology, in the sense that it represents the best application of theoretical and empirical psychology to the understanding of human behavior in industrial settings." It is my point that the need for, and the problems involved in, conceptualizing comprehensively man-system relationships is not a necessity for one kind of psychologist (e.g., school, industrial, etc.) but for any psychologist concerned with human behavior.

nothing more practical than a good theory. There are times when we would have settled for the illusory comfort of a bad theory. In any event, what follows in this paper is no more than a variety of thoughts which may serve only to convince others that the problem is important and requires thoughts better than our own.

THE PSYCHO-EDUCATIONAL CLINIC

Several years ago a Psycho-Educational Clinic was started at Yale as an integral part of our clinical training program. The origins, purposes and activities of the Clinic have been described in detail elsewhere (Sarason, Levine, Goldenberg, Cherlin, & Bennett, 1966). For the present paper it is necessary to state very briefly two of the purposes which have increasingly become the focus of our interest and concern. The first of these purposes is to describe and understand the educational setting as a social system, i.e., to view and study this setting as a subculture possessing a distinctive pattern of traditions, dynamics, and goals (Sarason, 1966). We are quite aware that this is a task far beyond the capacities of any single group of investigators. We are acutely aware that it is a task which involves almost every important problem and field in psychology. The complexity of the task in part reflects the fact that in the educational setting these problems have to be conceptualized in a way which erases artificial or arbitrary distinctions (e.g., learning, social psychology, clinical psychology, child development, etc.) and which truly reflects actual relationships. For example, it apparently (but inexplicably) makes sense to some people to talk of "curriculum" independent of who teaches it, why he teaches it, to whom he teaches it, his conceptions of children and the nature of learning, and whether or not he has had any voice in its selection or is given the freedom to depart from it. Elsewhere (Sarason, 1966) I have illustrated and discussed this problem in relation to the "new math," emphasizing the point that how a curriculum is introduced to (and even foisted upon) teachers affects children, teachers, supervisors, and the "curriculum." What I am saying is obvious to any thinking graduate student, i.e., any graduate course is a function not only of the formal curriculum for that course and the particular instructor but also of the particular department, relationships within it, and characteristics of the particular university.

The second purpose which I must briefly discuss is that we are interested in two kinds of change: that which is introduced and executed by those indigenous to the school, and that which represents primarily forces outside the social system we call a school. We know far more about the latter than the former kind of change and this is symptomatic not only of our lack of knowledge about what goes on in a school but also of the implicit assumption that it is a static and not particularly complicated kind of setting. There are many people, including most psychologists who should know better, who view the school as they do (or would) a so-called primitive society, i.e., life in it is simple, the people in it relatively uncomplicated and easy to understand, and the surface appearance of order and purpose can be taken pretty much at face value. There are times when those of us at the Psycho-Educational Clinic wish that such a view of the school setting could indeed be justified because the more we have gotten into the problem the more impressed we have become with its complexity. We sometimes look back nostalgically at the days when we could think of studying the school in terms of what seemed to be discrete problems such as learning, socialization, intellectual development, the process of teaching, the formal curriculum, and the like. This is not to say that one cannot study these discrete problems in a profitable way, but one runs the risk of becoming a prisoner of one's limited theories and methodologies. It is not always made clear that theories—containing as they do a defined but limited set of variables and their presumed relationships—constrict one's scope at the same time that they expand it. Nowhere is this more true than in the literature on the school setting.

But the school is only one of several settings in which we have been able to observe processes of change. In relation to all these settings we have also been in the role of "advice givers," a role which illuminates not only the processes of change as they are reflected in the "advice seeker" but in the advice giver as well. The remainder of this paper contains observations and thoughts about processes of change as we have seen them in the role of observer and advice giver.

CHANGE AND IMPLEMENTATION

Some of the most interesting and important aspects of the processes of change are revealed before the point of implementation of proposals for change. The importance of these aspects resides not only in how they affect implementation *but in the degree to which they result in no implementation at all.* It is not enough for the person interested in processes of change in various types of organizations or social systems to focus on ongoing or planned changes, although there is no question that such a focus can be a productive one. It is my contention, however, that an equally important part of the problem is the frequency of, and the contexts which surround, proposals for change which either do not get a hearing or never reach the stage of implementation. I have no doubt that these instances are far more frequent than those which reach the stage of implementation. Organizations—such as a university department, a professional school, a social agency—vary tremendously among and between themselves in the degree to which proposals and ideas for change never reach the stage of discussion or implementation.

In recent months I have taken to asking members of various types of organizations what their estimate was of the relationship between proposals made and proposals implemented. The most frequent response was embarrassed silence. In some instances the embarrassment stemmed from the feeling that the question touched on something which, if pursued, would be quite revealing of that organization, and the revelation would not be very pleasant. In other instances the embarrassment was a consequence of the realization that the individual had never been aware of what was implied in the question, although I tried to ask the question without stating what I thought its implications were.

The significance of the question I have been putting to individuals may be gleaned in the following opinion: the greater the discrepancy between the frequency of proposals for change which are never implemented, and the number of proposals which are implemented, the more likely that the implemented changes over time will increasingly lose whatever innovative characteristics they may have had or were intended. In other words, the more things change on the surface the more conditions remain basically the same.

The basis for this opinion brings us back to one of the major interests of the Psycho-Educational Clinic, i.e., the culture of the school and the processes of change. It has been in relation to our work in various school systems that we have become acutely aware of how implemented changes quickly lose their innovative intent.[3] Elsewhere (Sarason, 1966) I have indicated that one of the major reasons for this self-defeating process is the tendency for change proposals to emanate from on high without taking into account the feelings and opinions of those who must implement the changes, i.e., the teachers. What I emphasized was the interpersonal turmoil which such tendencies engender and its effect on the content and goals of change. My comments, however, were in relation to the history and consequences of a single proposal for change (e.g., new math, bussing, etc.) and neglected what I now think is the more general characteristic of the system: the marked discrepancy between the number of proposals to change the system and the number of proposals actually implemented. Put in another way: The fate of any single proposal for change will be determined in part by the number of changes which have been proposed but never implemented. If this is true, my observations suggest that it is because

---

[3] A colleague, Albert Myers, has well characterized urban school systems as the "fastest changing status quos."

those who have to implement any single proposal for change react to it in terms of their knowledge of and experiences with other proposals (implemented or not) for change in the system. If they are aware, rightly or wrongly, that there is a discrepancy between proposals made and implemented, and particularly if this awareness is associated with feelings of dissatisfaction, it often affects the implementation of the single proposal for change in a way so as to fulfill the prophecy that the more things change the more they remain the same. The fate of a single proposal for change cannot be understood apart from all other proposals for change if only because those who do the implementing do not understand or react to it in that way—and any theory of change and innovation must face this inescapable fact.

The above observations and formulations stemmed in part from repeated experiences in the role of advice giver in relation to personnel in the school system. More candidly, they stemmed from a variety of frustrating and failure experiences in which, as I look back over them, I underestimated how much of an advice seeker's behavior reflected the system of which he was a part. I could, of course, be criticized as naïve. The point is that my naïveté reflects well the naïveté of psychological theories (e.g., learning, psychoanalytic) which do not face the fact that individual behavior always takes place in the contexts of organizations or social systems. I am not maintaining that social systems "cause" behavior. I am only maintaining that any theory which purports to explain behavior and which does not come to grips with man-system relationships is a naïve, incomplete, and mischief-producing theory.

THE ADVICE SEEKER AND ADVICE GIVER

The behavior of advice givers, like that of advice seekers, reflect man-system relationships. With increasing frequency, in ours as well as other societies, the advice giver is outside the system of the advice seeker, a fact which can markedly influence change and innovation. Put in its most concrete form the question which I would like to raise is: If somebody is interested in studying a social system (e.g., a school, a company, police department, etc.) with the intent of devising ways of changing it in some ways, and that somebody comes to you for advice and guidance, how would you go about deciding how to respond? Let us assume that you are relatively unfamiliar with the particular setting the individual wishes to study and ultimately change in some large or small way. This assumption provides an easy out for many people who feel uncomfortable thinking about problems with which they are not familiar. It may well be that these are the kinds of people who discourage students and others from getting into unfamiliar territory. I do not intend this as an *argumentum ad hominem* but as a way of stating that an unfamiliar problem—be it unfamiliar to a single advice giver or to the field at large—tends to engender reactions which serve to change the problem or to discourage the advice seeker. It is not all necessary for the unfamiliar to be threatening in some personal way to the establishment. It is often sufficient that the proposal be unfamiliar, i.e., not capable of being assimilated by prevailing attitudes toward "important" problems.

Am I straying from the question by focusing initially on the response of an individual advice giver or field to an unfamiliar problem? There are at least two reasons why I do not think I have strayed. The first reason is that the fate of any proposal for change is not unrelated to the prevailing attitudes of the field to which the advice giver belongs. Although these attitudes may not always be decisive—the situation is much too complicated to permit one to focus exclusively on a single source or variable—they can or do play a role well before the time when the proposal for change reaches the point of implementation. It needs hardly to be pointed out that these prevailing attitudes can abort the proposed change even though the change involves a setting different from that in which the prevailing attitudes are found. The second reason I do not think I have strayed from the original question is, I think, less of a glimpse of the obvious than is the first reason. The relationship between the advice seeker, on the one hand, and the advice giver or field, on the other hand, is frequently identical to the relationship between the advice seeker and the setting which is the object of change. The point here is that a proposal for change far more often than not encounters an obstacle course and its ultimate fate, by whatever criteria this may be judged, must be viewed in terms of how the proposal changed as a function of each hurdle. We are far more aware of what happens once a proposal reaches the stage of implementation than we are of what happens to the proposed change (and changer) before that stage. A psychology of change and innovation cannot neglect these preimplementation events which, in my experience, frequently have the effect of insuring that changes will take place in a way so as to preclude innovation.

AN ILLUSTRATIVE CASE

A number of years ago in New Haven an organization was started the major aim of which was to develop programs and services for the inner city or poverty population. The name of this organization is Community Progress Inc. (CPI). Anyone familiar with community action programs is well aware that CPI was one of the first of such programs and is regarded as one of the, if not *the*, most successful and comprehensive of these ventures. CPI antedates many of the Federal programs and, in fact, a number of Federal programs are modeled on what CPI has done. In our recent book (Sarason et al., 1966) we described two of CPI's most pioneering and intriguing programs and the relationship of our clinic to these programs. One of these programs is the Neighborhood Employment Center and the other is the Work Crew Program for school dropouts. Most of the employees in these programs are nonprofessional personnel who are indigenous to the area and the population served. With very few exceptions no employee had previous experience in or training for the job he was doing. It is obviously impossible for me here to describe in any detail the nature of and rationale for these programs. Suffice it to say that the titles "Neighborhood Employment Center" and "Work Crew Programs" are distressingly ineffective in communicating the seriousness, variety, and complexity of the human problems which these programs encounter, cope with, and effectively handle. By "effectively handle" we mean that there is no reason to believe that the rate of success is any less than that in more traditional helping agencies. Our opinion is that when one takes into account the nature of the population served, the rate of success is somewhat short of amazing. It sometimes has offended some of our colleagues in the mental health professions when we have said that these two programs are truly mental health programs. But how can you call them mental health programs if they do not employ psychiatrists, clinical psychologists, and social workers? The obstacles to change or innovation—both in thinking and action—are many, and words and categorical thinking will be found high on the list.

How did these programs, reflecting as they do change and innovation, come about? Before answering this question I must tell you two things about CPI. First, the mental health professions had nothing to do with the beginnings of CPI. It would be near correct to say that CPI was begun and developed by a small group of individuals who had no previous formal training to do what they subsequently did. The second fact I must tell you is that today, a few years after CPI's existence, there is not a single mental health agency in New Haven whose thinking and practices have not been changed by what CPI has developed. This is not to say that these agencies have changed in a fundamental way but rather that to a limited extent they have adapted their way of thinking to new problems and new settings. This is not true for the Psycho-Educational Clinic and I hope it will not be taken as an expression of arrogance or presumption when I say that as in the case of those at CPI we at the Clinic are involved in problems and settings in ways which represent a deliberate break with our own pasts and professional training—as a result of which we have become quite knowledgeable about the interactions among the unfamiliar, anxiety, and resistances to change in self and others. I must add that the consequences of resistance are much less lethal to change, by which I mean here engaging in an activity one has not done before, than they are to innovation by which I mean sustaining the spirit or intent of change so that one recognizes that one has unlearned part of one's past and that the direction of one's future has thereby been influenced.

Now let us return to the original question via a fantasy I have sometimes had. Reformulated, the question is: what if CPI, as an advice seeker, came to me as an advice giver to respond to their initial plans to develop programs and services for the school dropouts and poverty population? In point of fact CPI did circulate a document containing a general statement of its aims in relation to its view of the problems with which it was to deal. This document was sent to me and I confess that I saw a lot in there that I considered presumptuous, if not grandiose, particularly in light of the fact that a program in "human renewal" was going to be attempted by people possessing no particular expertise in the dynamics of human behavior and the ways in which one goes about helping problem people. The fantasy I have had centers around the situation in which CPI learns that I think what they are planning to do is probably for the birds and that I was not prepared to give them my blessings. (In reality, of course, nobody was asking for my blessings or anything else I had to give them.) CPI comes running to my door and says, "O.K., you don't like what we want to do. You don't like the way we are thinking about the problems. What would *you* do?" That would have been the polite way they would phrase the question. The more legitimate way of phrasing the question—and fantasy is not noted for its close relation to reality—would have been: "What do you or your mental health colleagues who have not been involved with the poverty population have to suggest to us?" It is not important to relate in detail what I would have told them. Suffice it to say that what I would have recommended would have been an instance of translating an unfamiliar problem into familiar terms. I would have told them about clinics, diagnostic and treatment services, mental health professionals, and research and evaluation. The result, of course, would have been quite different from what they intended and subsequently implemented. Had they taken my advice some innovative programs which have had a pervasive and sustained effect around the country would have been scuttled, to the detriment of the populations served *and* the mental health fields.

SOME CONCLUDING COMMENTS

Social systems, large or small, are fantastically complicated. To describe and understand a single school, let alone a school system, presents staggering problems for methodology and theory. What I have attempted to do in this paper is to suggest that the complexity of these systems as well as some of their distinctive characteristics become quite clear as one focuses on how these systems change over time, particularly in relation to innovations which are sustained, or aborted, or in one or another way defeating of the aims of change. Perhaps the major import of this view is that at the same time that it illuminates features of the system it also makes clear how understanding of the behavior of the individual requires, in fact demands, conceptualization of man-system relationships. This is as true for the individual we call a psychologist as it is for anyone else. I tried to illustrate the point by focusing on the psychologist in the role of advice giver not only because the psychologist is so frequently related to processes of change in individuals or groups but because he so often is the contact point between different social systems or organizations, i.e., he illustrates the fact that processes of change frequently (if not always) involve interacting systems. An additional factor in focusing on the psychologist is that it is too easy to overlook that whatever conceptualizations we develop will have to be as relevant for psychology and psychologists as for any individual in any other social system.

At the beginning of this paper I ventured the opinion that there are probably no important facets of a psychologist's existence which do not reflect the influence of his relationship to one or another type of organization. I would at this point venture the additional hypothesis that there is not a single psychologist who has not at some time or another been involved in initiating or administering proposals for change in some organization. Whatever his role, I would predict that if we ever studied the psychologist in relation to processes of change in various types of organizations we would be impressed by two findings. First, psychologists are as good as anybody else in initiating change and as bad as everybody else in sustaining it in a way such that "the more things change the more they remain the same." Second, in relation to these changes the behavior of most psychologists will be found to be remarkably uninfluenced by knowledge of or concern for relationships between change and innovation, on the one hand, and complexity of social systems, on the other.

The distinction between processes of change and innovation as they occur in organized settings is fundamental to understanding how these settings work. It is a distinction which has profitably occupied the thinking of those interested in child development, e.g., the concept of stages implies a distinction between change and innovation. As this distinction is applied to the most important social systems with which we are or have been related, our understanding of these systems *and* the individuals in it will take on an innovative characteristic. I have no doubt that this will be particularly true in the case of the social system we call a school.

The last point brings me, finally, to a consideration to which I have only alluded earlier in this paper. One can characterize our society as one in which massive and deliberate attempts are being made to change aspects of the nature of groups, settings, and regions within as well as beyond our society. The schools, the Negro, the poverty population, Appalachia, the public mental hospital—these are only some of the more important objects of change. Being, as most of us are, for virtue and against sin we applaud and support these programs for change. We know something is being done because billions are being spent. For what it is worth, it is my opinion, based on some extensive observations, that much is being done but little of it in a way calculated to bring about changes which sustain the intent to innovate. I do not say this in the spirit of criticism, but rather as a way of suggesting that, among many reasons, two of them are: the absence of a psychology of change and innovation, and the tendency within psychology to develop molecular theories about molecular-sized problems. In relation to the latter reason it is necessary to state that however necessary it may be at times to restrict the scope of theorizing by grasping a part of the problem and sticking with it, there is the distinct danger that over time the part unwittingly becomes the whole of the problem.

References

Sarason, S. B. The culture of the school and processes of change. Brechbill Lecture, University of Maryland School of Education, January 1966.

Sarason, S. B., Levine, M., Goldenberg, I. I., Cherlin, D., & Bennett, E. *Psychology in community settings: Clinical, educational, vocational, social aspects.* New York: Wiley, 1966.

Stagner, R. Book review. *Contemporary Psychology*, 1966, *11*, 145–150.

Consulting with the System

The consultant understands and works with the social systems composed of the school, home, and community. He is an agent or architect of change and not an institutional agent (Kehas and Morris, 1971; Warnath, 1973). The consultant has as a major concern the well-being of people rather than things, and he acts to facilitate humaneness rather than the preservation of the institution. Research in pupil personnel work has not consistently nor conclusively supported current practices. This perhaps is because we have been remiss in intervening with the major source of dysfunction. As Sarason (1972), Satir (1972), Silberman (1970), and others have repeatedly pointed out, our clients are the "victims" of their environmental milieu. They have reached their current state as a result of interacting with or responding to their dysfunctional environment. Yet, in most cases, we have advocated and worked directly with the individual client instead of the milieu. It would seem that we have been involved with the symptom and not the source.

The writers in this section have developed alternative ways to establish comprehensive programs that encapsulate all aspects of an individual's world. The initial thrust of each paper is to help the reader look at his or her world in a different fashion. The authors are primarily concerned with the gestalt or whole and are secondarily interested in an analysis of the elements. The focus is on helping to create a humane, well functioning organization. This sometimes involves doing nothing and allowing a system to destroy itself rather than keeping a damaging or injurious system alive. Other procedures such as "judo," which involves using an organization's strength to defeat its purposes can be found in Postman and Weingartner's (1969) **The Soft Revolution.**

The consultant operates as a systems analyst (Blocher, Dustin, and Dugan, 1971). He has clear-cut goals as to what type of a system is desired and works to insure its creation and subsequent maintenance. He has developed a hierarchy and set of priorities for his or her strategies of change.

Dahl describes a myriad of institutional policies that prevent humaneness from prevailing. The necessity of **directly** dealing with pathological systems is fundamental to her position. She concludes her presentation by challenging pupil personnel workers to become solutions to the problem rather than parts of it.

Blocher discusses the role of the consultant as a change agent with the central theme being to treat the society as patient. He posits a goal of creating a developmental milieu that understands and supports developing individuals. He devotes much attention to the changes counselors must make to function in this capacity.

Aubrey emphasizes the necessity of attaining power to influence school policy makers. He presents a rationale, procedures, and examples that can be used by the consultant to establish power bases. He believes that if consultants do not establish power bases or sources of strength, they will sacrifice their jobs.

Blocher and Rapoza present a very specific ecological approach to organizational change. They have developed a systematic, step-by-step process that may be used with a variety of populations (e.g., single individuals, families, social organizations, and classrooms). The broad applicability of this approach is evidenced in the examples that supplement their presentation.

Murray and Schmuck postulate a radical role change for the school pupil personnel specialist. They contend that the consultant **must** become actively involved with the organizational process and development of the school and community. The consultant then visualizes a student's emotional problems as primarily the result of his response to his human (or inhuman) environment. They identify different approaches to bringing about organizational change and provide an outline of the stages necessary as well as examples that show the process applied.

As you read these articles consider the following:

● Is the consultant primarily interested in institutions or individuals?
● Identify **specific** methods of working with the "community."
● What are the results or effects of clients being integrated into an environment that is alien to them?
● Blocher feels that "boat rockers" or activists are often not viewed as helping people. Dahl, on the other hand, believes that consultants must be activists. What do you think? How can you incorporate activist principles into the consultant role?
● Discuss the inhumane occurrences that are happening in your school and community. What are some procedures that you could use to revitalize your school and community? What have you already done?
● What are the similarities between Dahl's "bridges," Blocher's "developmental milieu," Murray and Schmuck's "organizational development," and Aubrey's "power bases?"

● All of the articles in this section seem to place the consultant in the role of a catalyst or architect of change. Does a catalyst get directly involved with the change process? If your answer is yes, how does the consultant keep the system from becoming dependent on him? If your answer is no, how does the consultant initiate change?

REFERENCES

Blocher, D. H., Dustin, E. R., Dugan, W. E. **Guidance systems.** New York: Ronald Press, 1971.

Kehas, C. D., and Morris, J. L. "Perceptions in role change from teacher to counselor: intra-role conflict and motivation for change." **Counselor Education and Supervision,** 1971, **10,** 200–208.

Postman, N., and Weingartner, C. **The soft revolution.** New York: Delta, 1971.

Sarason, S. B. **The creation of settings and the future societies.** San Francisco: Jossey-Bass, 1972.

Satir, V. **People-making.** Palo Alto, CA: Science and Behavior Books, 1972.

Silberman, C. B. **Crisis in the classroom.** New York: Random House, 1970.

Warnath, C. F. "The school counselor as institutional agent." **The School Counselor,** 1973, **20** (3), 202–208.

7. POWER BASES: THE CONSULTANT'S VEHICLE FOR CHANGE

Roger F. Aubrey

The desires and aspirations of many elementary school counselors are constantly thwarted by many nonnegotiable factors within the educational system. These nonnegotiable factors are institutional constraints which have been ingrained and long-established by custom and tradition, e.g., the ultimate authority of the principal in instructional and noninstructional matters, the inviolate sovereignty of the teacher in his classroom, the rigid time schedule in schools, the inflexible methods in the grouping of children, the uniform expectations for boys and girls, the premium placed on docility and conformity, and so on. In the course of time, they become sanctioned and therefore present themselves to counselors as routine procedures, structural patterns, organizational practices, hierarchical processes, and conventional observances. Collectively, these school heirlooms represent tremendous impediments to counselors wishing to innovate programs and practices for children. Without power, a viable means of influencing the school policy makers, counselors have little or no chance of effecting changes for children.

In dealing with the established system in schools, elementary counselors face three immediate and serious obstacles. First, the functions of elementary counselors are frequently determined in advance by individuals outside the guidance and counseling profession, e.g., teachers and administrators. Second, many elementary counselors are powerless to implement new programs and practices without the consent and approval of numerous audiences, e.g., parents, teachers, school boards, and administrators. Third, counselors' initial access to children for any purpose is restricted by a physical separation of child and counselor, classroom and counseling office. As a consequence of these factors, the role and work of the elementary counselor is often prescribed in advance and narrowly limited to a relatively small number of options. Counselors lack leverage and credibility from

Source. Roger F. Aubrey, "Power Bases: The Consultant's Vehicle for Change" *Elementary School Guidance and Counseling*, 1972, Vol. 7–2, 90–97. Copyright 1972 by the American Personnel and Guidance Association and reproduced by permission.

the first moment they enter an elementary school. To date, counselors have been impotent in developing vigorous constituencies to assist them in their programs for children.

This article is primarily concerned with how elementary counselors develop constituencies and power bases to support programs, practices, and innovative changes in schools. More specifically, the core of this article is to help the counselor build support bodies among parents and teachers. This support is viewed as the key factor in unlocking closed doors and in endeavors calculated to offset institutional inflexibility and rigidity. Other audiences in addition to parents and teachers are potential power bases for counselors. These might include school boards, school administrators, local civic groups, and even students themselves.

WHY POWER BASES?

The need for the elementary counselor to build audiences of parents and teachers into power bases may appear self-evident. It obviously makes a great deal of sense to have the enthusiastic support of these groups. Additionally, parents and teachers represent two of the most powerful environmental factors in the development of youngsters. By directly affecting the attitudes and behaviors of these groups, the elementary counselor–consultant indirectly exerts tremendous influence over the major environmental figures in the lives of children.

The main reason for soliciting the support of parents and teachers is simple. Together they are a powerful and influential voice in "bucking the system" and confronting timid (or tyrannical) administrators and school boards. The need for creating strong and organized lobbying groups has long been ignored by educators because of political implications. However, no force is quite so potent as a series of parent phone calls to principals, superintendents, and school board members. There is nothing quite so unnerving as a combined group of parents and teachers packing a school committee room and demanding action. Finally, there is nothing so unsettling to establishment personnel as the thought of hundreds of irate voters on election day. Harnessing this support for guidance programs is long overdue among members of our profession. If we are to have a voice in educational policy matters, especially in those areas related to psychological well-being, it behooves counselors to establish supportive constituencies among many audiences.

POWER FOR WHAT?

If the elementary counselor is successful in building a power base among teachers and/or parents, to what use does the counselor put this power?

What is it within the system that can be changed only through the strong and vigorous backing of parents and teachers? Can't the counselor work within the existing system to obtain guidance objectives? Won't these power bases threaten and antagonize school administrators?

The answers to these questions can be discovered in large part by an examination of two phenomena. First, the counselor–consultant is an educational maverick, a newcomer to the school without portfolio or testimonials. As such, the counselor may choose to gradually gain confidences and eventualy suggest minor modifications in policies and practices. This route is slow and laborious and forces the conselor to enter the school, hat in hand, hoping someone will recognize his talents. As a newcomer the counselor must prove his worth while not rocking the boat.

The second phenomenon affecting the counselor–consultant relates to power and role. Like the principal, the counselor has a longitudinal view of the total educational process and its impact on students. Like the principal, the counselor assumes responsibility for the well-being of all students in a given building. Like the principal, the counselor interrelates with all faculty in a given building. Unlike the principal, the counselor does not possess authority to instigate immediate changes when needed. The power of the counselor to effect change does not reside in delegated authority; rather, the counselor's power stems from persuasion and acquired supportive audiences.

The dilemma facing all counselors stems from the ambiguous posture of any full-time school personnel classified as neither teacher nor administrator. Without a classroom of students or an office conferred with authority, how does one intervene for students with maximum impact? Must one always cajole, persuade, and convince the stubborn and skeptical? Cannot the counselor build systematic and ongoing support groups to aid in the initiation of constructive changes and modifications in schools?

Power therefore should not be sought for its own sake. The acquisition or creation of power bases among parents and teachers is merely a necessary step in launching new thrusts within the educational system. Power for the elementary counselor is a means of counteracting the forces of timidity and orthodoxy rampant in any long-established institution. Power is the key to unlocking closed doors and allowing innovation, vigor, and vitality into the musty corridors of education.

MAXIMIZING POWER BASES

The ideal type of power base involves a combination of parents and teachers. The alliance of these groups neutralizes any possible future antagonism and assures the counselor that home and school influences converge on shared objectives. The elementary counselor must develop a program broad and inclusive enough to accommodate the interests of both groups. Teachers and parents must be sold on the worth of the proposed program and feel their contribution to its success is essential. Their active involvement in planning such a program is as important as their contribution in implementing the program.

In some cases, the elementary counselor may wish to work with only one power group. Quite frequently this occurs with his teaching colleagues, but it may also involve a parent or community group. It is therefore critical when working with just one power base to remember not to antagonize another potential power group. Counselors cannot afford to build strong support among parents if this threatens teachers and hampers everyday relationships in the school. By the same token, elementary counselors cannot ally themselves totally with teachers if this results in further distance from parents and community.

The simplest and most effective manner of maximizing power bases is the construction of ongoing programs involving one or more influential groups. An example would be a joint committee investigating open classrooms or a training program for parents to become paraprofessionals. Parents and teachers, under the leadership of the counselor, could also work cooperatively for programs in learning disabilities, human development training, and so on. Once these programs are accepted and operationalized they become established practices and therefore legitimatize the program within the system. The system therefore absorbs the program, but in so doing has to make adjustments and accommodations. These accommodations allow the elementary counselor a foothold and wedge for further innovations by loosening the educational structure and allowing fresh and novel approaches into the schools.

ESTABLISHING POWER BASES

An example at this point might clarify the intention and purpose of power bases. We will examine a recent program in an actual school system and the multiple advantages of building power bases for elementary guidance into the school structure. To appreciate the scope of this program, consider the following questions that faced the elementary counselors in this system:

1. How can the counseling staff develop an early identification system to detect emotional problems, learning disabilities, developmental deficiencies, and medical concerns as early as possible in the child's school history?

2. How can the elementary counselor play a role in the assignment and grouping of kindergarten children to maximize this first school experience?
3. How can the elementary counselor develop a child study group involving mothers of kindergarten children on a weekly basis?
4. How can the elementary counselor maximize involvement and participation with primary grade teachers?
5. How can the elementary counselor cope with principals who wish the bulk of the counselor's time spent with older children with severe problems or crisis situations?

All were legitimate issues in need of resolution. Each would involve staff members in seemingly different directions. Each would require inordinate amounts of time and energy. Each would require support and assistance from numerous groups and individuals outside the area of elementary guidance. All would at some point demand the support or acquiescence of the school administration. The guidance staff was in need of strong support from collective groups of teachers and parents in order to successfully resolve these issues.

Through weekly meetings, the counselors in this school system eventually recognized a number of similarities in their desires for improvement throughout the system. These commonalities included:

1. A current lack of program support from any segment of the school or community
2. A desire for a major focus on preventive intervention measures
3. A central emphasis on the child's total environment, especially those aspects monitored by teachers and mothers
4. A need to develop credibility and intimacy with teachers
5. Greater influence on administrative decisions involving primary grade children

VEHICLES FOR CHANGE

By discovering their mutual interests and concerns, the elementary counselors also developed a plan inclusive enough to achieve most of their objectives. Their immediate weakness appeared to be a lack of support and communication with teachers and parents. The plan began with a meeting of kindergarten teachers, school psychologists, elementary counselors, and school health personnel. The purpose of the meeting was to draw up a confidential questionnaire to be administered by counselors to all kindergarten mothers in the spring preceding their child's entrance to kindergarten. Ostensibly, the purpose of the questionnaire was to gather sensitive and delicate information for the kindergarten teacher to provide for special needs in the fall of the year.

Once the kindergarten teachers were involved with committees led by counselors, the preparation of a kindergarten questionnaire took on a new light. The preparation required considerable exchange between counselors and teachers and allowed both parties an opportunity to share values and ideas. The questionnaire provided a safe target for views on parents, guidance, children, and early education.

As the questionnaire took shape, the counselors and teachers as a group approached building principals and requested time during April registration for an announcement to parents. This announcement asked fall kindergarten mothers to make appointments with elementary counselors during the months of April through June for a private interview. Parents were told that the interview was to explain the resources of the school and to gather data on their children for placement purposes.

The interviews with mothers ranged from 30 to 45 minutes. During this period of time the mothers were administered a questionnaire.

The use of this questionnaire opened many doors and allowed counselors a new entree to parents and teachers. The spin-offs and ripple effects of this easy device resulted in the attainment of the following objectives:

1. An assessment instrument for obtaining sensitive and vital information about the early developmental history and life style of a student prior to formal entrance to school
2. Data and information on medical and psychological factors allowing better placement, grouping, and special services for new students
3. Closer relationships between counselors and kindergarten teachers, and an immediate access to children and teachers in the fall of the year through the use of material uncovered in the questionnaire
4. A legitimate means of meeting new mothers in an intimate setting to inform them of school and community resources and the function of the counselor
5. A vehicle for recruiting mothers into a once-a-week child study seminar, chaired by the counselor, in the fall of the year

Obviously, one simple questionnaire did not actually accomplish all these aims. Nonetheless, the questionnaire did legitimate the counselor's accessibility to teachers, parents, and children. The questionnaire presented a safe means of counselor–teacher—counselor–parent interaction on issues of vital concern to children. The questionnaire also enabled the counselor to deal with the school administrator through the utilization of a valid instrument for gathering school information. However, in the process of obtaining this information the counselor was able to secure power bases and confidence among teachers and parents. Once these power bases have been obtained, counselors may try even more imaginative programs with the active support of parents and teachers.

Kindergarten Parent Interview

Child's Name: _____ Date: _____
Nickname: _____ Sex: _____ Birthdate: _____
School: _____ Counselor: _____

How does your child feel about starting kindergarten?
_____ looking forward to it.
_____ doesn't want to go.
_____ doesn't seem to care one way or the other.
_____ doesn't know he's going to be starting.
_____ don't know.

Does your child have any special friends who will be entering the same kindergarten?

Does your child *primarily* play with:
_____ younger children   _____ older children or adults
_____ children his own age   _____ siblings
_____ limited opportunity to play with other children
_____ age doesn't seem to matter

How physically active is your child?

When your child plays alone what type of play or activity does he prefer?

When he plays with other children, what activity does he prefer?

How much does your child talk around home?
_____ He talks all the time; it's hard to get a word in edge-wise.
_____ About average for children his age.
_____ He doesn't talk much.

Does your child like to be read to? _____

If so, by whom? _____

How often? _____

Does your child like to watch T.V.? _____

What programs? _____, _____, _____

Does he watch Sesame Street regularly? _____

Approximately how much time does he spend watching T.V. each day? _____

Which of the following experiences has your child had?

___ pre-school or nursery
      Name _____
___ having friends over to play
___ going to a friend's house to play
___ moving: how many times _____,
      where (rural, urban) _____
___ a long visit with relatives
___ living with someone other than parent
___ staying overnight away from family
___ eating in a restaurant
___ camping (not day)
___ time in a foreign country
___ experience with another language
___ an airplane ride
___ a train ride
___ a boat ride
___ surgery
___ a serious accident
___ visiting an airport
___ visiting a doctor regularly
      e.g. pediatrician or other

___ a long illness
___ a great fright
___ a death in the family
___ a parent with a long illness
___ a parent away from home for an
      extended period of time
___ caring for or having a pet
___ raising plants or having a garden
___ going swimming
___ cooking (his own)
___ dancing lessons
___ music lessons
___ children's museum
___ visiting a farm
___ aquarium
___ going to the zoo
___ downtown Boston
___ going to the circus
___ extensive eye or hearing examinations
___ any other significant experience in
      your child's life.

Mother's Name _____

Occupation _____ Working hours _____

Father's Name _____

Occupation _____ Working hours _____

Your child's household includes:

Mother _____ Father _____ Grandmother _____ Grandfather _____

Aunt _____ Uncle _____

Other (including babysitters or others who spend a significant amount of time with your child)

Siblings: Names and ages

_____

_____

Parents are: Married _____ Divorced _____ Separated _____

Widowed _____

Is your child adopted? _____ If yes, does he know? _____

In comparison with your other children, or other people's children, has this child been easier, or more difficult, to rear, or about average?

_____ This child has been especially easy to get along with; very easy to rear.

_____ This child is about average.

_____ This child is hard to handle, and gives me more trouble than most other children.

When your child goes to sleep at night does he:

_____ Take a long time to get to sleep.

_____ Awaken during the night.

_____ Have nightmares. Occasionally _____ Frequently _____

_____ Walk in his sleep.

_____ Wet his bed. Occasionally _____ Frequently _____

What is your child's usual bedtime? _____

At what time does he usually arise? _____

How much help does he need at bedtime and in the morning with undressing, dressing, and toileting? And who usually helps him?

Does he eat breakfast? _____

Does he take a nap? Regularly _____ Occasionally _____ Never _____

Which of the following might describe your child?

— affectionate   — outgoing
— aggressive   — physically active
— calm   — prefers to play alone
— cries easily   — prefers to play with one other child
— demanding   — prefers to play with small group
— easily frightened   — prefers adult company
— even tempered   — quiet
— happy-go-lucky   — shy
— moody   — nervous
— noisy   — talkative

What else would you like us to know about your child so that we can help your child have a good year in kindergarten?

THE BASIS FOR CHANGE AGENTRY

A great deal has recently been said regarding the role of the counselor as an agent for change within the educational setting. Unfortunately, little has been written concerning the manner whereby significant changes can occur. This article suggests that without power bases among teachers and parents, the elementary counselor–consultant has little chance of effecting meaningful change in schools. These individuals ultimately control our access to children and exert tremendous influence on children's attitudes and values. As a consequence, counselors can ill afford to neglect or work around these groups. They must be actively solicited for their support and use in assisting children.

Major shifts in school structure, organization, curriculum, and treatment of children do not require a major revolution. In fact, change does not even require the support of a majority of parents and teachers. However, it does require individuals willing to take risks when the educational system is unresponsive to the needs of students. In these moments the counselor requires supportive clusters of parents and teachers to bulwark his stand. This article suggests that these supportive groups of parents and teachers be formed and organized, through constructive efforts, in advance of conflictive situations.

If elementary school counselors wish to "buck the system" (and buck it they must if they see it with their eyes open) and innovate changes and programs for students, it is imperative that they seek support within and outside the school. Counselors must assume leadership positions among parents and teachers if they truly desire better schools and more humane environments for children. We can avoid these leadership positions only at peril to our jobs and to our relationships with children. It is time for new approaches and purposes in guidance. We must all become more ambitious for our profession and for the children we serve. Let us begin.

Bibliography

Aubrey, R. F. Intervention strategies for guidance. In H. Peters, R. Dunlap, and R. Aubrey (Eds.), *The Practice of Guidance.* Denver, Colo.: Love Publishing Company, 1972.

Blocher, D. Can the counselor function as an effective agent of change? *School Counselor,* 1966, *13,* 202–206.

Brown, D., & Pruett, R. P. The elementary teacher views guidance. *School Counselor,* 1967, *15,* 195–203.

Cheikin, M. Counseling: activist or reactivist? *School Counselor,* 1971, *19,* 68–71.

Duncan, W. L. Parent counselor conferences do make a difference. Paper presented at the American Personnel and Guidance Association Convention, Las Vegas, Nevada, 1969.

Eckerson, L. The White House Conference: Tips or taps for counselors. *Personnel and Guidance Journal*, 1971, *50*, 167–174.

Kehas, C. D. Administrative structure and guidance theory. *Counselor Education and Supervision*, 1965, *4*, 147–153.

Postman, N., & Weingartner, C. *Teaching as a subversive activity*. New York: Delacorte Press, 1969.

Postman, N., & Weingartner, C. *The soft revolution*. New York: Delacorte Press, 1971.

Sarason, S. B. *The culture of the school and the problem of change*. Boston: Allyn & Bacon, 1971.

Shertzer, B., & Stone, S. The school counselor and his publics: A problem in role definition. *Personnel and Guidance Journal*, 1963, *41*, 687–695.

Walz, G., & Miller, J. School climates and student behavior: Implications for counselor role. *Personnel and Guidance Journal*, 1969, *47*, 859–867.

8. CAN THE COUNSELOR FUNCTION AS AN EFFECTIVE AGENT OF CHANGE?

Donald Blocher

The school counselor is faced increasingly with the challenge of effecting change in educational institutions. Students, parents, and writers, both professional and popular, see the counselor as a person who can actually change the educational environment. The need for dramatic change in American education seems so overwhelmingly apparent that it would be difficult to cast any sophisticated argument against it. A great many of the cases which are continually referred to counselors in hope of some kind of remediative or palliative treatment are themselves simply products of the gross imperfections in the social systems represented by the school and community.

A central thesis of my own approach to counseling is that the counselor's primary professional responsibility is to facilitate human development. We know that development represents an interaction process between the individual with his own inherent dispositions and his environment, particularly that part of his environment which we call society and culture.

Source. Donald Blocher, "Can the Counselor Function As An Agent of Change" *The School Counselor*, 1966. Vol. 13–4, 202–205. Copyright 1966 by the American Personnel and Guidance Association and reproduced by permission.

In their attempts to intervene in the transactional process between the individual and society, educators, physicians, judges, social workers, and other professional persons almost invariably assume that their intervention must be addressed solely to the individual. They tend to assume that it is always the individual who must be changed, adjusted, or manipulated to bring him into conformity with the unquestioned and unquestionable demands of groups, institutions, or other socially sanctified components of the culture.

Nearly thirty years ago Lawrence Frank, in an article entitled "Society As the Patient," summed up the cultural myopia of the helping professions in these terms:

"In every department and aspect of our social life we find the same pattern of thought about our society: that our social ills come from individual misconduct that must be corrected and punished so that these supposed social forces and social laws can operate without hindrances, thereby solving our social problems. . . .

"If, then, we abandon this social mythology, as a growing number of individuals are urging, what have we as an alternative? . . . The conception of culture and personality, emphasizing the patterned behavior of man toward his group and toward other individuals offers some promise of help, for it indicates at once that our society is only one of numerous ways of patterning and organizing life and that what individuals do for good or evil is in response to the cultural demands and opportunities offered them." [2]

Unfortunately, in the nearly thirty years which have intervened since these words were written, the promise which Frank saw has not been fulfilled. Education, as a social institution, has been particularly slow to adjust itself to the needs and demands of developing individuals and has instead settled back comfortably within the mythology of its own omniscience and moral rectitude.

In only one area of social welfare of which I have become aware have thorough and systematic attempts been made to abandon the myth of social inviolability and to attempt to conceptualize human problems within the model advocated by Frank thirty years ago. The area of which I speak is the movement called milieu therapy or sometimes social psychiatry which has already demonstrated its usefulness in mental health settings throughout the country. Characteristically, however, we are behind several European countries in this approach.

The concept of milieu therapy seems to me to offer a useful model from which education can learn. Cohen [1] writes of the hospital as a "therapeutic instrument" in which patterns of human relationships, physical environments, and interactions with the large society are consciously and systematically attuned to the treatment needs of patients.

In a similar vein, the counselor is interested in creating the school as a "developmental instrument" attuned to the developmental needs of youth. Goldsmith, Schulman, and Grossbard in an article on milieu therapy with disturbed children stress the point that a clinical process such as psychotherapy cannot be integrated into an environment which is alien to it. They say:

"To achieve a schematicized environment which can be consistent and therapeutic in all its aspects, there must first and foremost be a common denominator in the functioning of all staff—clinical and non-clinical—beginning with the acceptance of a common formulation for the treatment of those disturbed children. The common bond, the thread which runs through the institution, must be the understanding of the nature of the child. It is this understanding which extends the clinical process into all aspects of the environmental setting. This understanding creates identification, sympathy and tolerance. It permits individualization in the handling of children by all concerned. It is this which creates the basic milieu for and of therapy." [3]

The creation of a *developmental* milieu for clients is one of the goals of the counselor. The developmental milieu may not be quite the same as the therapeutic milieu, but it, too, would seem to rest on the common denominator of understanding human development. Unless the developing individual can exist in a milieu within family, within school, and within community where some rather high degree of understanding of developmental needs and processes can be found, much of the work of the counselor will be hopelessly difficult.

Can the counselor operate as an effective agent of change to produce this kind of developmental milieu? I raise a number of questions about this role for the counselor not to be a voice of doubt, but to focus upon some real considerations which must be faced before we can glibly undertake this role for the counselor as we have glibly taken on so many others in the past.

1. *Is the counselor qualified by training background and experience to be an effective agent of change?*

To be such an agent the counselor, I believe, must be a behavioral scientist in the best sense of the term. He must be able to view human behavior as phenomena, phenomena that are potentially understandable and modifiable. He cannot be merely shocked, or frightened, or angered by behavior. He must also be able to get outside the cultural cocoon which encapsulates most members of a society to view human behavior and human institutions objectively and cross-culturally. These requirements, I believe, mean that the counselor must have a broad and rigorous background in fields such as anthropology, sociology, political science, economics and social psychology (particularly group dynamics), as well as a thorough grounding in humanities.

I am afraid that at the present time neither most counselors nor most counselor education programs stack up very well on these criteria:

2. *Does the role of the counselor permit him to operate as an effective agent of change?*

The counselor's primary role in the school is as a helping person. His effectiveness depends largely on being perceived as such a person by parents, students, teachers, and administrators. One of his greatest assets is that because he is perceived as a helping person, the counselor has access to a great deal of "feedback" from people about how their needs are being met or not met that is available to no one else.

The counselor who is openly and strongly committed to controversial changes may no longer be perceived as a helping person, at least by many to whom such changes may be disturbing and threatening. The "boat-rocker" often is not seen as a helping person even when the boat may need rocking very badly.

3. *Is the counselor's position in the organization of the school such that he can become an effective agent of change?*

The counselor is typically neither fish nor fowl insofar as his organizational relationships in the school are concerned. He is typically not a full-fledged administrator with well-defined responsibilities, nor is he viewed strictly as a teacher who operates without administrative authority or responsibility. The concept of staff roles in educational organizations is presently so poorly developed that the counselor must operate in a virtual organizational "no man's land." For the counselor to operate directly and consciously as a change agent in the school can lead to threat-inducing situations for both administrators and teachers.

One of the real enigmas to me is why those that consistently urge change in education have bypassed the school administrator, who is the only person in the school vested with the authority and responsibility to promote valued change.

Has the school administrator lost his identity as the educational leader? Has he become so identified with buses, buildings, and bands, that he is not identified with pupils, parents, and programs? Has the school administrator been so laden down with such a diversity of tasks that a leadership vacuum is forming under the increasing demands of a kaleidoscopic culture? Milieu therapy models would suggest that schools might be moving closer to the hospital model in which the administrator is essentially the office manager and the responsibility for professional treatments—the dominant mission of the organization—rests finally in the hands of the active practitioners rather than the professional administrator?

This movement, indeed, may already be underway. Perhaps counselors should continue to play quasi-administrative roles and concern themselves more and more deeply in curriculum, pupil grouping, and the many other areas in which vital changes are needed. Such is the challenge thrown out by Shoben when he says:

". . . willy-nilly, the school represents a society-in-little. The challenge before it is whether it can transform itself into a developmentally productive one on an articulate and informed basis and, by a regular and planful process of self-appraisal, maintain itself as a true growth-enhancing community. In such an effort to sharpen the impact of the school and to give it greater cogency for individual students, guidance workers can play a key role, forging in the course of it, a genuine new profession for themselves." [4]

If this is the challenge which counselors wish to undertake, they must accept it with a clear vision of the demands which it will place upon them as individuals, with awareness of the scope of preparation which it will require, and with knowledge of the new organizational relationships which will inevitably emerge from it.

References

1. Cohen, R. *The hospital as a therapeutic instrument.* In Milton, O. *Behavior disorders, perspectives and trends.* New York: J. B. Lippincott, 1965, pp. 290–298.
2. Frank, L. Society as the patient. *American J. Sociol.* 1936, *42*, pp. 335–344, also in Vinacke, W. Edgar and Wilson, Warner R. *Dimensions of social psychology.* Chicago: Scott, Foresman, 1964, p. 50.
3. Goldsmith, J. Schulman, R. & Grossland, H. Integrating clinical processes with planned living experiences. In Gorlow, Leon & Katkovsky, Walter (Ed.) *Readings in the psychology of adjustment.* New York: McGraw-Hill, 1959, p. 483.
4. Shoben, E. J., Jr., Guidance: remedial function or social reconstruction? *Harv. educ. Rev.* Guidance—an examination (A special issue), *32*, No. 4, Fall 1962, p. 442.

9.   A SYSTEMATIC ECLECTIC MODEL FOR COUNSELING—CONSULTING

•‑••‑••‑‑•‑•

Donald H. Blocher and Rita S. Rapoza

One way to look at the emerging role of psychological workers in educational settings is from an essentially ecological view (Blocher, Dustin & Dugan 1971; Danskin, Kennedy & Friesen 1965). From such a view the major professional goal of the student personnel worker (or consultant) is to help create and to maintain a network of learning environments in family, school, and community that will nurture the optimal development of every student. Most of the learning environments that presently exist within our families, schools, and communities are clearly not designed to provide the kind of psychosocial interaction that will optimize human development, so that the role of the personnel worker often becomes that of an agent of environmental change (McCully 1965). The counselor or personnel worker in effect becomes an applied social scientist and uses the tools afforded him by social and developmental psychology to facilitate positive change in those human systems that become his clients (Berdie 1972; Blocher 1969).

Within this framework the client may be seen as a single individual or as a social system, such as a family, classroom, or school organization. The kinds of treatments or interventions available to the counselor may include consultation techniques, small group work, or laboratory learning procedures, as well as the more traditional individual counseling approaches. Counselors may be engaged in process consultation within classrooms, teaching parent or teacher effectiveness courses, or running academic improvement or interpersonal skills groups. They could be involved with vocational decision making groups with students, or engaged in consultation and staff development activities with school administrators, as well as being occupied with individual counseling cases.

A major problem for counselors in developing this new ecologically based role has been the fact that traditional counseling theories and approaches were derived primarily from personality theories. These approaches have not been flexible enough to provide the conceptual underpinning neces-

Source. Donald H. Blocher and Rita S. Rapoza "A Systematic Model for Counseling-Consulting" *Elementary School Guidance and Counseling*, 1972, Vol. 7–2, 106–112. Copyright 1972 by the American Personnel and Guidance Association and reproduced by permission.

sary for the wide range of problems and settings in which the ecologically oriented counselor finds himself. Many such approaches are based primarily on clinical experiences with middle class adult neurotics engaged in insight-oriented psychotherapy. For several years leaders in the field have called for systematic eclectic approaches that will provide the flexibility needed to apply the kinds of specific interventions that have proved effective for specific problems of specific clients (Carkhuff 1966). The profession has almost abandoned its search for panaceas.

One attempt at developing a systematic eclectic approach for use by counselors in educational settings is described very briefly here. The method is systematic in that it presents a specific sequence of activities in which the counselor engages. It is eclectic in that it utilizes several different sources of gain based upon relationship, cognitive, behavioral, and social psychological theories. The model is presented in flowchart form in Figure 1. It seems useful to comment briefly on its practical use. The rationale involved is described more fully elsewhere (Blocher & Shaffer 1971; Blocher, in press).

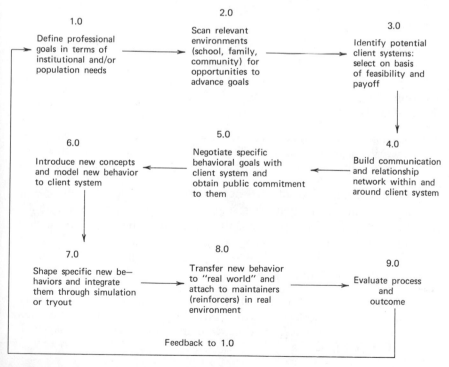

FIGURE 1
Facilitating change in human systems.

The systematic eclectic model assumes that the first step for the counselor in the process of intervening in a positive way with a client system (school, family, or individual) is to clearly understand his own professional identity and goals. These need to be clarified in relation to the needs and perceptions of the institutional framework and potential client population with which the counselor works. This may be expressed in a basic postulate:

1. The counselor understands himself and the systems within which he operates before he intervenes actively.

Now the counselor can actively scan the relevant learning environments with which he works to find opportunities to advance his professional goals. He operates from a proactive rather than a reactive stance. As he encounters groups and situations that may represent potential opportunities to facilitate growth in key human systems, he begins to build communication and relationship networks. These networks will allow open, honest, and important messages to be transmitted in many directions. This phase may be summarized in a second postulate:

2. The way to begin to help any human system is to listen to it and help it listen to itself.

After successfully establishing that relationship and communication network, the counselor becomes involved in open and direct negotiation. The counselor focuses on the specification of goals in behavioral terms, and the securing of open client commitment to these goals. A third postuate can be summarized:

3. Change in human systems occurs most readily when goals are clearly and mutually agreed upon and when public commitment is obtained in a contractual way.

Upon the completion of the negotiation phase, a whole-part-whole learning sequence is initiated. This sequence uses principles of information dissemination in order to obtain cognitive change coupled with social learning and operant shaping procedures, as well as simulation techniques drawn from laboratory learning wherever appropriate. This sequence can be summarized in the following way:

4. Human systems learn best when presented with clear general concepts and models, followed by error correction and discrimination training, followed by supervised practice with the newly acquired complex behaviors in safe settings.

The next sequence of activities is aimed at the transfer of learning and the maintenance of new learning in the actual environment of the client.

The counselor follows up the client system as it attempts to respond to real problems in new ways. He attempts to arrange for the new behavior to be supported and encouraged by significant individuals or subsystems. The basic postulate follows:

5. The help-giving process is not complete until the client system has successfully utilized its learning in the real situation and has experienced rewards for doing so.

The final sequence involves evaluation and is shown in Figure 2. Essentially, this phase involves the computation of success ratios for specific treatments with specific client problems and populations. This information is then used to improve performance and goal setting. The final postulate is simple:

6. Professional practice can only improve where accurate and immediate feedback is available about results.

The preceding discussion of this systematic eclectic model for counseling practice is necessarily very brief and abstract. It seems very complex and perhaps cumbersome. It has been employed successfully, however, in many practical counseling situations. The following is an example of its use in a junior high school.

The counselor's first function in the school was to write the following job description; this statement clearly defined her areas of expertise in relation to her personal needs and the needs of the educational institution she was

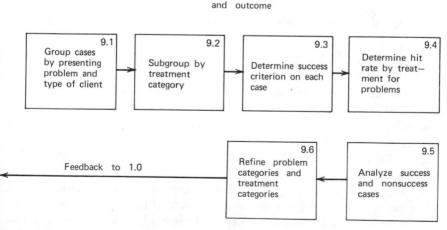

FIGURE 2
Breakdown of evaluation procedures.

about to enter. Administrators, supportive staff members, teachers, and parents used this outline as a stimulus for further negotiation and clarification of the school's and counselor's goals.

    I. Expertise in staff development and consulting with teacher-advisers in the following areas:
        A. Group dynamics
        B. Communications skills
        C. Decision making skills
        D. Study skills
        E. Student development
        F. Individual differences
        G. Vocational development
        H. Parental and/or family counseling
    II. Training and expertise in consulting with staff and administration concerning problems of:
        A. Human relations
        B. Organizational development
        C. Curriculum development
   III. Expertise and experience in organizing and conducting:
        A. Academic improvement groups
        B. Interpersonal skills groups
        C. Vocational-educational planning groups
   IV. Skills in individual counseling with students who have special problems.
    V. Ability to perform assessment and diagnostic activities in regard to the following types of problems:
        A. Learning difficulties
        B. Special referral problems (personality disorders and learning dysfunctions)
        C. Vocational aptitudes and interests

EXAMPLE 1

An example of how this approach can be implemented is described in a consultation with a first year teacher, who had previously worked with the counselor. General dissatisfaction with what was happening in one of her classes brought the young teacher in contact with the counselor. Her request for help came in the form of asking the counselor to observe the class as she taught.

    Before agreeing to enter the classroom, the counselor asked the teacher to define some specific behaviors that she wanted the counselor to observe during the process observation (Step 1, Figure 1). A set of group rating scales was used as a basis for negotiation in this particular case, because the teacher had some difficulty in defining these specific behaviors (Blocher,

Dustin & Dugan 1971). After the behaviors were written down and explicitly agreed upon, the teacher and the counselor decided on the day and time of the classroom observation (Steps 2, 3, 4, 5, Figure 1). Throughout this preparation period the counselor was very much aware of the relationship she was trying to establish with the teacher. Her goal at this point was to insure the flow of expressive, instrumental, positive and negative communication (Step 4, Figure 1). This climate needed to be established before the results of the process observation could be given to the teacher.

Sensing that the teacher was nervous after her classroom presentation, the counselor tried to help her stay with some of the feelings she was experiencing (Step 4, Figure 1). With the communication open once more, the two studied the results of the observation and again negotiated until they agreed upon a plan of action (Step 5, Figure 1).

During the ensuing two sessions the counselor introduced her client to new ways of thinking about her students and herself, reinforced the teacher's attempts at new behaviors, and played the role of a student as the teacher tried out some personally difficult behaviors in the counselor's office (Steps 6, 7, Figure 1). The counselor was invited back into the classroom for a follow-up observation. Afterwards, in their evaluation session, the counselor asked the teacher if there was any one staff member that she liked and respected and could talk to about the skills she was trying to acquire. This person turned out to be a veteran teacher in another department. In a meeting where all three were present, the counselor served as a facilitator to insure that the goals were feasible and clearly defined and that the communication between the two teachers was direct and open (Step 8, Figure 1). Before terminating that session, the counselor and the new teacher once again reviewed the value of this particular approach and agreed upon another time to re-evaluate the situation (Step 9, Figure 1).

EXAMPLE 2

Another example of the effectiveness of the systematic eclectic model is provided by six students who wished to increase their study skills in an academic improvement group. During the individual intake interviews, the counselor clearly defined her goals for the group and helped the students decide if their goals were appropriate for this particular group. Once this was determined, the counselor requested that the potential group member (a) declare his behavioral objectives to the group in either the first or second session; (b) commit himself to assisting other members in the group; and (c) let the group know of his decision to sever his relationship with them if he should find the group inappropriate for his needs after the first two meetings.

Even before the counselor met with the group, she showed evidence of following the first three postulates: She knew her own goals, tried to secure the right people for the right group, and obtained an oral commitment to individual and group goals. When the group convened, the objectives were redefined through the sharing of expectations. During the negotiation of group and individual goals, the counselor modeled the honest communication that she wanted the students to be using with each other. She also reinforced personal and relationship statements emitted throughout all of the group sessions. Students were paired up at the end of each meeting in order to jointly draw up a learning contract for the week. Each co-signed the other's written agreement (Steps 3, 4, 5, Figure 1).

Group members were soon able to congratulate each other on successes, no matter how small, and confrontations especially between partners over unfulfilled contracts were common (Steps 6, 7, 8, Figure 1). At the last session, the counselor had the students draw a picture of the group in terms of how they saw each member's participation and the group's movement toward its goals. This served as a departure point for a general evaluation and feedback session to the entire academic improvement group (Step 9, Figure 1).

EXAMPLE 3

Knowing of her special interest in conducting inservice training for the staff, the principal called upon the counselor to design a workshop for 10 teachers to take place during the summer. The eight-day workshop ran for four hours daily and had several objectives: (a) to help the teachers meet community members with some degree of ease; (b) to compile a community resource directory for the school; and (c) to devise a plan that would assist these workshop teachers in encouraging other teachers in the school to make community contacts and to add to the community resource directory.

After hearing the principal's institutional goals defined, the counselor met with the teachers to obtain their professional and personal objectives for this project (Steps 1, 2, 3, Figure 1). In these discussions, the counselor functioned as a group facilitator and carefully listened to what was being said and helped the members to listen to each other (Step 4, Figure 1). Once the professional goals were clearly defined in terms of institutional needs, specific behavioral goals were agreed upon both in the large group and between those pairs who decided to work together (Step 5, Figure 1).

Group members, as well as the counselor, introduced new concepts and practical skills to each other (Steps 6, 7, Figure 1). This allowed the group to draw on the expertise of all of its members. Simulated task sessions coupled with a sharing of the previous day's field work experiences gave each member a chance to evaluate, critique, and reinforce others as well as himself (Steps 8, 9, Figure 1). The group began to pull together and collaborate on many decisions, such as the setting of goals for each meeting.

On days when some teachers were meeting with community members, the counselor remained in the school to keep the communication open and to get to know each staff member in the workshop better. This also proved to be an excellent opportunity for re-teaching small units involving concepts and skills on an individual basis. Another advantage of having some free informal time for the teachers came in the form of having the occasion to encourage and reinforce those relevant behaviors that had just been practiced in the community (Steps 7, 8, Figure 1). The counselor reinforced the teachers, and the teachers in a very short time were reinforcing each other.

At the closing session of the workshop the members reviewed their original goals to evaluate their progress. They then modified their project guidelines and appointed a committee to organize the information obtained from more than one hundred community contacts. They committed themselves to a jointly determined strategy for introducing and teaching their skills to the rest of the faculty. This strategy required that each project member identify one other member to serve as a support system to help share this project with his department. After filling out an evaluation questionnaire, members shared their evaluation of the entire workshop with each other. Personal feedback was given to every member of the group with communication open enough by this time for expressive, critical, and positive messages to be given and received (Step 9, Figure 1).

The counselor found all of the steps in the systematic eclectic model necessary in order to effectively work with various human systems. Although she had performed some of the steps intuitively before being introduced to the model, the conceptual framework provided her with an objective criterion against which to analyze her progress. This proved especially helpful when resistance and opposition appeared to be blocking further advancement of goals. She was then forced to study the sequenced steps and retrace some steps when necessary before proceeding.

In conclusion, the authors have discussed the systematic eclectic model and illustrated its use in the daily duties of a school counselor. The model described provides a systematic conceptual framework flexible enough to be used in a wide range of situations and interventions, including individual and group counseling as well as consultation and organizational development. The model also draws upon sources of gain in facilitating behavior change that include relationship conditions, public commitment, cognitive learning, social modeling, and operant shaping and reinforcement. The model attends to problems of transfer and maintenance of behavior usually ignored in therapeutically oriented systems.

References

Berdie, R. F. The 1980 counselor: Applied behavioral scientist. *Personnel and Guidance Journal*, 1972, *50*, 451–456.

Blocher, D. H. Counseling as a technology for facilitating and guiding change in human systems. *Educational Technology*, 1969, *9*, 15–18.

Blocher, D. H. Counseling process variables. In C. Pulvino (Ed.), *Proceedings of counseling workshop*. Madison: University of Wisconsin Press, in press.

Blocher, D. H., Dustin, E. R., & Dugan, W. E. *Guidance systems: An introduction to student personnel work*. New York: Ronald Press, 1971.

Blocher, D. H., & Shaffer, W. F. Guidance and human development. In D. R. Cook (Ed.), *Guidance for education in revolution*. Boston: Allyn & Bacon, 1971.

Carkhuff, R. Counseling research, theory and practice—1965. *Journal of Counseling Psychology*, 1966, *13*, 467–480.

Danskin, D., Kennedy, C. E., & Friesen, W. S. Guidance—the ecology of students. *Personnel and Guidance Journal*, 1965, *45*, 130–135.

McCully, H. The counselor: Instrument of change. *Teachers College Record*, 1965, *66*, 405–412.

10.   WHO IS BUILDING THE BRIDGES?

•-●--•--●--•

Alexandra Robbin

YOU WANT ANSWERS. At what level do you come seeking? Why are you reading this: merely curious? keeping up? fed up and pessimistic? fed up but optimistic? Who are you, now?

Let me speak from the South, from the schools. I've known the Northwest. I cannot assume what you have experienced elsewhere; but, rural or urban, in school or agency, I'll bet it's a variation of what's happening here:

Source. Alexandra Robbin, "Who Is Building Bridges?" *Personnel and Guidance Journal*, 1971, Vol. 49–9, 693–697. Copyright 1971 by the American Personnel and Guidance Association and reproduced by permission.

• A 14-year-old, deserted by his mother and his alcoholic father, sitting in jail 32 days without a lawyer after throwing a crumpled sheet of paper into his principal's face.

• Married teenagers being expelled from high school at the suggestion of their school superintendent, who in turn is backed by the school board. A board member, assuming he is in the business of deciding who deserves what, laughs, "Let them get some jackleg lawyer to challenge it!"

• A principal expelling a hyperactive brain-damaged seven-year-old from special education on the first day of class, advising the counselor that the boy is "just a happy little moron" and that there are "some cases we have to look the other way for."

• A principal giving the long-haired leader of a teen rock band an ultimatum: "Either you cut your hair, or your poem doesn't appear in the school's literary magazine."

• A teacher ignoring one-third of his students, assuming, "There's nobody dumber than a colored kid." (In the Northwest, I heard "There's nobody dumber than an Indian or an Eskimo.") . . . other thousands of school-age minority children left sitting at home, tacitly assumed not to exist.

• Principals forbidding some students to see the counselor.

• Frustrated, underachieving white youths playing cat-and-mouse games with their black teachers and peers; white teachers self-consciously clamping down on white students, and black teachers clamping down on black students; while their administrators declare, "We haven't had problems with desegregation *here!*"

• Principals still paddling elementary and high school students (sometimes with the intercom on) and teachers trying to show adolescents who's boss by refusing them permission to go to the toilet.

• The poor denied free breakfasts because extra meals would mean extra bother to school personnel.

• State funds for the handicapped turned down by superintendents who dread the administrative chores required.

• Architects still designing classrooms in straight, sterile rows, and lavatories without showers in schools serving the poor.

• School boards and administrators still defining a good teacher or a good counselor as a good child: industrious, but reverent and compliant.

• Teachers and counselors *still defining themselves the same way.*

BENEVOLENT ACCOMPLICES

These destructive acts and attitudes—this subtle violence—we condone through our own behavior. Ill-trained and ill-at-ease, we busy ourselves with scheduling and we hide our eyes, our ears and our hearts behind office doors and piles of paper. Some of us prostitute our profession by trying to shape students as schoolmen see fit. We've been gullible; we've been used; we've been muzzled promoters of authoritarian doctrine, subtly threatened against speaking out—in fact, deluded into believing we have neither right nor reason to. We are part of the pathology, and we are sick unto death.

I don't know at what level you've come searching. Or whether you have even begun to trace the implications of your own experience. It makes a difference.

Let's assume you're aware, you're concerned, and you're looking for answers.

I don't have the answers. Education already has enough seven-day wonders with answers for everyone. I do have some comments and questions about schooling.

As professionals who presume to educate, we are impostors. We are frauds. We are dinosaurs! Even worse, we are dangerous, because we have made ignorance and self-delusion our style of life.

AN ALTERNATE FOCUS

Within a pathological system, one's task seems to be threefold: to aid the ailing, to support the healthy, and to deal with the pathology itself. However, by concentrating on the ailing and the healthy—the losers and the winners among our students—we have unwittingly intensified the pathology of the system itself. Our attention has been deflected from the nature of the human relationships *which define the entire system.*

Without taking time fully to understand what a *system* is, a counselor can initiate counteraction to illness within it. Of course there is danger that such amelioration will be more harmful than helpful, if it fools members of the system into thinking relationships have basically improved when they have not.

Choices of strategy depend partly on one's definition of change. To define it as the emergence of a new stage of the same system is certainly different from regarding it as a totally new condition. One must also decide whether impetus and leadership for change need to come from within, from without, from either, or both, or whether the locus matters at all.

Considering the tacit purposes and powers of our schooling system, most counselors aspiring to be change agents are more likely to make headway by defining change as emergence of new states of being. They will work toward metamorphosis of the present system by establishing their credibility and working within the system.

A counselor's intuitions about readiness, timing and appropriateness are crucial. One needs to understand how school people think and what their unwritten priorities and behavior guides are.

Some teachers and most administrators, including school boards, impede basic change. They fear or resent persons who welcome alternatives, and they muster defenses against them. Especially vocal against "change for the sake of change," they tend to interpret most change as that type. They are also wary of persons with "overbearing manners." Surely one can empathize with their predicament, expressed by the country song, "It ain't my world and it ain't my time . . . My song won't sing and my words won't rhyme."[1] There is a fine distinction between patience and hurry. Such people require patience. To force a sense of urgency upon them is to provoke their reflexive repression and shutting out.

How, then, can one reconcile a sense of urgency with realities of the system's rate of response?

GEARING FOR CHANGE

One needs to consider: Are the guardians of the status quo malicious? unenlightened? Do they need to be threatened? coerced? Do they need psychologically safe conditions for growth? The tools of suppression are handily theirs. But what if this were not the case?

A school system is a network; a web of relationships wherein a change in one affects all. Reverberating, messages multiply. I-Thou Dialogue (Buber, 1958) is therefore essential to achieving humaneness. "When the dialogue stops, the I's and Thou's become Its, and they are subject to manipulation, coercion, and exploitation" (Buchanan, 1970). This fact points up the ethical dilemma we enter when we attempt to solve a problem by weighing the rights of one group (students) against the rights of another (the people who wield power over them).

I am reminded of a high school principal to whom I reported, "A group of students wants to establish dialogue with you." Students had complained that he wouldn't listen.

Reddening, the principal blurted, "We already have a dialogue going, and they know what the rules are! Those boys are troublemakers."

Strategically I had bungled. I had hurried to the core of a problem, disregarding my listener's readiness to hear. I had rushed the encounter in an inappropriate place (outside safe territory for him). Most devastating, undermining one's effectiveness with the people who presently hold power. I had regarded the person as It, not as Thou, and he had reacted accordingly.

An activist counselor must square his shoulders sometimes, of course. But "activism" does not imply power struggles with showdowns in which someone must win and someone must lose. Angry personal exchanges It's no less honest to confine hatred to *issues*, and it's immensely more

---

[1] "Pathways of My Life," written by Red Lane, sung by Hank Thompson on Dot Records. Published by Tree Publishing Co.

practical, because it encourages one's own self-respect while providing for the saving of face.

STRATEGY AND LEVERAGE

Once I talked with a small-town superintendent about the reluctance of our state legislature to fund certain programs for handicaped students. I couldn't understand why the lawmakers did not feel compelled to do something about the evidence presented. With a shrug he explained, *"It depends on who says it and who agrees with it."*

Obviously this insight can be useful in planning for change. The activist counselor needs to establish credibility and working relationships with people to whom the "power structures" listen.

School administrators are sensitive to public opinion, a type of force which a counselor can use legitimately. They react to "numbers" and "tax-payers." If they believe that sufficient numbers of taxpayers support a proposal, they will usually give it provisional try-out. They feel safety in numbers. They also respond to published evidence that other administrators are behaving in ways you are trying to promote. Paradoxically, they like to be regarded as up to date, and will unexpectedly adopt innovations considered safe by their peers. Information about trends in your own geographic region, or in population areas similar to your own, is even more effective than evidence from outside, unless the administrators are jealous or distrustful of each other. (This you need to find out.)

An activist counselor must be willing to use community resources for students and faculty whose civil liberties have been violated (for example, the American Civil Liberties Union, Legal Aid Societies, and neighborhood law offices manned by advanced law students).

Likewise, it's important to identify like-minded colleagues and citizens who can help establish a humane subsystem within the larger system: supporting each other's morale, making alternatives visible, and providing observable numbers at appropriate times.

However, one must be aware that such talk about "strategy" smacks of the manipulation which is bound to begin when true dialogue stops.

BUILDING THE BRIDGES

The foregoing remedies are short-range, palliative, superficial. They can assist change, but they are not equivalent to the *basic* changes we need.

Products of the schooling system ourselves, we anticipate easy answers. We resent speakers and writers who cannot provide solutions. We applaud those who would delude us into thinking they can.

We Haven't Even Formulated Good Questions Yet

It's hard to know where to begin. There is such a void of knowledge and understanding—such a lack, even, of *will* among us. We sidestep evidence that answers await inside ourselves. We plug our ears when someone insists that we need philosophy. With tunnel vision we focus on the obvious, inattentive to the subtle. We stay situation-bound, grossly uninformed of larger social issues. We observe the world changing, but we don't perceive it *really*, because we wouldn't know what to do if we did. All in a bundle, we are anti-intellectual, anti-rational, anti-irrational. Incredible! What are we *for*?

For pupils. For people.

Then, what are we *doing*?

Who in Education is building bridges? Bridges between cowardice and courage; between past, present and future; between violence and humaneness, repression and freedom; between thinking, feeling and doing; between schooling and education? Who is recognizing the primacy of the self caught in conflict?

Let's listen:

"Man is now in the position of actually creating the total world in which he lives. . . . In creating this world, he is actually determining what kind of organism he will be. . . ." Hall, 1969, p. 4)

"The future potential for "genetic engineering" seems incredible. But then so does our lack of consideration of just what kinds of human beings we want to engineer, and to what purposes." (Ehrlich, 1969, p. 30)

"The age of nations is past. The task before us now, if we would not perish, is to shake off our ancient prejudices, and to build the earth." (Teilhard de Chardin, 1969, p. 67)

"NOW is one of those times in history when a tremendous transformation could take place with dramatic rapidity . . . a transformation which could accelerate and encompass mankind with a new and exciting purpose." (Dunn, 1970, p. 59)

In our schools, who is considering these and other insistent messages? Is any group trying to assist a humane evolution? or humane personal *revolutions*?

ALONG WITH THE RHETORIC: WORK

For the activist counselor in a pathological system, there can be no pat answers. Seeking remedies, he knows his quest must be radical in the dictionary sense of the term. He realizes that his job is often a mission: to save the individual's right to know. He finds courage to recognize social suppression when he would rather feel freedom. He senses that he must function on at least two levels: dealing with immediacies, while searching tirelessly for transcending insights.

The activist counselor realizes the implications of Gandhi's belief that "broadly speaking (there are) five stages in every movement: first, indifference; second, ridicule; third, abuse; fourth, repression; and, finally, respect. . . . If a movement does not survive the fourth stage, it has not even begun to count" (Iyer, 1970, p. 61).

Who is building the bridges? Assuming that it's not too late, *will we?*

References

Buber, M. *I and Thou.* (2d ed.) New York: Charles Scribner's Sons, 1958.

Buchanan, S. "Second edition/Civil disobedience: Martin Buber." *The Center Magazine*, 1970, *3*, 3.

Dunn, H. L. "Evolution of the mind and human potential." *Fields Within Fields . . . Within Fields: The Methodology of the Creative Process*, 1970, *3*, 1.

Ehrlich, P. R. "The biological revolution." *The Center Magazine*, 1969, *2*, 6.

Hall, E. T. *The Hidden Dimension.* New York: Anchor Books, 1969.

Iyer, R. N. "Second edition/Civil disobedience: Gandhi." *The Center Magazine*, 1970, *3*, 3.

Teilhard de Chardin, P. *Building the Earth.* New York: Avon Books, 1969.

11. THE COUNSELOR–CONSULTANT AS A SPECIALIST IN ORGANIZATION DEVELOPMENT

•–•··•–•·

Donald Murray and Richard Schmuck

"The number of persons presently afflicted with some form of mental disorder may be as high as one in three [Wechsler, Solomon, & Kramer 1970, p. 3]." If we add to this calculation another large number of "normal"

Source. Donald Murray and Richard Schmuck, "The Counselor–Consultant as a Specialist in Organization Development" *Elementary School Guidance and Counseling*, 1972, Vol. 7–2, 99–104. Copyright 1972 by the American Personnel and Guidance Association and reproduced by permission.

people who lack positive mental health (Jahoda 1958), the social problem of a lack of psychological well-being becomes staggering. Since school counselors have emphasized the mental health area as their primary province, it is natural to think of them as being associated with this social problem. At the same time, it seems that the counselor's lack of success in dealing with student mental health is due to the overwhelming challenges he faces. Not only are counselors overloaded with students who need help, but they are expected to work effectively in the midst of outrageously conflicting expectations from students, colleagues, and administrators. Counselors are expected to act on the same day as a sympathetic listener, disciplinarian, friend, coordinator, trouble-shooter, and public relations officer. This inevitably leads to personal role conceptions that are fragmented, inconsistent, and full of confusion, and reduces the interpersonal effectiveness of the counselor.

In the face of such impossible working conditions, what is the school counselor to do? We believe that a radical change in role is needed. Not only is there a great need for more consistency in what the counselor does, but the counselor should focus his mental health work differently. The change should involve moving away from attempts to improve the mental health of individual students through counseling toward attempts to improve the climate of the school organization by consulting with all members of the school. In short, he would become a specialist in organization development.[1]

The organizational specialist considers a student's emotional problems to be due primarily to his reactions to the school as a human (or inhumane) culture. Referring a student to the counselor currently implies that the student is not adjusting to the school culture and that he should change his behavior appropriately. The traditional counselor is charged with helping the student to adjust to the school as it now exists. In contrast, the organizational specialist views the school as having organizational problems. He takes the position that personal, emotional problems are strongly influenced by interpersonal environments and that the interpersonal relationships of the staff and student peer groups represent especially potent environments for students. He queries, "What are the deficiencies in the interpersonal dynamics of the school?" before he asks, "What is psychologically wrong with this student?"

Unlike one-to-one or small group counseling relationships, the organiza-

---

[1] This article omits much of the theory and practice (as well as research) of organization development. For more information about organization development in schools, the interested reader should look at Schmuck and Runkel (1970), Schmuck and Miles (1971), and Schmuck, Runkel, Saturen, Martell, and Derr (1972).

tional specialist works with all members of the school or at least with key subsystems of the school such as grade levels, classroom groups, or the student government. Instead of reacting to individual disturbances as they arise, the organizational specialist initiates diagnostic meetings and training sessions when he believes the organization needs to change itself. The energy that counselors spend on a few students is used instead to work with large groups of students and staff. Recent applications of training in organization development indicate that it can indeed have salutary effects on both the adult staff and the student peer culture (Bigelow 1971). It is legitimate to say that the new role of organizational specialist can help schools to develop more emotionally supportive climates for working and learning.

HOW TRAINING IN ORGANIZATION DEVELOPMENT WORKS

Training in organization development aims at improving communication among administrators, teachers, and students, at making their respective resources more available, and at increasing their effectiveness in collaborative problem solving. It strives to help the members of a school develop the skills, norms, roles, procedures, and group structures that will enable them to change their modes of operating in order to cope effectively with changing environments. Specifically, the objectives of organization development training include: increasing understanding within the school of how the different participants affect one another; establishing clear ways of defining goals and of assessing goal achievement; uncovering organizational conflicts and confusions so that they can be dealt with constructively; improving the group procedures used at large meetings; introducing new procedures for effective problem solving in small groups; and involving more participants at all levels in decision making.

There are five central assumptions and principles that guide the work of the organization development specialist. First, the organization development training will be more effective if it is carried out with all the members of a working subsystem (an organizational family) rather than with individuals who do not work together closely. We assume that since role-taking in the school is done in interaction with others, changes in a school's procedures will be brought about as the training offers new ways for the role-takers to act in relation to one another. Thus by being trained together the participants can see that their colleagues are accepting the new patterns of behavior and are acting upon them.

Second, the organization development consultation should generate valid data for the members of the school to use in understanding their functioning. This data, along with the specialists' observations, should offer a mirror that the trainees can look into to see themselves clearly as a group.

Third, discrepancies between current performance and the goal achievement of a school can be used as leverage points for change. The dissonance experienced by falling short of objectives can motivate participants to become involved in changing their modes of operating.

Fourth, the organization development training should make available the resources that already exist within and between the members for problem solving and innovation. In other words, the consultation should help participants to conceive of a number of alternatives for future functioning and a number of ways of putting some of the alternatives into action.

Fifth, the organization development specialist will have a higher likelihood of being objective and neutral as a consultant if he is not a member of the subsystem being trained and if he works as part of a consulting team rather than alone.

THE COUNSELOR AS AN ORGANIZATIONAL SPECIALIST

The counselor can perform his role as an organizational specialist either as a group process consultant within his own building or as a member of an external team of organization development consultants.

The Internal Process Consultant

There are primarily three ways in which a counselor, performing as an organizational specialist, can strengthen the organization development of his own school. All three of these types of consultation share some of the benefits of acting as an external consultant because they involve serving as an objective third-party consultant.

1. Consulting with staff groups. The counselor as a process consultant during faculty meetings observes the group in action, gives it feedback on how it is functioning, helps the group to check out how the members feel, and leads the group in discussions about its norms and methods of operating. He encourages the airing of problems and conflicts that would probably remain hidden; he helps the group to discuss its communication patterns, problem solving competencies, and decision making procedures. Perhaps most importantly, the process consultant teaches members to share in these diagnoses and helps them to discuss their own processes even when he is not present. (For elaboration on these points, and for several examples of procedures for uncovering problems in meetings, see Chapter 6 of Schmuck, Runkel, Saturen, Martell, and Derr [1972].)

2. Consulting with classroom groups. Another way that the counselor

can help to improve his school's interpersonal processes is to serve as a consultant to classroom groups. In this sort of consultation, the client is the entire learning group (not just the teacher) and the target is to improve the climate of the group. By employing such training techniques as observation and feedback, communication skills, simulations and games, and innovative group procedures, the consultant strives to help the class improve on group issues such as influence, attraction, norms, communication, and cohesiveness.

This definition of a positive classroom climate from Schmuck and Schmuck (1971) describes the kind of goals the counselor as a classroom consultant is after:

"A positive classroom climate is one in which the students share high amounts of potential influence—both with one another and with the teacher; where high levels of attraction exist for the group as a whole and between classmates; where norms are supportive for getting academic work done, as well as for maximizing individual differences; where communication is open and featured by dialogue; and where the processes of working and developing together as a group are considered relevant in themselves for study [p. 18]."

(For more information about working with classroom groups, see Schmuck and Schmuck [1971].)

3. Consulting with school groups. Most consultation to improve the system functioning of schools to date has been aimed either at the staff or classroom levels. There is now considerable interest in bringing students and teachers into more effective collaboration, especially concerning the development of educational alternatives and individualization.

The External Organization Development Team

Another way in which a counselor can perform as an organizational specialist is as the member of a consulting team which intervenes in another school in the district. Cadres of organizational specialists can be formed within districts to conduct organization development training throughout the district. Such cadres can be constituted not only of counselors but also of teachers, principals, curriculum specialists, school psychologists, and assistant superintendents. Each cadre member receives training in such substantive topics as communication, effective meetings, conflict and interdependence, problem solving, and decision making, as well as a supervised practicum and lengthy training in the theory and techniques of organization development. Counselors clearly bring special and unique skills to the cadre. Their knowledge of social psychology and group dynamics, previous roles as third party links between teachers and students, and skills in interpersonal communication and conflict contribute significantly to the resources of the cadres. (For detailed reports on cadres of organization development specialists, see Schmuck and Runkel [1971] and Wyant [1972].)

EXAMPLE OF COUNSELOR AS INTERNAL PROCESS CONSULTANT

The following hypothetical example denotes some typical actions that the counselor might take as an internal process consultant:

1. The counselor senses considerable force and irritation behind some referrals from the sixth grade teachers about student vandalism around the school. The counselor interprets these referrals as indicating an organizational problem involving the fifth and sixth grades rather than a disciplinary issue involving only a handful of students.

2. In starting the consultation, the counselor interviews the fifth and sixth grade teachers, several students, the principal, and even one cook and the custodian to assess the nature and magnitude of the problem of vandalism.

3. Next the counselor puts together a planning committee made up of some fifth and sixth grade teachers and students and the custodian (who the counselor has discovered is involved in the problem). This group helps the counselor plan some steps for working both with sixth grade classes and their teachers on the vandalism problem.

4. The planning group establishes an informal contract with the sixth grade classes having to do with goals of the consultation, procedures, times, etc. In turn, this contract is approved (or rejected) by the sixth grade teachers and students.

5. Next the counselor collects more diagnostic data from the sixth grade classes. He observes a few of their class sessions and interviews an assortment of the class members.

6. A two-day training session is scheduled for the sixth grade classes. The training involves communication skills, improving group functioning, uncovering conflicts, and feeding back data collected previously. The counselor leads the classes through exercises and procedures to improve their interpersonal relations.

7. On the last half day of the training, the classes move through a problem solving sequence that helps to define the situation (the nature of the vandalism), to delineate the objectives, and to generate several proposals for action.

8. The counselor initiates a half-day follow-up session with the sixth grade classes to determine if the proposals are being tried and to build some agreements for working on similar problems in the future.

MAJOR STAGES OF ORGANIZATION DEVELOPMENT

Organization development consultants typically proceed through three major stages:

1. *Improving communication skills through simulation.* The specialists build increased openness and ease of interpersonal communication among the trainees by using simulations of typical school situations to train them in such communication skills as paraphrasing, describing behavior, describing their own feelings, checking their impressions of others' feelings, taking a survey, and giving and receiving feedback.

2. *Changing norms through problem solving.* After the specialists help the participants to identify their most central organizational problems, they present a sequence of problem solving. By using real school problems, they help the participants to proceed through the steps of problem solving in an orderly fashion.

3. *Structural changes through group agreements.* The specialists help the participants to transform the results of their problem solving into new functions, roles, and procedures. These new organizational patterns can be formally decided upon by the participants, and agreements can be made about the action steps for carrying them out. Some structural changes might include a faculty senate with well-defined decision making powers, some procedures for teachers and students regularly giving feedback to one another about teaching, and some new teamwork procedures for helping students with special problems.

SUMMARY

Counselors are trapped in a professional situation very much analogous to the knight who jumped on his horse to ride off in all directions. The multiple demands and confusing expectations of counselors need to be reexamined. Rather than viewing the role of organizational specialist as still another expectation, we see it as a natural fit between the preventive approach to mental health and a systems orientation to human behavior. Counselors should modify their targets to improvements in organizational and interpersonal processes and should act more as consultants either as a group process expert within a single building or as a member of a district wide cadre of organization development consultants. The traditional role of counselor and that of the organizational specialist can be made to fit into a single job description that we believe should be the emerging role of the counselor of tomorrow.

References

Bigelow, R. Changing classroom interaction through organizational development. In R. A. Schmuck, and M. B. Miles (Eds.), *Organization development in schools.* Palo Alto, Calif.: National Press Books, 1971.

Jahoda, M. *Current concepts of positive mental health.* New York: Basic Books, Inc., 1958.

Schmuck, R. A., & Miles, M. B. (Eds.) *Organization development in schools.* Palo Alto, Calif.: National Press Books, 1971.

Schmuck, R. A., & Runkel, P. J. *Organizational training for a school faculty.* Eugene, Ore.: Center for the Advanced Study of Educational Administration, 1970.

Schmuck, R. A., & Runkel, P. J. *Integrating organizational specialists into school district.* Eugene, Ore.: Center for the Advanced Study of Educational Administration, 1971.

Schmuck, R. A., & Schmuck, P. A. *Group process in the classroom.* Dubuque, Iowa: William C. Brown Co., 1971.

Schmuck, R. A., Runkel, P. J., Saturen, S. I., Martell, R. T., & Derr, C. B. *Handbook of organization development in schools.* Palo Alto, Calif.: National Press Books, 1972.

Wechsler, H., Solomon, L., & Kramer, B. (Eds.), *Social psychology and mental health.* New York: Holt, Rinehart & Winston, Inc., 1970.

Wyant, S. *Organizational development from the inside: A progress report on the first cadre of organizational specialists.* (CASEA Tech. Rep. No. 12) Eugene, Ore.: Center for the Advanced Study of Educational Administration, 1972.

III Consultation Processes and Procedures

Consultation is a process in which the consultant and the consultee meet to discuss a concern regarding a client and to consider more effective ways for the consultee to function. In a school setting this usually refers to the consultant's working directly with teachers, parents, and administrators. The consultation process (like counseling and psychotherapy) is subject to all of the basic principles and necessary conditions for a helping relationship (Carkhuff, 1971, Combs, Avila & Purkey, 1971). The effectiveness of the consulting contract is, therefore, related to the extent that the consultant is perceived as possessing Roger's (1959) facilitative conditions or Combs et al. (1969) perceptual characteristics of good helpers.

The consultant operates in a planned, purposive, and deliberate manner. The consultant begins by determining his goals and objectives based on need, and then develops specific processes and practices to meet those ends. He determines his method of operation in the following fashion.

Step 1. Analyzes the entire social system in which he or she will be working. This involves what has been called a psychoecological approach (Kuriloff, 1973).

Step 2. Identifies areas of strengths and weaknesses. Particular attention is paid to assets that can be built on and problems that are creating systematic breakdown.

Step 3. Develops a plan of action that clearly delineates his priorities of hierarchy of functions.

Step 4. Implements his plan.

√ **Step 5.** Evaluates or monitors process to provide feedback with regard to effectiveness.

To operate in this fashion, the consultant needs to be a specialist in human relations, group process, and communication.

The consulting contact should be direct or on a personal basis. As Baker (1965) observed in his research on teacher consulting:

"Results suggested that a teacher's willingness to carry out the recommendations and the psychologist's willingness to make specific recommendations was directly proportionate to the quality of face-to-face relationships existing between these two professionals." (p. 41)

The qualitative nature of the relationship helps determine the impact of the contact as does the quantity or number of contacts (Kaplan and Sprunger, 1967; Tyler and Fine, 1973). The consulting contact would seem to be most effective if it is meaningful and on a regular or planned basis.

This collaborative relationship always involves the consultant, the consultee (the one asking for help), and the consultee's client. The consultant functions as a model for effective communication. He listens and responds to the words, feelings, and gestures of the consultee.

The specific processes and practices utilized in consulting are as numerous as the people using them. The specific procedures employed should be dependent on their "fit" to the consultant. As Combs et al. (1969) states:

"It occurred to us then that perhaps the question of methods in the helping professions is not a matter of adopting the "right" method, but a question of the helper discovering the right method **for him.** That is to say, the crucial question is not "what" method, but the "fit" of the method, its appropriateness to the self of the helper, to his purposes, his subjects, the situation, and so forth." (p. 75)

The effectiveness does not lie in the tool but, instead, in the user and how comfortable he or she is with the procedure.

Mayer presents several very specific procedures to be used in the consulting relationship. Using a behavior modification approach, he presents a specific definition and illustration of each procedure.

Kennedy, also of the behavioral orientation, describes the use of learning principles (which are the basis of most personality theories) in consulting. This powerful approach is well demonstrated through the application of basic learning principles to typical school problems. (Kennedy and Mayer and Dinkmeyer all emphasize the crucial necessity of a good relationship.)

Dinkmeyer approaches consulting from an Adlerian or socioteleological frame-work. He posits an operational theory of human behavior as it applies to con-sulting. A transcript of these principles and procedures applied to consulting help in clarifying Dinkmeyer's approach.

Fine and Tyler present a survey of the literature on consulting. They touch on the excellent work of Caplan, Rogers, and Lippitt on the consulting process. The writers advocate a direct consultant-consultee contact as opposed to be-havior modification, written reports, or prescriptive teaching. These are viewed as problem areas in the search for effective procedures. They add further empirical support to the importance and crucial nature of the consultant-consultee relationship.

Hagens identifies the commonalities between counseling and consultation. She differentiates these approaches from therapy and explains how they can compliment one another.

As these articles are read, consider the following:

● What are the common elements in these approaches? Specifically, compare Dinkmeyer and Mayer.

● Each of the authors in this section places a high value on the consulting relationship. Is it possible to have an effective consulting contact without a good relationship? Is it more important to have a good relationship or an effective repertoire of modification procedures?

● What do Fine and Tyler mean when they describe written reports, prescrip-tive teaching, and behavior modification as problem areas? Discuss how Mayer or Kennedy would respond to their position.

● How do you envision the consulting process? Prepare a personal step-by-step plan for consultation from the initial contact to termination.

● List some of the variety of procedures that are used within the consulting interview? List some procedures that can be utilized outside of the interview in the modification process?

● How do counseling, psychotherapy, and consultation differ? How are they similar?

REFERENCES

Baker, H. L. "Psychological services: From the school staff's point of view." **Journal of School Psychology,** 1965, **3,** 36–42.

Carkhuff, R. R. **The development of human resources.** New York: Holt, Rinehart and Winston, 1971.

Combs, A. W., Avila, D. L., and Purkey, W. W. **Helping relationships: Basic concepts for the helping professions.** Boston: Allyn & Bacon, 1971.

Combs, A. W. et al. **Florida Studies in the helping professions.** Gainesville, Fla.: University of Florida Press, 1969.

Kaplan, M., and Sprunger, B. Psychological evaluations and teacher perceptions of students. **Journal of School Psychology,** 1967, **5,** 287–291.

Kuriloff, P. J. The counselor as psychoecologist. **Personnel and Guidance Journal,** 1973, Vol. 51-5, 321–327.

Rogers, C. R. Significant learning: in therapy and in education. **Educational Leadership,** January, 1959, **16,** 232–242.

Tyler, M. M., and Fine, M. J. The effects of limited and intensive school psychologist-teacher consultation. Mimeo from University of Kansas, 1973.

12. BEHAVIORAL CONSULTING: USING BEHAVIOR MODIFICATION PROCEDURES IN THE CONSULTING RELATIONSHIP

G. Roy Mayer

The use of behavior modification procedures by counselors is not new. Many recent articles and books have described how such procedures have been used to effect desirable student behavior changes (Blackham & Silberman 1971; Engelhardt, Sulzer & Altekruse 1971; Farber & Mayer 1972; Krumboltz & Thoresen 1969; Skinner 1968; Sulzer & Mayer 1972; Whitley & Sulzer 1970). In several of these recent writings, counselors and school psychologists, or behavioral consultants, consulted with teachers to help the teachers become more aware of the effects that their behaviors and classroom environments were having on student behavior. The consultant also helped the teachers to use this behavioral information in formulating objectives and in selecting behavioral procedures to facilitate student learning and personal-social development. By enhancing the teachers' competencies in managing student behavior, the consultant sought to reduce the number of children needing counseling. Such consultation is both preventative and problem-oriented. The teacher learns behavioral strategies and procedures from the consultant which can be used not only to handle immediate problem situations, but also to influence the behaviors of all her students. Such documented outcomes of behavioral consulting are of major importance to the practitioner. Other consulting approaches have yet to produce such supportive data (Kranzler 1969).

THE CONSULTING RELATIONSHIP

Although there is outcome evidence supporting the use of behavioral consulting, there is at this time very little research or writing describing the

Source. G. Roy Mayer, "Behavioral Consulting: Using Behavior Modification Procedures in the Consulting Relationship," *Elementary School Guidance and Counseling*, 1972, Vol. 7(2), 114–119. Copyright 1972 by the American Personnel and Guidance Association and reproduced by permission.

behavioral consulting relationship. Yet, it is this relationship that often determines the degree of success achieved in helping the student. It is through this relationship that the behavioral strategy and procedures are transmitted to the students, teachers, and parents. Thus, though behavioral consulting is an important area of investigation, most researchers have neglected it up to this time.

CONSULTANT OBJECTIVES FOR THE CONSULTEE'S BEHAVIOR

The behavioral consultant has several objectives for those with whom he consults. The two most common objectives are (a) to help the teacher or parent (consultee) specify desired terminal behaviors for the student (select goals); and (b) to facilitate the consultee's acquisition and implementation (decrease acquisition time and increase rate of usage) of the mutually agreed upon behavioral procedures (use behavioral approaches).

BEHAVIOR MODIFICATION PROCEDURES

The behavioral consultant seeks to effectively enhance teachers' competencies in managing student behavior toward the attainment of educational and social objectives. In order to do so, he uses the same basic learning procedures in his consulting relationship that he uses in counseling, and which he suggests be used in the classroom or home. In other words, behavioral or operant learning procedures are as applicable to the counselor-teacher relationship as they are to the teacher-pupil, counselor-client, or any interpersonal relationship. It is the specific stimuli used within each behavioral procedures that may change among relationships. For example, the consultant is more likely to use verbal praise than hugs or candy as a reinforcer on teachers or parents, though he might recommend the use of hugs or candy with a particular child. The reinforcement procedure, as well as other behavioral procedures, is applicable to all interpersonal relationships. A few of the behavioral procedures frequently used for attainment of consultation objectives, such as the two above, are illustrated below.

POSITIVE REINFORCEMENT AND EXTINCTION

Defined

Positive reinforcement occurs when a stimulus which follows a behavior (i.e., a consequential event or object) results in the behavior being maintained or increasing in frequency. Extinction is a procedure in which reinforcement is withheld from a previously reinforced behavior.

Discussed and Illustrated

School counselors and psychologists frequently use both positive reinforcement and extinction procedures with their consultees. For example, Moore and Sanner (1969) note that during the consulting relationship, the behavioral consultant "responds verbally or non-verbally in order to reinforce the teacher's descriptive statements of behavior [p. 256]." General statements by the teacher, such as wanting the student to "be happy," or become a "better student," or become less "hyperactive" and "aggressive," are not reinforced. However, statements such as "he seldom smiles," "he seldom completes his homework," "she is frequently out of her seat," and "I wish he would stop hitting Mary," are reinforced. These are behavioral statements which facilitate goal selection for the student. They are also usually the behaviors which the consultee used to infer that the child was unhappy or hyperactive. Thus, for clarity of communication and to help all concerned zero in on the specific behavior or concern, behavioral statements are selectively reinforced.

Positive reinforcement and extinction procedures can also be used to aid the consultee in consistently using agreed upon behavioral approaches. One commonly held explanation of the reason that teachers and parents continue to use the agreed upon behavioral approach is that the child's progress reinforces them (Panyan, Boozer & Morris 1970). However, such reinforcement is often delayed or not immediate enough; in that case, the consultant may follow Krumboltz and Thoresen's (1969) suggestion that "the counselor's best strategy is to help the teacher select a specific workable behavior problem where results can be observable within a short period of time [p. 154]." Consultants, however, are not always able to follow such a strategy. Consequently, numerous investigators have reported the importance of reinforcing the consultee's use of appropriate behavioral procedures if such usage is to be maintained or increased. MacDonald, Gallimore, and MacDonald (1970) noted that parents and relatives needed support (reinforcement) in the form of a face-to-face meeting or a phone conversation at least twice a week. Such a procedure was found necessary if the parents were to maintain the behavioral contracts made between them and their adolescents to increase school attendance. Cooper, Thomson, and Baer (1970) reported that the provision of feedback to teachers, in the form of charted observational data as to how they were doing in attending to or reinforcing appropriate student responses, selectively increased such attending by the teachers.

Another means of reinforcing the consultee's use of the procedures has been through the means of charts and graphs which depict the student's progress. As Mayer (1973) has noted, "When the teacher and/or parents can see from a graph that the procedure *is* bringing about the desired change, they are in essence, reinforced." Such an approach is frequently helpful, since often during the early phases of a behavior change program a small behavior change may be overlooked unless data is collected and graphed. This is particularly true with disruptive behavior. For example, a reduction from 80 percent disruption to 60 percent can be easily overlooked and the procedure dropped prematurely, unless such data is presented.

Other investigators (Whitley 1970; Zeilberger, Sampen & Sloane 1968) report having verbally commended teachers and parents following their usage of an appropriate behavioral procedure. For example, the counselors in Whitley's study (1970) commended teachers for attending to the student following a desirable response or for withholding their attention following an undesirable response. Inappropriate teacher responses were usually ignored or placed on extinction.

DISCRIMINATIVE STIMULI

Defined

Discriminative stimuli are events, objects, or behaviors which occur prior to the occurrence of the behavior and serve to bring about the behavior's occurrence. They are the antecedents to the behavior and might include directions, prompts, cues, and models.

Discussed and Illustrated

Modeling is frequently used by behavioral consultants. As Goodwin (1969) notes, "In effect, the counselor can model a strategy, in his work with the teacher, which serves as an example of how the teacher, in turn, can behave when problems arise [p. 260]." In addition to modeling a behavioral strategy (Sulzer & Mayer 1972) he might also model or roleplay the procedure to be used by the consultee. The consultant might demonstrate the application of various social reinforcers (Sulzer & Mayer 1972, p. 31) that the teacher could use in the classroom.

Questions are also used to bring forth operational statements of behavior and involve the teacher in the behavioral strategy. Such questions might include: What did he do? What does he spend the most time doing? What happened prior to and following the occurrance of the behavior? What is usually happening when the behavior does not occur? What has worked or is working as a reinforcer?

Written or oral directions to the consultee have been used by most investigators in order to get the consultee to use appropriate behavioral procedures. However, some behavioral consultants also have reported using other forms of discriminative stimuli to get the teacher to use their described approaches effectively. For example, in-service education workshops and seminars have been used by some consultants (Madsen, Becker & Thomas 1968; Ward & Baker 1968). Others, such as Hall, Lund, and Jackson (1968), had classroom observers hold up a small square of colored paper, in a manner not likely to be noticed by the pupil, whenever the pupil was engaged in the goal behavior of study. This served as a signal for the teacher to reinforce the student. Zeilberger, Sampen, and Sloane (1968) also found it necessary to cue parents in assisting them in reducing their child's aggressive behavior. Often a simple nod of the head can serve such a function. Mandelker, Brigham, and Bushell (1970) have reported that sometimes a reinforcer can serve as a discriminative stimulus for the delivery of another reinforcer. They found that the use of tokens by teachers served to increase the teachers' use of social reinforcement such as praise.

Discriminative stimuli then are also used in the behavioral consulting relationship to facilitate the attainment of the objectives the consultant has for the consultee. However, there seems to be a general consensus among behavioral consultants that the use of discriminative stimuli must be associated with reinforcement and vice versa. Several investigators' findings indicate that the combination of discriminative stimuli and reinforcement is more effective in achieving our previously stated objectives than either used alone (Ayllon & Azrin 1964; Herman & Tramontana 1971; Whitley 1970). Thus, in addition to instructing the consultee in the use of behavioral procedures, the occurrence of reinforcement must also be assured.

FADING

Defined

Fading is a procedure in which discriminative stimuli (prompts, guidelines, directions, or other behavioral antecedents) are gradually and progressively withdrawn (Carlson & Mayer 1971; Sulzer & Mayer 1972).

Discussed and Illustrated

As the consultee acquires the skill of specifying behavioral goals, the consultant gradually reduces or fades out his usage of questions such as "What did he do?" Likewise, as the consultant acquires proficiency in using appropriate behavioral procedures, the consultant gradually fades out his directions, roleplaying activities, and use of cues. Similarly, the activity of pointing out similarities between two situations is used less frequently as the consultee acquires proficient use of the procedures.

Fading then is a procedure used by the consultant to assure that the consultee's behavior does not become dependent upon his assistance. Thus, it fosters goal or objective mastery and independent action.

SCHEDULING

Defined

Whereas fading involved the gradual removal of antecedents, or more precisely, discriminative stimuli, scheduling involves the gradual removal of reinforcing consequences.

Discussed and Illustrated

To get a behavior to increase in occurrence to the desired level, the best procedure is to reinforce it as frequently as feasible. Ideally, one should immediately reinforce the behavior each time it occurs until it is established. Once established, however, the reinforcement should be gradually thinned out; intermittent reinforcement schedules should be selected (Sulzer & Mayer 1972).

As was pointed out in the discussion of reinforcement, the consultant often finds it necessary to reinforce the consultee's use of appropriate behavior. This immediate and frequent reinforcement is necessary until the student's progress begins to reinforce the consultee's behavior. At this point, the consultant's reinforcement can be gradually reduced. For example, once it has become apparent to the teacher that the behavioral procedures he is using are effectively reducing the disruptive behavior in his classroom, the consultant's frequent praise and his use of charts and graphs can be gradually reduced.

Scheduling, like fading, assists the behavioral consultant in fully acquiring the prespecified objectives for his consultees. Ideally the consultee should eventually be able to specify his own behavioral goals and effectively use behavioral approaches without the consultant's assistance. Scheduling and fading are procedures used by the behavioral consultant to promote such proficiency.

DISCUSSION

The applicability of behavioral procedures to the consulting relationship has been demonstrated. However, this article should be considered as only an introduction to behavioral consulting. Numerous other behavioral objectives and procedures are applicable to consulting in the schools. Furthermore, much was omitted about each discussed procedure. For example, I did not discuss how to identify or develop reinforcers and discriminative stimuli, and presented little as to how to use the discussed procedures with maximal effectiveness. Such knowledge, much of which can be found elsewhere (Sulzer & Mayer 1972), is of vital importance to the behavioral consultant.

As we come to understand how behavioral procedures can be applied to achieve our consulting objectives, the student will benefit. Thus as noted before, it is the consulting relationship which often determines the degree of success achieved toward helping students—a goal to which we all subscribe.

References

Ayllon, T., & Azrin, N. Reinforcement and instructions with mental patients. *Journal of the Experimental Analysis of Behavior,* 1964, *7,* 327–331.

Blackham, G. J., & Silberman, A. *Modification of child behavior.* Belmont, Calif.: Wadsworth Publishing Company, 1971.

Carlson, J., & Mayer, G. R. Fading: A behavioral procedure to increase independent behavior. *School Counselor,* 1971, *18,* 193–197.

Cooper, M. L., Thomson, C. L., & Baer, D. M. The experimental modification of teacher attending behavior. *Journal of Applied Behavior Analysis,* 1970, *3,* 153–157.

Engelhardt, L., Sulzer, R., & Altekruse, M. The counselor as a consultant in eliminating out-of-seat behavior. *Elementary School Guidance and Counseling,* 1971, *5,* 196–204.

Farber, H., & Mayer, G. R. Behavior consultation in a barrio high school. *The Personnel and Guidance Journal,* 1972, *51,* in press.

Goodwin, D. L. Consulting with the classroom teacher. In J. D. Krumboltz and C. E. Thoresen (Eds.), *Behavioral Counseling Cases and Techniques.* New York: Holt, Rinehart & Winston, 1969.

Hall, R. V., Lund, D., & Jackson, D. Effects of teacher attention on study behavior. *Journal of Applied Behavior Analysis,* 1968, *1,* 1–12.

Herman, S. H., & Tramontana, J. Instructions and group versus individual reinforcement in modifying disruptive group behavior. *Journal of Applied Behavior Analysis,* 1971, *4,* 113–119.

Kranzler, G. D. The elementary school counselor as consultant: An evaluation. *Elementary School Guidance and Counseling,* 1969, *3,* 285–288.

Krumboltz, J. D., & Thoresen, C. E. (Eds.) *Behavioral counseling cases and techniques.* New York: Holt, Rinehart & Winston, 1969.

MacDonald, W. S., Gallimore, R., & MacDonald, G. Contingency counseling by school personnel: An economical model of intervention. *Journal of Applied Behavior Analysis,* 1970, *3,* 175–182.

Madsen, C. H., Jr., Becker, W. C., & Thomas, D. R. Rules, praise and ignoring: Elements of elementary classroom control. *Journal of Applied Behavior Analysis,* 1968, *1,* 139–150.

Mandelker, A. V., Brigham, T. A., & Bushell, D., Jr. The effects of token procedures on a teacher's social contacts with her students. *Journal of Applied Behavior Analysis,* 1970, *3,* 169–174.

Mayer, G. R. Achieving student behavior change: A rationale and model. In W. H. Van Hoose, J. Pietrofesa, and J. Carlson (Eds.), *Elementary school guidance and counseling: A composite view.* Boston: Houghton Mifflin, 1973.

Moore, R., & Sanner, K. Helping teachers analyze and remedy problems. In J. D. Krumboltz and C. E. Thoresen (Eds.), *Behavioral counseling cases and techniques.* New York: Holt, Rinehart & Winston, 1969.

Panyan, M., Boozer, H., & Morris, N. Feedback to attendants as a reinforcer for applying operant techniques. *Journal of Applied Behavior Analysis,* 1970, *3,* 1–4.

Skinner, B. F. *The technology of teaching.* New York: Appleton-Century-Crofts, 1968.

Sulzer, B., & Mayer, G. R. *Behavior modification procedures for school personnel.* Hinsdale, Ill.: Dryden Press, 1972.

Ward, M. H., & Baker, B. L. Reinforcement therapy in the classroom. *Journal of Applied Behavior Analysis,* 1968, *1,* 323–328.

Whitley, A. D. Counselor-teacher consultation including video analysis to reduce undesirable student responses. Unpublished doctoral dissertation, Southern Illinois University, 1970.

Whitley, A. D., & Sulzer, B. Reducing disruptive behavior through consultation. *Personnel and Guidance Journal,* 1970, *48,* 836–841.

Zeilberger, J., Sampen, S. E., & Sloane, H. N., Jr. Modification of a child's problem behaviors in the home with the mother as therapist. *Journal of Applied Behavior Analysis,* 1968, *1,* 47–53.

13. CONTRIBUTIONS OF ADLERIAN PSYCHOLOGY TO SCHOOL CONSULTING

Don Dinkmeyer

THE NEED AND THE SETTING

It is increasingly apparent that teachers require a type of professional assistance that enables them to function more effectively with the child who is difficult to teach. The present provision of specialists in pupil personnel services who diagnose and develop reports or who develop a therapeutic experience for the child outside of the classroom, is often not a solution for the concerns of the teacher.

The teacher is concerned with practical problems. She asks, "What do I do when he wanders from his seat, annoys other children, starts fights, and

Source. Don Dinkmeyer, "Contributions of Adlerian Psychology to School Consulting," in Harold H. Mosak (Ed.) *Alfred Adler: His Influence on Psychology Today.* Park Ridge, N.J.: Noyes Press, 1973, pp. 212–220.

even sulks and refuses to move his pencil when kept after school? It is interesting to know that he has low ability, a bad home situation, and should be treated as an individual; but specifically, what do I do?"

Specialists in pupil personnel services often spend extensive time in diagnostic appraisal only to summarize in psychological language what the teacher has already suspected. Furthermore, recommendations are often developed in the office without any consideration of the teacher's capacity to execute such recommendations. In some instances, children are assigned to counseling experience with little expectation that the counselor and teacher should communicate. Occasionally it is even suggested that if the child's behavior became more difficult that the teacher should take this as a sign of improvement. This type of assumption is not easily accepted by the teacher who has a large group of children to educate. The type of assistance that teachers have received has made them suspicious that psychology has little to offer the harried teacher. Occasionally, it has encouraged them in desperation to adhere to authoritarian practices, even though this tends to increase the conflict and reduce the communication with the child.

A possible solution to the communication gap between counselors and teachers exists in a new approach to consultation.

"Consulting is the procedure through which teachers, parents, principals, and other adults significant in the life of the child communicate. Consultation involves sharing information and ideas, coordinating, comparing observations, providing a sounding board, and developing tentative hypotheses for action. In contrast to the superior-inferior relationship involved in some consultation with specialists, emphasis is placed on joint planning and collaboration. The purpose is to develop tentative recommendations which fit the uniqueness of the child, the teacher, and the setting." [2]

This approach has long been advocated by leaders in the field of counseling. [7, 8, 9, 10]

A national committee of the American Personnel and Guidance Association identified consultation as one of three major responsibilities of the counselor. [1] However, little can be found in the literature which suggests procedures for school consultation. The failure of counselors to consult effectively with teachers can probably be traced to three factors:

1. Lack of understanding of a rationale of human behavior which enables them to comprehend the purpose of a child's behavior and develop hypotheses regarding corrective actions.
2. Inability to develop a program which structures their role as a consultant who collaborates in contrast to a crisis manipulation.

THE CONSULTANT RELATIONSHIP

The consultant relationship is based upon mutual trust and mutual respect. The teacher comes with a problem which requires additional professional skills and insights. The consultant recognizes that he cannot solve the problem without the complete collaboration of the teacher. There must be an alignment of goals and purposes. This can only be established as educational jargon is deleted and they communicate their perceptions clearly.

The consulting relationship is collaborative, a joint venture in which both contribute to understanding the problem and developing solutions. An atmosphere for cooperative problem-solving must be developed. This is not a superior-inferior relationship, and the teacher must be made aware that she has something to contribute to the consultant through: (1) her access to daily observation of the child; (2) feedback regarding the efficacy of the ideas. The consultant has no one who can provide this information and without it, meaningful consultation is impossible.

It is apparent that well educated counselors are effective in listening to students and in promoting self-understanding and decision-making. However, work with teachers frequently deteriorates to advising and vague generalizations. This is valuable professional time and the counselor must listen, be empathic, and focus on the teacher's perception of the situation. He hears what is said and not said, while noting the tone and affect. He is concerned with what the teacher believes about children, and this child specifically. He is more concerned about how she converts her belief into transactions with the child. He helps her to clarify what the child's actions and her actions mean.

While the relationship with teachers is similar to the counseling relationship, it is also a teaching relationship. There is a concern for helping to develop principles which can be applied to other situations. The truly effective consultant helps the teacher build her competencies. Skilled consultation may result in less referrals from a teacher as she understand the specific application of principles.

PROPOSITIONS FOR UNDERSTANDING BEHAVIOR

Adlerian psychology has some specific contributions to make to the school consultation. The increased interest of teachers in Adlerian procedures indicates their efficacy for use with classroom problems. [3, 4] Teachers find the procedures are effective in meeting the challenge of the child who resents typical attempts to secure his cooperation.

The consultant process immediately takes on new meaning in terms of the conceptualization of man as an indivisible, social, decision-making being whose psychological movements and actions have a purpose. The consultant is less concerned with the pattern that emerges from the data. He is interested in how the passive resistance in the classroom relates to the child's aggressive behavior on the playground. Perhaps both are indications that the child is interested in controlling others and believes the best way he can do it in school is through forcing the teacher to notice him. He always searches for the relationship between the data.

Some assumptions basic to consultation:

1. *Behavior is goal directed and purposive.* Consultation time is not lost on attempting to determine the causes of the behavior. Too many of the causes (i.e. physical handicap, broken homes and poverty) are beyond the capacity of the school to change. In contrast to looking backward to determine a cause, focus is on the "here and now" behavior and understanding the goal. If Johnny is not working at mathematics, the first procedure is not to start a lengthy child study. The focus is on the consequences of not accomplishing math. The consultant is always interested not only in what the child does, but more specifically, what do peers, parents and teachers do about the refusal to work? Dreikurs made a major contribution to school consultation in his description of the four goals of misbehavior: attention-getting; the struggle for power; the desire to retaliate; and the display of disability. [4]

The teleoanalytic approach is a unique contribution to school consultation. While different in theoretical premise, it is similar to the Behavioral approach in its emphasis on the consequences of the behavior. [6]

2. *Motivation can be understood in terms of striving for significance.* The striving receives direction from the child's uniquely conceived goal or self-ideal. The emphasis then is on how is the child seeking to be known. There is less concern with what he is doing and more with the direction in which he is moving. The child's refusal to cooperate in the classroom which results in punishment and penalties may not make immediate sense. However, if it enables him to become known with the peers as one who dares to challenge the teacher, it may help him to establish a reputation. If the child is to be changed, a method of helping him increase self-esteem in relationship to the peers must be found. The consultant team is always questioning how does this behavior help him to be known?

3. *All behavior has social meaning.* Behavior is always understood in terms of its social context. Thus, the consultant must rely on the teacher's classroom observations. He requests that anecdotes are kept which describe the action of the child, reaction of others, and the response of the child to these reactions. This enables the team to infer social meaning and establish tentative hypotheses. The consultant comes to the classroom to observe

and here the teleoanalytic frame of reference enables him to record observations he shares with the teacher. The consultant becomes another pair of eyes for the teacher.

The following anecdote provides data for consultation:

"As Bill came to the front of the room to give his report, Jack got up to sharpen his pencil. The teacher ignored Jack, but Dave and Sam laughed. The teacher corrected all three of the boys."

The anecdote shows the social rewards Jack receives. Adlerians recognize that social striving is not secondary, but primary. It is not suggested that decisions about the meaning of behavior should be made from one anecdote, but several may reveal a pattern.

4. *The individual is understood in terms of his phenomenological field.* We are not concerned with how the events appear externally, but seek out the meaning the events possess for the individual. This enables the consultant to recognize that the teacher may be operating from a model in which she sees herself as a source for all information and controls. This will certainly affect recommendations if the teacher is afraid to make a mistake or permit the child to learn from the consequences of misbehavior. Too many professional recommendations do not result in changes because the consultant does not understand the teacher's frame of reference. Until the verbal message that is sent by the consultant is the same as that received by the teacher, and vice versa, no communication or consultation will have transpired.

This principle obviously applies to understanding the child's private logic. The child who believes "It is safer to withdraw than try and fail"; "I am not as able as others"; or "I only try if I can be perfect" will function on the basis of these assumptions, regardless of their validity. The consultant's training in this specific rationale of human behavior enables him to "guess what the child is thinking." Guessing in the right direction is an acceptable procedure in establishing hypotheses, and is always presented to the child in a tentative fashion for confirmation. The disclosure of goals is discussed extensively by Dreikurs. [4]

5. *The individual has the capacity to assign personal meanings to experiences, to decide.* Adler was the first to call our attention to the biased apperception. This principle is particularly important insofar as it cautions against any simple stimulus-response interpretation of behavior. It recognizes that the teacher cannot predict the child's response to her behavior. Behavior is more than reactive; it is creative. On one occasion the child is kept after school, and he immediately gets to work and completes his assignments. The next time he is kept he refuses to pick up the pencil. He had the capacity to decide how he will respond. However, the teacher can

learn to observe her response to his behavior and his responses to correction in order to understand the behavior. The psychological movement will become apparent. She will recognize the child has this capacity to choose ultimately. Once this is acknowledged, then choice can be utilized as a therapeutic agent insofar as the teacher is willing to permit the child to experience the natural and logical consequences of his behavior. [5]

6. *Failure to function relates to the psychodynamics of discouragement.* The extremely discouraged individual, teacher, or child assumes he cannot function or that it is not worthwhile to function or that he will fail or that if he succeeds, others will only demand more. He does not even attempt to see alternatives. He believes his is not as capable as others and refuses to accept his inevitable imperfections.

Changes in human behavior are based on alterations in concepts, beliefs, attitudes, and expectations. Corrective efforts must be directed toward altering the individual's anticipations, the strongest human motivations.

Consultation cannot be a theoretical exchange but must be planned to alter specific behaviors. The focus is on action by the child which will change the individual's opinion of self. This may require manipulation of the environment so the child receives different feedback.

"Bill's transfer to school was preceded by a lengthy letter describing him as incorrigible. The new principal decided to treat Bill as if he could function. He did not wait for him to earn a place through misbehavior, but he gave him a responsible job and relayed his anticipation that Bill would succeed. Bill was confused at first, but in the new environment found he could be recognized for active-constructive behavior."

However, the process of encouragement is difficult, and the child is often better equipped to discourage the adult than the teacher is to encourage. [3]

7. *Belonging is a basic need.* Man can only be actualized as he finds his place and belongs to someone, or something. Fear and anxiety, often cripplers of the learning process, arise out of the fear of not being acceptable.

The school often generates the environment for the feeding of the neurotic process. Demands are set high, standards are frequently irrelevant to individual differences, and the teacher is perceived as primarily concerned with diagnosing mistakes or liabilities. Teachers do not use the potential power which comes from involvement and belonging, and in many instances even work to suppress social development not directly related to academic progress. They are often at war with the socially powerful students.

When the significance of belonging is recognized, various sociometric procedures can be used to identify social needs. Corrective procedures then might consist of revised seating, new study groups, group discussion, or group counseling. The focus then would be on activities which facilitate belonging.

8. *Adlerians are less concerned with what a person has than what he decides to do with what he possesses.* The schools are overconcerned with testing and the accumulation of data. This preoccupation with identification of traits and abilities has led to many studies of underachievement.

Frequently the test data in the school records provide only the skeleton, and do not reveal anything of importance for the teaching process. Pupil personnel records, to be functional, should acquaint one with the child's attitudes, beliefs, motives, and convictions. There should be data which helps to clarify his purposes and interests. This data may consist of anecdotes, autobiographies, sentence completion forms, and other procedures which permit access to his private logic. Each teacher should be required to describe "what works" with this child.

This brief excerpt from a case may clarify some of the practical applications of Adlerian psychology in school consultation.

Action	*Analysis*
Mrs. Smith contacted the consultant regarding Jane, a second grade student. The complaint centered around the child's causing a disturbance in the classroom and failing to work up to ability. The consultant, after listening to the general complaint, asks the teacher to describe the situation which she finds most difficult.	Attack a specific problem, not generalities.
MRS. SMITH: Well, if she is given an assignment, rather than doing it she first visits with 5 or 6 children in the room.	
CONSULTANT: What do you usually do about this?	Seek to clarify. Focus on the psychological movement and the transaction between teacher and child.
MRS. SMITH: I usually say, "Jane, get busy and take your seat."	
CONSULTANT: What does Jane do?	
MRS. SMITH: In a few minutes she's back to the same pattern. She never seems to be bothered and readily recognizes she shouldn't do this.	
CONSULTANT: It seems teacher and Jane have an agreement about their roles—Jane misbehaves and you remind her. Is it possible she does this to get your attention?	Seek to identify the child's purpose.

MRS. SMITH: That's probably true!

CONSULTANT: Do you have any idea of what might be done differently when she gets out of her seat and starts wandering around the room?

Consultant seeks teacher's perceptions and her collaboration.

MRS. SMITH: I've thought about ignoring her, but I feel this is not fair to the other children to ignore her when she is disturbing them; and if they enjoy her company everything gets out of hand.

Teacher poses first potential solution.

CONSULTANT: You feel ignoring wouldn't change the situation in this case?

MRS. SMITH: No, Jane enjoys people too much.

(At this point the teacher was encouraged to explore other remedies. After some exploration, the consultant poses tentatively a new procedure.)

CONSULTANT: I wonder how you would feel about giving Jane a choice about whether she'd rather sit in her seat when there's work to be done, or if she'd rather stand up.

MRS. SMITH: That might work. I've never thought of that!

CONSULTANT: My idea is that frequently with children like Jane we are forced to react to her. I'm wondering if, instead, we could get her to cope with you by giving her a choice. The next time in a private conference you could pose to her the alternatives of working at her seat or standing for the morning. This must not be relayed as a punishment, but as a choice.

Utilize the therapeutic agent of choice and the child's capacity to decide by changing the consequences.

(At this point the teacher and consultant explore other examples of misbehavior. Emphasis is placed on observing closely times when Jane is functioning and commenting positively. Consequences are to be balanced with encouragement.)

This transcript from a consultation situation provides a snapshot of the consulting procedure with teachers.

THE CONSULTANT PROCESS

Adlerian psychology makes a specific contribution to the actual consultant process through:

1. A focus on dynamics and psychological movement rather than upon labels and static entities.
2. A concern for the pattern of behavior, the life-style, or characteristic pattern of responses.
3. A recognition that misbehavior and failure to function convey a non-verbal message.
4. Awareness that the consequences of the behavior point to the purpose.
5. Analysis of the relationship and interaction between teacher and child.

These principles influence the type of information collected from the teacher and the child. They give direction to the consultation interview.

References

1. ACES-ASCA Committee on the Elementary School Counselor, Preliminary Statement. Minneapolis: American Personnel & Guidance Association Convention, April 1965.
2. Dinkmeyer, D. "The counselor as consultant: rationale and procedures." *Elementary School Guidance and Counseling*, 1968, *2*, 187.
3. Dinkmeyer, D., and Dreikurs, R. *Encouraging children to learn: The encouragement process*. Englewood Cliffs, N.J.: Prentice-Hall, 1963.
4. Dreikurs, R. *Psychology in the Classroom*. 2nd ed. N.Y.: Harper, 1968.
5. Dreikurs, R., and Grey, D. Logical Consequences, Des Moines: Meredith 1968.
6. Krumboltz, D., and Hosford, R. E. "Behavioral counseling in the elementary school." *Elementary School Guidance and Counseling*, 1967, *1*, 27–40.
7. Oldridge, B. "Two roles for elementary school guidance personnel." *Personnel and Guidance*. 1964, *43*, 367–370.
8. Patouillet, R. "Organizing for Guidance in the Elementary School." *Teachers College Record*, 1957, *58* (8).
9. Smith, H., and Eckerson, L. O. "Guidance services in elementary schools: a national survey." Wash., D.C.: U. S. Government Printing Office, 1966.
10. Wrenn, C. G. *The counselor in a changing world*. Wash., D.C.: American Personnel and Guidance Association, 1962.

14. CONCERNS AND DIRECTIONS IN TEACHER CONSULTATION

•–•

Marvin J. Fine and Milton M. Tyler

The role of the school psychologist as a consultant has not been ignored in the literature. Newman (1967), for example, presented a strong and illustrative treatise on effective consultation, arguing the need for continuous and on-the-spot contacts and for the development of a trusting relationship among the people involved as being central to effective consultation. Gray (1963) also treated consultation extensively, presenting the early consultation model of Caplan (1956) as a viable framework. Other recent publications (Fischer, 1969; Mannino, 1969; Berkowitz, 1968; Losen, 1964; Farnsworth, 1966; Handler, Gerston, & Handler, 1965; Reger, 1964; Capobianco, 1967) have examined the parameters of psychological and psychiatric school consultation, and it would be accurate to conclude that almost all models or conceptions of school psychology view the psychologist-teacher relationship as the pivotal point for effective service.

Despite this apparent plethora of attention to consultation, many school psychologists seem unresponsive to the interpersonal dimensions of their functioning, preferring to operate out of a narrow, insulated tester-reporter model, or substituting technological knowledge for human relations skills. It is hoped that the ensuing discussion of concerns and directions in consultation will prove helpful and stimulating to the practicing school psychologist who is struggling to mediate the demands of his position with the existing needs of teachers and children and with theoretical advances in the fields of psychology and education.

CURRENT CONCERNS IN CONSULTATION

Several areas of the psychologist-teacher relationship have been identified as having special pertinence to the consultation process; these areas need examination. The substitution of written reports for vis-a-vis teacher contacts has been and still is of concern to school psychologists. Additionally, the more recent thrusts by school psychologists into the realms of behavior modification and prescriptive teaching, though potentially quite productive, possess some inherent dangers for the psychologist-teacher relationship.

Source. Marvin J. Fine and Milton M. Tyler, "Concerns and Directions in Teacher Consultation," *Journal of School Psychology*, 1971, Vol. 9–4, 436–444.

Psychological Report

The school psychologist's report historically has been quite enigmatic; psychologists have debated what should go into it, who should read it, and what it accomplishes, and yet many school psychologists still seem content for the report to represent their main communication with the teacher. The image of the "hit and run" school psychologist who tests and weeks later sends a jargonish or abbreviated report to the schools is only too prevalent.

The psychological report, however descriptive and prescriptive, is highly subject to individual teacher interpretation. By itself, a report may suffice for the disseminating of objective data; it is questionable, however, how effective an unaccompanied report would be in leading to some significant behavior change in teacher or child.

Similar thoughts prompted Bardon (1963) to query, "Instead of testing a child and writing a report with recommendations for the teacher to follow, what would happen if a psychologist tested or observed a child and then sat down with the teacher to exchange views?" [p. 25] Bardon's question was tentatively answered in a study of school psychological services in an Ohio county (Baker, 1965):

"Results suggested a teacher's willingness to carry out recommendations and the psychologist's willingness to make specific recommendations was directly proportional to the quality of face-to-face relationship existing between these two professionals." [p. 41]

The excessive use of written reports as substitutes for personal contacts may be tied in with the pressures for handling many cases. Also, the demand for the testing and retesting of retarded children with the emphasis on obtaining scores seems to be another logical culprit in this situation. The probability that reports alone may be a highly ineffective way of helping individuals should prompt school psychologists to reconsider the function of reports.

Prescriptive Teaching

This orientation places extensive and somewhat esoteric data in the hands of the school psychologist, who must translate this information into educationally relevant concepts. The psychologist's attempts to communicate the existence of specific language or sensory motor deficits to a teacher and then to develop an appropriate in-class program may meet considerable resistance from the teacher: the teacher may hold an opposing rationale for the child's lack of achievement (the child is just being lazy, or "he could succeed if only he would try"), or the teacher may accept the definition of the child's problem but then protest that there is not enough time to work with the child.

A rhetorical question can be raised regarding the teacher's right to his own beliefs about the child and whether or not he can program for the child in his classroom. However, in many situations the teacher's position is a reflection of anxiety or threat, and a phase of the school psychologist's consultant role should be to deal with these feelings. The curricular emphasis upon prescriptive teaching can represent a source of threat to the teacher. Curriculum know-how is supposedly the teacher's area of competence, but now the teacher finds himself confronted by a non-teacher who is very knowledgeable about unfamiliar curricular concepts and materials.

The prescriptive teaching recommendations should be in terms that the teacher can understand and accept. The psychologist may be impressed by elaborate terminology and concepts, but the teacher will only be threatened or disgusted if the psychologist's recommendations are unfathomable.

If the psychologist is unable to obtain the teacher's support for the prescriptive teaching program, then diagnostic testing time has been wasted, the child remains with his problem, and the teacher has not been assisted in broadening his skills and understanding his students. It is important that the psychologist attempt to introduce his recommendations in a sensible way and be prepared to deal with the teacher attitude variable. The psychologist should assume an approach to consultation that reduces the likelihood of threat and that includes provisions for helping teachers become more sensitive to themselves and to their relationship with the child.

Behavior Modification

The procedures encompassed under the rubric of behavior modification represent an effective technology for changing behavior, and the literature abounds with testimonials to this observation. But the zeal and certitude of the behavior modification-oriented psychologist may not be matched by the teacher's readiness to participate in a program. As with the area of prescriptive teaching, the teacher might be threatened by the newness and technical aspects of this approach. Also, the ethical questions pertaining to actively manipulating behavior via reinforcement, resolved by the psychologist, might still concern the teacher.

In some cases the psychologist may erroneously interpret the absence of verbalized resistance as meaning that the teacher endorses a behavior modification approach. In order to satisfy the psychologist, the teacher may have selected certain behaviors for modification that really were not the vital ones. Not only does a teacher usually have ambivalent feelings about a misbehaving child, he also may not clearly recognize which behaviors or combinations of behaviors constitute the problem.

In planning a modification program there can be a great deal of teacher-psychologist communication, but these contacts might be primarily in terms of the teacher being used as an observer, recorder, and contingency manager. The perceived insensivity of the psychologist to the teacher's feelings and concerns over the child may prompt the teacher to reject the psychologist and the modification techniques. A paradox lies in the frequently found contrast between the amount of attention given by the psychologist to the easily objectified classroom variables, compared with limited attention to the teacher's feelings about himself in relation to the child.

DIRECTIONS IN CONSULTATION

The components of a successful consulting relationship have been discussed by a number of writers and common themes are easily detected. Rogers (1959) suggested that a productive and satisfying relationship between teacher and school psychologist will ensue when (*a*) the teacher perceives himself as having a problem (e.g., a child with whom he has been unable to cope successfully); (*b*) the school psychologist is a congruent, genuine person in the relationship; (*c*) the school psychologist feels a high degree of positive regard for the teacher; (*d*) the school psychologist experiences an accurate, empathic understanding of the teacher's experiences, and communicates this; and (*e*) the teacher, to a degree, experiences the psychologist's congruence, acceptance, and empathy.

In a similar vein, Lippitt (1967) described a fruitful, helping situation as one characterized by:

"(1) mutual trust, (2) recognition that the helping situation is a joint exploration, (3) listening, with the helper listening more than the individual receiving help, and (4) behavior by the helper which is calculated to make it easier for the individual receiving help to talk." [pp. 73–74]

The psychologist's sensitivity, ability to communicate, and non-dominative attitude were valued in both orientations. The two orientations also appear to have a common goal to consultation, that of strengthening the teacher personally and professionally. Magary (1967), while generally supporting Rogers' orientation, cautioned that the skills of diagnosis, assessment, and evaluation are also needed by the school psychologist along with the psychologist's characteristics described by Rogers.

Caplan's (1964) discussion of consultee-centered case consultation is extremely germane to the school psychologist. This approach focuses on the teacher and his relationship with the child. Caplan is concerned that, as a professional person, the teacher may be impeded in working effectively with children. The school psychologist's entree into the situation will probably be through a teacher's referral, but if the psychologist "listens" carefully to the teacher he may conclude that a major portion of the difficulty lies in some way with the teacher's perceptions or handling of the situation. This approach to consultation does not preclude the possibility that the child may be experiencing a "real" problem; it simply emphasizes how a better classroom adjustment might be affected for the child through a change in teacher understanding and behavior, and through the teacher altering aspects of the classroom environment.

The four major categories of difficulty identified by Caplan as potentially interfering with a teacher's ability to deal effectively with a child were: lack of understanding, lack of skill, lack of objectivity, and lack of confidence and of esteem.

Lack of understanding. The teacher may have drawn erroneous conclusions or may simply lack the psychological skill to draw any conclusion regarding a child's behavior that she finds unusual or disturbing. Caplan (1964) illustrated this point by describing how a teacher believed that a child was going "bad" or delinquent as a result of his beginning to steal. The clarifying information the teacher received was that the boy's mother was pregnant and that his stealing was associated with feelings of loneliness, loss of love, etc. This information gave the teacher a new understanding of the child, and she changed her behavior accordingly.

The psychologist's insights into the teaching-learning process as well as his understanding of child development may be shared with the teacher. The problem situation may exist simply because the new teacher is unaware of what constitutes normal behavior for a group. Or a teacher may have misinterpreted some data from a child's cumulative folder, such as the IQ score. Or perhaps a teacher is using noncontingent reinforcement with a child, in which case a simple explanation of systematic, contingent reinforcement would be sufficient to increase the effectiveness of the teacher. In such situations, when the teacher lacks basic psychological insights, the consulting relationship could carry a needed didactic dimension.

Lack of skill. In this instance the teacher has adequate insight into the child's behavior but lacks specific skills or information pertaining to a course of action. For example, a teacher may be aware that a child has visual-perceptual problems but is unaware of how to program for the child within the classroom. Another teacher might be working with a socially alienated child and may not know how to "break the ice" and establish communication. Or the teacher may have an adequate awareness of the complexity of a child's problem and the child's need for psychotherapy, but may be unfamiliar with the community's psychiatric resources.

As with "lack of understanding," the psychologist's approach can be almost of a supervisory or didactic nature: "telling" the teacher would be the effective consultative strategy.

Lack of objectivity. Caplan gave relatively more emphasis to this category of difficulty, and school psychologists attempting teacher consultation will probably agree with this emphasis. The teacher through training and experience may have the understanding and skills necessary to work with a particular child, but he is in some way inhibited from using his professional skills. Caplan used the term "theme interference" to describe how certain problem themes interfere with a person's professional functioning. An illustration of this phenomenon (Fine, 1970) involved a psychologist advising a teacher to positively reinforce specified behaviors of a child and ignore other behaviors. The teacher's reluctance to accept this program was subsequently discovered to be based on her moralistic beliefs about the need to punish misbehaving children. She believed that the recommended program was the reverse of what it should be on moral grounds.

Some anxiety and faulty stereotyping can be expected from a teacher who has been unable to cope satisfactorily with a child. Examples of faulty stereotyping would be statements such as, "his older brother had the same problem, no one in that family can learn" or "you have to expect retarded kids to get in fights, they just don't know any better." In each of these examples the objective of the teacher's rationalization was to allay the threat and anxiety associated with being unable to cope with the child's behavior, and with the symbolic meaning that the child's behavior held for the teacher.

Caplan emphasized that the separation of the teacher's personal life from the work difficulties should be respected by the consultant. The consultant's concern should be with reducing the theme interference by focusing "on defining the nature of the theme by a careful examination of its manifestations in the work context. The consultant then reduces the theme interference by influencing the consultee to adopt a reality-based expectation for the client." [1964, p. 225]

The psychologist must be careful not to provoke teacher compliance through his inferred authority. The earlier discussed difficulties in implementing behavior modification and prescriptive teaching programs are sometimes brought about because, to use Kelman's (1958) terms, the teacher feels she must "comply" but has not really "identified" with or "internalized" the basic rationale of these programs.

Interpersonal sensitivity, ability to communicate, and a nondominative attitude, already mentioned in the context of Rogers (1959) and Lippitt (1967), would be vital for the school psychologist working with a teacher who lacks objectivity. Teacher trust in the psychologist should increase as it becomes apparent that they are working together toward common goals, rather than trying to dominate or control each other. As the psychologist and teacher discuss the child, simultaneously unveiling the teacher's distorted perceptions, the psychologist can periodically highlight and reflect the teacher's feelings and comments, giving the teacher a conscious opportunity to re-evaluate them. The psychologist can also introduce reality variables through looking objectively at the child's strength and limitations and at how the educational environment psychologically matches or mismatches the child. This kind of interaction is likely to dissipate the teacher's distorted stereotyping, and he can be expected to contribute ideas for altering his own behavior or altering classroom variables. The psychologist can also introduce possible avenues of change, but these too should grow logically out of the shared analysis of the situation and agreement as to the basis of the child's problem. This kind of teacher-psychologist interaction will usually not be obtained in just one visit, but will require several sessions and occasional follow-up.

Lack of confidence and self-esteem. Teachers who are challenged daily by the disparate personalities of their children, bombarded with literature describing technological advances in curriculum materials, and subjected to mass media criticisms of education, periodically experience a lack of confidence and self-esteem. Consequently, in some consultant situations the teacher may be seeking ego support rather than specific help with a child.

The ego support can be offered just through the consultant's willingness to sit and listen while the teacher describes his approach to dealing with the child. An approving and admiring comment such as, "that sounds like a great idea" or "I'll have to remember to suggest that to another teacher" can be a tremendous ego booster. In other situations the consultant may need to allude to the progress the teacher has made or to the value of the teacher's efforts under difficult circumstances. Overly sympathizing with the teacher's despondency may tend to reinforce these feelings, while focusing on the teacher's strengths and accomplishments with the child, without sounding artificial, can energize the teacher.

Some consultants are ever-ready to contribute a suggestion or a totally different program even when this kind of advice is not needed, and in this way they further weaken the teacher's self concept. These consultants seem in need of reaffirming that they are the experts who give final approval on a course of action and that the teacher cannot independently arrive at an accurate perception of a situation or a viable solution. Such people lower the teacher's self-esteem and sense of adequacy. The ideal consultative experience should leave the teacher feeling more capable and confident.

POSTSCRIPT TO THE CONSULTATIVE PROCESS

The structure and content of consultation are going to vary from situation to situation, and in this regard Caplan's (1964) consultee-centered case consultation, including the four categories of teacher difficulty, seems to represent a viable framework. In some situations, giving specific clarifying information to the teacher will suffice, while in other situations reduction of theme interference or teacher ego boosting may be required. Sensitivity to the teacher's feelings, flexibility, and an ability to establish a trusting relationship are tremendously important in consultation. Under most circumstances the school psychologist would be naïve to believe that he could analyze and remediate a child's problem without the co-operation of the child's teacher.

In an ideal situation, all teachers would be able to respond to school psychological consultations as this one did: "Although my feelings were mixed and varied, they were all vital to my growth as a teacher. They made me more sensitive and aware of my role. They gave me direction and, perhaps most important of all, the conviction that I was a good teacher." [Williams, 1967, p. 90]

CONCLUSIONS

The intent of this paper was to examine some problems and directions in teacher consultation will school psychologists. Writing reports and implementing behavior modification and prescriptive teaching programs were identified as potential problem areas. Rogers (1959), Lippitt (1967), and especially Caplan (1964) were seen as offering meaningful insights into the consultative process.

Though there is general agreement that teacher consultation is important, this seems to remain a questionable area in the practice of school psychologists. One frequent defense against extensive teacher consultation has to do with the time factor: other demands being more pressing, there simply is not enough time for adequate teacher contacts. This position is often suspiciously viewed as being a self imposed limitation by those who would rather not spend the time with teachers. Related to the disinclination toward consultation is the possibility that many practicing school psychologists, master's level trained, have not been adequately prepared in interviewing and counseling skills or the consultation process. As Gray (1963) observed:

"Consultation, when broadly interpreted, is one of the major roles of the school psychologist today. It should even be a larger role in the future. Yet unfortunately there is little available published material that treats this topic directly in relation to the school psychologist's functioning; there is little direct teaching or practicum experience in consultation current in training programs for school psychologists." [p. 118]

Her observations are still generally accurate: curricular changes are needed in school psychology training programs.

As to the time factor argument, Starkman's (1966) discussion of the decision-making paradox in school psychology is most apt. If school psychologists value teacher consultation and consider it a viable avenue for reaching many children, they should communicate this professional posture to the appropriate administrators and begin a program of educating administrators as to what constitutes effective service. Constructive changes in the nature of school psychological services cannot realistically be expected to emanate from the "top." The importance of teacher consultation needs to be articulately expressed to administrative people, with as much documentation as is available, including the results of surveys of teacher opinions on psychological services and the testimonials of teachers who received satisfactory consultation.

Ideally, the school psychologist should be one of the most competent consultants in the schools in terms of his skills in interpersonal relations and his understanding of human behavior. Most of the other school consultants (speech clinicians, remedial reading teachers, guidance counselors, etc.) tend to focus on the child and usually work with him independently of the teacher and classroom. In a period of increasing role diffusion among these various consultants, when testing, counseling, and remedial skills are claimed by different professional groups, perhaps the school psychologist can establish himself as the person concerned about the teacher and the classroom and enthusiastically available to consult with the teacher.

References

Baker, H. L. Psychological services: From the school staff's point of view. *Journal of School Psychology*, 1965, *3*, 36–42.

Bardon, J. I. Mental health education: A framework for psychological services in the schools. *Journal of School Psychology*, 1963, *1*, 20–27.

Berkowitz, H. The child clinical psychologist in the schools: Consultation. *Psychology in the Schools*, 1968, *5*, 118–124.

Caplan, G. Mental health consultation in the schools. In *The elements of a community mental health program*. New York: Milbank Memorial Fund, 1956. Pp. 77–85.

Caplan, G. *Principles of preventative psychiatry*. New York: Basic Books, 1964.

Capobianco, R. J. The psychologist collaborates with other school staff. In J. F. Magary (Ed.), *School psychological services*. Englewood Cliffs, New Jersey: Prentice-Hall, 1967. Pp. 99–120.

Farnsworth, D. L. Psychiatric consultation in secondary schools. *Psychology in the Schools*, 1966, *3*, 17–19.

Fine, M. J. Some qualifying notes on the development and implementation of behavior modification programs. *Journal of School Psychology*, 1970, *8*(4), 301–305.

Fischer, H. L. School consultation in a special education setting. *Psychology in the Schools*, 1969, *6*, 12–17.

Gray, S. W. *The psychologist in the schools*. New York: Holt, Rinehart and Winston, 1963.

Handler, L., Gerston, A., & Handler, B. Suggestions for improved psychologist-teacher communication. *Psychology in the Schools*, 1965, *2*, 77–81.

Kelman, H. C. Compliance, identification, and internalization, three processes of attitude change. *Journal of Conflict Resolution*, 1958, *2*, 51–60.

Lippitt, G. L. The consultative process. *The School Psychologist*, 1967, *21*, 72–74.

Losen, S. M. The school psychologist–psychotherapist or consultant? *Psychology in the Schools*, 1964, *1*, 13–17.

Magary, J. F. Emerging viewpoints in school psychological sources. In J. F. Magary (Ed.), *School psychological services*. Englewood Cliffs, New Jersey: Prentice-Hall, 1967. Pp. 671–755.

Mannino, F. V. *Consultation in mental health and related fields. A reference guide.* Chevy Chase: National Institute of Mental Health, 1969.

Newman, R. G. *Psychological consultation in the schools*. New York: Basic Books, 1967.

Reger, R. The school psychologist and the teacher: Effective interpersonal relationships. *Journal of School Psychology*, 1964, *3*, 13–18.

Rogers, C. R. Significant learning: In therapy and education. *Educational Leadership*, 1959, *16*, 232–242.

Starkman, S. The professional model: Paradox in school psychology. *American Psychologist*, 1966, *21*, 807–808.

Williams, M. E. Help for the teacher of disturbed children in the public school: The use of consultation for problem solving and personal growth. *Exceptional Children*, 1967, *34*, 87–91.

15.   CONSULTATION AND COUNSELING

Loyce McG. Hagens

Two types of helping relationship are labeled in similar fashion. These are *client-centered counseling* and *consultee-centered consultation*. There is a

Source. Loyce McG. Hagens, "Consultation and Counseling," *Elementary School Guidance and Counseling*, 1969, Vol. 3–3, 155–163. Copyright 1969 by the American Personnel and Guidance Association and reproduced by permission.

difference in these two that appears, at first glance, to place the two systems of dyadic interaction in philosophical opposition to each other. This is particularly true in regard to the position held by Rogers (1951) and those who have used his general philosophy to develop their own approach. The most blatant difference centers around the apparently manipulative, devious approach of the consultant in endeavoring to affect change in the behavior of his consultee as opposed to the open engagement of the counselor in the process of attempting to achieve the same goal with the complete knowledge of his client.

The client-centered therapist, Rogerian or otherwise, assumes that his client will have to make his own decisions, and that the counselor's task is to help his client understand himself more honestly and openly so that he may work his problems through. Although he may be exerting certain influences over him consciously or unconsciously, the counselor disclaims responsibility for his client's decisions. The consultant, on the other hand, presents himself as an expert in a specific area, ready to work with the consultee about problems he is having in relation to a third person, the client. He does not tell the consultee that he needs to change, but this change is his non-verbalized goal if the consultant is operating in the Caplanian (1959, 1964) or consultee-centered framework.

The difference between the two points of view is not nearly as great as the last few sentences imply. In reality, the counselor is also attempting to change the way the client views himself and his functions in life. Some counselors will deny that they are setting out to change or even to help others, but this is a question of semantics, not actuality. Most counselors who deny that they are attempting to change others are leaning over backwards to assure themselves that they are not being authoritarian, advice-giving, or disrespectful of the rights of others. The consultant, on the other hand, is more open in stating that he is an expert. He is willing to accept the responsibility that goes with making decisions. The counselor who denies the responsibility for influencing decision-making is evading the fact that—although the final decision is made by the client—he is a part of the process.

Both approaches require that the professional person have a real respect for the other as a human being, that he possess the ability to be flexible, to make tentative hypotheses, and to change when the evidence changes. Both are earnestly engaged in teaching the client or the consultee a *process* he may use. The process is not a one-time solution, but something that can be used over and over. Counseling and consultation are alike in this regard. Both hold that the process is the most important part of the interaction;

if the person learns the process of thinking-through and problem-solving, then this same process can be used in many situations.

The kind of process taught is different in the two cases. The counseling process requires the utmost self-honesty from the client. The consultant may teach the consultee the process of thinking about clients, but never touch upon the consultee's own problem. Yet by his messages the consultant will be constantly striving for change in his consultee. These may be called indirect ways of pointing out alterate methods the consultee may use to cope with life, or alternate ways of responding to different problems.

The material presented in the following case analysis may be understood better if the specific techniques employed in consultation in a school setting as described here are defined. The consultant is a professional who comes into the school with a body of knowledge differing from that of the teacher or administrator. His role is to act as a resource, supplementing the knowledge of the educator with his own expertise in the behavioral sciences. The relationship is established with mutual respect for the different areas of competence each contributes and that can be pooled to aid the child.

Since the role of the consultant is new, and the needs of the consultee variable, the consultant attempts to be accessible in informal settings when the teacher may have the time and the need to discuss a particular case. Thus the consultant tries to be aggressively available, present where needed, not waiting for others to seek him. This involves participation in whatever ways may be feasible in the non-instructional program of the school. One of the most useful places for unstructured contacts is frequently the teachers' lounge. The ethical problem of discussing individual cases with a group of teachers may be resolved through the discretion of the consultant. The discussion may be used as a learning session when the material is not of a confidential nature. When the material is particularly confidential a more private location may be necessary.

Once contact has been established between himself and the consultee or teacher, the consultant typically functions on the basis of Caplan's (1964) formulations, with the assumption that individuals tend to overreact to certain types of behavior on the part of others, and thus to be not as effective with them. If the consultee can be assisted in removing this kind of emotional blocking he will be able to deal more effectively with all similar clients, or (in the case of teachers) with all similar children. The consultee's behavior is assumed to emerge from his own dynamics, but the consultant does not attempt to deal with it in a direct manner. Through a combination of increased cognitive understanding of the nature of the child's difficulty and covert messages directed at changing the consultee's way of responding to internal dynamics, change is expected. The consultant attempts to identify (covertly) the underlying theme being presented by the consultee or teacher, and to give an appropriate message. A theme may be quite simple. A strong involvement with bright underachieving boys, for example, may be based on the consultee's concern over his own bright underachieving son. Without making reference to the consultee's son—perhaps even without knowledge of this problem—the consultant might explain that the passive resistance of the underachieving child can be dealt with through less pressure on the child and increased communication emphasizing the child's ability to handle his own problems. The parent or teacher may also need to assume a supporting role when the child is receptive, offering assistance only as the child indicates a desire for help. Another example of a simple theme might be a lack of security on the part of the teacher about a planned course of action, particularly about the psychological implications. Simple reassurance might be the most appropriate message that could be given.

Experienced teachers will recognize the frequency with which certain types of children are upsetting to a particular teacher. The same teacher will tend to bring up several cases all stemming from the same basic dynamics. The objective of the consultant is to lower the teacher's emotional involvement with such cases, thus freeing him to think more objectively about them. More than one case may be worked through by the consultant and teacher before this occurs.

Along with change in the individual's coping techniques, the whole process of problem-solving is stressed in consultation interaction. The consultant attempts to assist the consultee to (1) focus on all the relevant data, (2) understand the possible meaning behind specific behaviors, (3) hypothesize concerning basic causes, (4) tentatively think through what kind of need may be evidenced, and (5) see how this need can be met by the teacher in the classroom. Further, he helps the consultee determine whether referral to more sophisticated diagnostic agencies or treatment centers is needed. Once the consultant and the teacher have worked out a tentative hypothesis (going deeper than the symptoms) the consultant will usually suggest the general area of focus concerning what needs are involved but not the specific classroom procedures required to meet those needs. The teacher is usually more knowledgeable about ways of applying the curriculum materials, the behavior controls, or whatever is needed than is the consultant. She may need some help in mentally reviewing her store of possible approaches, and may find it useful to discuss these, but the decision about particular tactics should be her own. Her style of teaching, her personality, and the particular characteristics of the child will determine which tactics will be most effective for her at this time.

Case Analysis

Type of school   The school was in a high socioeconomic area; the atmosphere of the entire school was a little hyperactive and rather permissive. The level of instruction was generally high. The faculty was small—at least small enough that they were nearly all on a first-name basis with each other and given to quite a bit of informal teasing and visiting.

Administrative influences   The principal was held in affectionate esteem. He was extremely earnest and worked frequently and well with both parents and teachers. He used practical, everyday, and rather firm approaches, usually without much depth of psychological insight.

The morale of the teachers was generally high. There *School climate* were a few interpersonal conflicts between certain teachers, but none were serious enough to disrupt the faculty.

Mrs. Johnson, a fourth grade teacher, had contacted a consultant for a one-session interview early in the year. The consultant's impression was that at that time she did not accept the message given. The theme had centered around Mrs. Johnson's over-identification *Initial contact* with a child from a very difficult background—a kind *with consultee* of underdog. She was ineffective because she felt too much pity for the child. The message given her by the consultant was that sometimes one needs to get tough with children to allow them to work out their suppressed hostility against a strong adult who is in control (safe) but not emotionally rejecting.

Since that time Mrs. Johnson had been in and out of the lounge, lunchroom, etc., when the consultant was present, but she had not directly entered the group interaction. She had frequently listened while the conversation centered around the informal problem-solving the consultant did in the lounge.

During the morning of the interview to be described *Consultant strives* below, the consultant was in the lounge working in- *to be aggressively* formally with several teachers about the general area *available—and* of sexual delinquency, telling an anecdote designed to *to show self* convey the message that behavior is caused, that chil- *to others* dren who deviate from middle-class standards in this area frequently have other problems and can be helped. Mrs. Johnson, in the lounge for a quick cup of coffee, asked the consultant in an unobtrusive way for a conference, saying that she did not have a real break that morning but would try to arrange her classroom schedule so that she could leave the children for a time to confer.

The consultant suggested that, although she usually did not lunch at the school, she could arrange her schedule so that they could talk during the lunch hour. This was agreed upon.

Consultant respect teacher's needs, adapts plans, communicating respect

When they arrived at the lunchroom, they chose a table apart from the other teachers where the conversation between Mrs. Johnson and the consultant could not be overheard, assuring privacy sufficient for confidentiality.

Presentation of case: Teacher displays knowledge and competence

The teacher gave a full and careful analysis of a child who had been known as a severe acting-out behavior problem for years and with whom she had succeeded in achieving rapport during the early part of the year. She covered the case well and paused only occasionally to check her evaluation of the way she had proceeded and how she saw the dynamics of the case operating.

Background of case

Essentially, she had established an accepting atmosphere with the boy and then set rather firm limits on his behavior. Past psychological and medical work had indicated that he was mildly impaired neurologically but that his parents had refused the opportunity to place him in special classes. His mother appeared, from these reports, to be an overtly over-protective but covertly rejecting person.

Teacher expresses trust in consultant through type of material, and affirms confidence in her own ability

Mrs. Johnson had "played it by ear" in adapting her treatment to fit the particular situation. She had helped the boy find for himself that he was neither stupid nor bad, as he had classified himself to her early in the year. His success had been apparent not only to her but to other teachers in the school, since his acting-out behavior in other situations had changed considerably. Returning to school after an illness, however, he had again experienced a sense of failure and had regressed in his behavior as a result of the

*Deeper theme
of teacher's
emotional
commitment*

frustration. The teacher was working out the problem in her own way—holding firm to controls on the acting-out behavior but giving additional support in the area of learning when the mother came into the picture. Probably as a result of her own defensive overprotective reactions, the mother conferred with the principal about the firm controls the teacher was exercising. The principal in turn conferred with the teacher, supporting the mother's position for more lenient disciplinary procedures. The teacher had to modify her controls to some degree, although she was aware that the child needed firm controls to protect him against his own impulses. The teacher felt that she had recovered from this intrusion as far as her relationship with the boy in the classroom was concerned but had discovered that he had begun to act out in other settings, e.g., with sexually hostile behavior (vulgar gestures, words) directed toward the girls in the music and P. E. classes.

The teacher felt that through enlisting the cooperation of the other two teachers and some of the more mature girls in the classes she would be able to help the boy surmount this outburst. She did not want to involve the principal as yet, since she felt he would be forced to discipline the boy.

*Consultant
analyzes total
contact in
terms of teacher
growth*

The consultant reviewed the teacher's evaluation and actions and was in agreement that her plan to ignore the vulgar gestures and words could be a somewhat hazardous procedure: Parents of little girls tend to be rather hyper-sensitive about sexual matters when their daughters are the targets. The consultant and teacher also agreed that the offenses were not severe enough to damage the girls and that this plan would be the best way for the boy to work out the hostile feelings he had been forced to repress in front of his mother.

Generally, the theme presented by the teacher was that of asserting her own strength and judgment in this situation, working to assist a child who was an underdog, but not to the point of being too easy or coddling him. She was accepting her own right to act firmly and to take responsibility. In the earlier case she had been unwilling to express her own strength. The consultant was used as confirmation of her own judgment.

Summary of this case

Problems: The consultant wondered if her support of the teacher's actions were, in fact, reinforcing the teacher's over-identification with the underdog. Yet the teacher had improved over her previous case in that she was not handling the child over-permissively but in an accepting and quite realistic way. She had been supporting the major idea that a child must learn to accept responsibility for his own actions.

Outcomes: The message given the teacher early in the year regarding the need to be less permissive with hostile children who were "underdogs" appeared to have been absorbed. The actual behavior of the teacher toward a similar child had become modified.

Consultation tends to follow certain patterns. The consultant usually focuses on the presenting problem of the teacher and gives professional support by reinforcing appropriate behavior; or discouraging by withholding praise or by negative reinforcement of the activities deemed not appropriate in the view of a behavioral scientist. At the same time messages or pressures of various kinds are used in an attempt to change or modify the teacher's perception of environment, other people (children), or internal emotional reactions. The modification does not attempt depth personality change in the consultee but uses the existing structure of the person, attempting to modify only certain portions of the perception of the child and his behavior.

The approach of a client-centered counselor would probably have focused from the beginning on the teacher's own feelings and would have encouraged exploration of the reasons behind this over-identification with hostile, underdog-type children. Consultation does not seek depth of self-understanding but attempts to achieve behavior modification on the part of the consultee in the most efficient way possible. When professional help is limited, short-term work (perhaps from one to six sessions, with the goal of unblocking certain specific coping behaviors) may be more economical than long-term—that is, one to two years of work done through direct counseling. Granted, while the teacher with two years' growth through counseling should be a more effective teacher with all children, the overall benefit of enhancement of the learning environment for children may be more drastically changed in a positive direction through intervention with a number of teachers. If the individual teacher's most gross blockings in relation to children are modified, the overall impact may be much greater. Currently, this point is debatable, since no research data relating to this comparison is available as far as the author is aware.

The two techniques may be used in complementary fashion. The same consultant or counselor may elect to use the counseling approach with one specific teacher while using a consultation approach with another, depending upon the needs of the particular situation. Faust (1968) dislikes combining the roles and points out the dangers or limitations inherent in situations where the consultant also acts as counselor. The depth of the trust relationship that needs to be developed between counselor and counselee (with the explanation of how day-to-day interaction on a normal socially competitive basis in such situations as the lounge, lunchroom, etc., may inhibit the depth of the trust relationship) is used by Faust as the justification for recommending the separation of the two roles. His suggestion of the use of two counselor-consultants who perform alternating roles in two different schools is excellent. But given the shortage of highly trained personnel, the complexities of administrative assignments, and the size of some schools, many elementary counselors may need to devise ways of lessening the social threat of what Faust has called the "propensity for interpersonal homeostasis" (in reference to normal social competition), while at the same time remaining aggressively available for consultations. This may be a lonely role, but it has been achieved by some elementary counselors known to the author; at least this appears to be true as far as subjective evaluation can discern. Ideally, a separation of the two roles is desirable. The major concern of the counselor-consultant who is functioning in both roles revolves around the need to remain in a professional relationship of trust in all interactions.

References

Caplan, G. *Concepts of mental health and consultation.* Washington, D.C.: U. S. Children's Bureau, 1959.

Caplan, G. *Principles of preventative psychiatry.* New York: Basic Books, 1964.

Faust, V. *The counselor-consultant in the elementary school.* Boston: Houghton Mifflin, 1968.

Rogers, C. *Client-centered therapy: Its current practice, implications, and theory.* Boston: Houghton Mifflin, 1951.

IV *Consulting with Individuals*

Consulting was originally done on an individual basis, and the skills of individual consulting are basic to the diagnostic and change goals of the consultation. The focus of consulting is on the consultee and processes for helping him work more effectively with his clientele. The consultant processes must be based on empathy, congruence, open communication, encouragement, commitment, and all of the essential elements in counseling. However, the process begins by considering the external unit, the client, and then determines the effect the client's behavior and attitudes has on the consultee.

The relationship between consultant and consultee must be one of equals who work collaboratively. Unfortunately, many supervisors in curriculum and special educational areas have operated as if they were in a superior position and, by definition, the consultee was deficient or inferior. A realistic understanding of consulting relationships would indicate that the consultee has much to contribute, and that without his full cooperation, little of value can be attained. In school consulting, the teacher is a critical resource who not only supplies information on the situation but feedback on the efficacy of procedures. Without this detailed picture of the interaction and feedback, the consultant is limited in his ability either to understand or to change the relationship.

The selections that follow present a variety of approaches to the consulting process. It is important to view consulting in terms of its human elements as well as its technical procedures. The careful reader will note some similarities in procedures that appear to come from opposite theoretical orientations. For example, although behavior modification is described extensively, the motivation modification approach of Grubbe is similar in the sense that both he and the behaviorists utilize the consequences to shape or change behavior. Our hope is that the reader will begin to synthesize an individual consulting approach that operationalizes his theory of human behavior and the consulting relationship processes.

The consultant should consider the consulting relationship in terms of the following.

1. System demands from administration on staff.
2. Cultural expectations placed on and internalized by teachers.
3. The authority dilemma and the general lack of awareness of democratic procedures.
4. The images and stereotypes of pupil personnel specialists that teachers bring to the consulting relationship.
5. The type of communication and dialogue that is generated with consultees.

Abidin emphasizes that behavior modification is not a panacea and is often used naively without considering the teaching style and personality of the teacher or the necessity of providing an extensive amount of in-service time to establish behavior modification procedures in a single classroom.

He notes the frequent failure to obtain baseline data, behavioral descriptions of the problem, and the teacher's feelings about the problem. Without these data, it is impossible to accurately determine the response contingency event that modifies the behavior. He makes a plea to be both scientific and realistic in applying behavior modification.

Bowers' article in a satirical vein clearly outlines "how not to consult." Because we can often learn more from an example of ridiculously ineffective behavior and generalize to more effective procedures, Bowers has some cogent suggestions for consultants. In reading this article, anyone who has been a teacher or consultant will relate to, at least, one of the relationships illustrated in the impotent and ineffectual 12, "Principles of Consulting."

Krumboltz and Hosford confront us with the painfully real situation that consultants have a reputation for being ineffectual. They propose that we evaluate success on the degree to which the consultant can help teachers engage in more appropriate behavior. They illustrate how this can be achieved through the application of learning principles to two actual cases. The consultant works directly with the child in practicing and role-playing behavior so that ability is progressively increased through systematic positive reinforcement and via extinction. The procedures are similar to Grubbe's in the sense that they are idiographic and tailored specifically for the individual. They provide an extensive list of procedures whereby specialists might work directly with children to change their behavior.

Peterson presents a unique mediation role for the specialist. It is one that involves a certain amount of risk or willingness on the part of the specialist to put his skills "on the line" and to work in direct intervention. Although there are countless classrooms where the teacher and students are in conflict, we suspect few specialists have intervened directly. This rule enables consultants to get into the mainstream of the educational process to improve relationships and upgrade teacher skills.

Sulzer, Mayer, and Cody provide a wide variety of procedures for changing undesirable student behavior. The article, in systematic fashion, presents and evaluates procedures such as punishment, extinction, time-out, satiation, modeling, and reinforcing incompatible behaviors. They supply a list of factors to consider in selecting the appropriate procedure.

The Grubbe's present a practical application of individual or Adlerian psychology. They indicate the importance of looking at the patterns and goals of the child and of determining the purpose of behavior. A specific case demonstrates how to apply Adlerian procedures.

As these articles are read, consider the following.

● What are some of the factors to consider in choosing which techniques to introduce to teachers?

● Abidin indicates that it is reasonable to expect to expend 150 hours of professional time in a school year to assist a teacher in setting up a token economy in the classroom. What problems do you see emerging from such a demand on time, and how might you engineer a more effective use of this time?

● Why is it important to ascertain the teacher's feelings about the situation and how might Abidin and Grubbe utilize the data on feelings differently?

● Bowers has provided a list of ineffective consulting behaviors. Role play in class the ineffectual behaviors and later model more effective ways to handle the same concerns.

● Krumboltz and Hosford advanced a number of procedures for working directly with the child. How could you train teachers in the use of these procedures? What are the skills necessary to effectively conduct mediation in the classroom? How might Krumboltz and Hosford have handled differently the case of Fred that is presented in Grubbe? What approaches do you believe Grubbe would have used with the problems of Mickey and Don?

16. WHAT'S WRONG WITH BEHAVIOR MODIFICATION

Richard R. Abidin, Jr.

All professional activity, be it educational, legal, medical, or psychological, has its excesses and abuses. It seems that whenever a new and worthwhile tool or technique comes along, many members of a professional group jump on the bandwagon and ride it into the ground. This is especially true when the new technique is not well understood and its users have little experience with it. With the technique excessively and often ineptly applied, disenchantment sets in. One hears: "It doesn't work," and "I have read the articles but when you apply it to real life it doesn't work." Behavior modification appears to be currently undergoing such a fate. I am sure that in the future it will find its appropriate place in the range of techniques available to school and clinical psychologists and, hopefully, to classroom teachers.

To my knowedge no profession has a universally applicable procedure; penicillin, for example, is great for bacterial pneumonia, but it fails in the case of acute appendicitis.

As with all remediation or intervention procedures, in all professions, there are certain parameters within which techniques are applicable. This article is addressed to the consideration of some of the parameters, issues, and problems which must be evaluated and dealt with before and during the application of behavior modification techniques. It focuses primarily on issues related to behavior modification in the classroom. The issues raised have developed out of the author's experiences with behavior modification over the past six years and out of his students' experiences as they have attempted to apply the techniques to the classroom. The conclusions, therefore, are not empirical facts; they are experientially developed hypotheses (opinions).

Source. Richard R. Abidin, Jr., "What's Wrong with Behavior Modification." *Journal of School Psychology*, 1971, Vol. 9–1, 38–42.

PRELIMINARY CONSIDERATIONS

Often a psychologist encounters a child or a situation which was "made for behavior modification," and so on the basis of the child's needs and the psychologist's understanding of these needs, he attempts to institute a behavior modification program. Now, as is generally known, he doesn't institute the behavior management program; he essentially recommends it and helps set it up. The teacher is supposed to carry it out. Here the problem begins. The school psychologist with his new-found tool may fail to conduct the necessary evaluation and training of the teacher prior to the use of the technique. What neuro-surgeon would have a pediatric nurse assist in surgery without some training specific to the job's demands? Further, not every nurse has the personal characteristics, needs, and motivation to be an assistant in surgery.

Pre Conditions

Step 1. The psychologist must evaluate the teacher's teaching style and personality in relation to the demands of the behavior modification program to be instituted. Our experience has indicated that in order for a teacher to work successfully in a behavior modification program she must have average or above average organizational ability; in fact, being mildly compulsive is generally helpful. Teachers who tend to be very non-directive, highly intuitive, or very existentially oriented generally do not work out well in the application of a behavior modification program.

Step 2. The psychologist must train the teacher in basic concepts as well as in psychomotor skills necessary in the behavior modification program. Failure to meet this preliminary condition is the single most common cause for failure of behavior modification programs. Although the basic concepts and the behavioral demands on the teacher appear simple, in practice the simplicity turns out to be quite elusive. In one program, for example, the teacher assumed that if the child was rewarded with tokens for good behavior, she would take tokens away for bad behavior. The "bad" behavior was unrelated to the target behavior; the program turned out to be a capricious system whereby the teacher threatened to take back tokens whenever she felt it was appropriate.

The recognition of the selection and training requirements will hopefully prevent the psychologist from approaching the use of behavior modification off-handedly. Our experience has indicated that it is reasonable to expect a school psychologist to expend 150 hours of professional time in a school year to assist a teacher in setting up a token economy in a classroom. This time includes planning sessions, teaching the teacher, classroom observation, weekly follow ups, crisis consultation, etc. When the teacher has no prior knowledge, training, or experience in behavior modification, we have found that assisting her in instituting a behavior modification program for one child will take approximately 30 hours.[1] It is our belief that if the psychologist recognizes how much time is involved, he would be more discriminating in recommending the institution of a behavior modification program.

Step. 3. The school psychologist must, after discussion with the teacher, decide how she is to be reinforced for her efforts. A teacher experienced in using behavior modification may need little reinforcement. However, since most teachers are not experienced in this area, there is a definite need for frequent and positive reinforcement. We have found that for most teachers weekly or daily verbal encouragement by the psychologist and principal is a powerful reinforcer. Comments recognizing the teacher's effort, work, interest in her children, and the progress of her children are but some of the obvious and natural reinforcers. It has been our experience that the teacher should be assisted in the collection of baseline data and verbally reinforced for plotting and recording countable behavior on a daily basis. We have found that without baseline data teachers will frequently become discouraged, since frequently the first *jnd* is usually a rather large step, requiring several days. For example, if a child's baseline for out-of-seat behavior is 50 to 55 incidences per day, and after the institution of a contingency management program that behavior is reduced to 40 incidences by the end of the first week, the average teacher will be ready to give up. There is just not sufficient difference between 50 and 55 out-of-seat incidents, in terms of the emotional demands on the teacher. However, we have found that seeing the tangible proof of the downward trend in the plotting of curve frequently becomes a reinforcing event. Further, when these changes are suitably paired with verbal reinforcements from the psychologist, the changing frequency curve can itself become a reinforcing event.

COMMON PROCESS ERRORS

Error 1. Failure to Define the Problem Behavior on Both an Operational Level and on a Feeling Tone Level.

A teacher's initial statement of a problem might be, "Johnny disrupts the class and he is hostile to me. He doesn't like me." Hopefully, after

---

[1] These time demands may be cut to one-quarter with the same teachers in subsequent years.

observation the school psychologist might be able to help the teacher see that "disrupts class behavior" may be operationally defined by the number of times Johnny is out of his seat when the teacher is not standing next to him. Further, he might point out that the hostility issue turns out to be an inference that the teacher makes because she feels the child rejects her, and this despite the fact that he gets more individual attention and instruction than any other child. The school psychologist can reassure the teacher that the child seems to like her very much, that her attention is so rewarding to him that he has learned that he can gain her attention by his out of seat behavior. The failure to deal with the teacher's feelings about the child or situation prior to the development of a behavior modification plan frequently results in miscommunication and resistance. Having met or at least recognized the teacher's needs and feelings, the psychologist may then help the teacher select a specific behavior or set of behaviors which are communicable to and understandable by the child. Often the teacher's natural inclination in setting up a contingency program is to tell the child that she doesn't want him to "disrupt the class." The child may find this difficult to understand: is talking loudly or softly to a friend disrupting the class, is sitting up and looking mad disrupting, or is his getting his books too rapidly or too slowly disruptive, etc.? The target behavior must be clearly defined.

Error 2. Failure to Collect Baseline Data

Many school psychologists and teachers tend to feel this step is unnecessary, but from a technical standpoint and from our experiences with behavior modification, we have come to feel that it is crucial. We have found that collecting baseline data often leads to a redefinition of the problem. The teacher may believe she recognizes the problem, but in the course of having to attend closely to the child's behavior she will often find that the behavior she is counting may not be the one that is most disturbing to her or that it occurs so seldom as to be less important than some other behavior.

Having a baseline and then noting changes from the baseline, once a response contingency contract has been developed, tends to provide a clear picture of the reinforcers' efficacy. For example: (*a*) M & M's are not necessarily reinforcers for middle class children who have access to all the candy they want; (*b*) Model Airplanes may turn out to be a punishment if the child's father makes him work on the model at home under his direction. The only way that we know that a response contingent event is reinforcing is the extent to which it modifies the behavior in relation to the baseline.

Error 3. Ineffective or Inappropriate Reinforcement

Often a teacher or a school psychologist assumes he has a reinforcer and makes this "reinforcer" contingent upon some behavior. Nothing happens. It is felt that three steps must be taken in attempting to locate reinforcers for a given child: (a) observe what the child does and what he likes; (b) ask him what would be reinforcing for him; and (c) set up a reinforcing menu, not just one item.

Both the psychologist and the teacher must remember that reinforcers change in their reinforcing strength with time. This expected change must be fully recognized in advance.

Error 4. The Attitude of the School Psychologist

Often the behavior most destructive to any given behavior modification program is the naively simplistic attitude of the school psychologist. He over sells his idea. The school psychologist must recognize that behavior modification is merely a tool to support good teaching. Many emotional components of teaching which do not lend themselves to a behavior modification program are essential for good teaching. "Positive regard," "love," "affection," etc. are but some of the complex behaviors which set the tone and determine the learning atmosphere. The school psychologist must recognize that there are many good teachers who do a good job by using less formalized approaches. We must realize that a child's life goes on outside of the behavior modification program and that the teacher's and psychologist's expectancies must be tempered with reality. No behavior modification program controls all of the contingencies of a child's life; often it doesn't control the most important contingencies. A child's generalized feelings of inadequacy and inferiority may lead to school failure. Behavior modification may change the school failure and help alleviate the problem, but those circumstances and contingencies which created the generalized feelings of inadequacy and inferiority outside of the school will continue to operate and to have their effect.

Certainly behavior modification principles and programs have been demonstrated to be highly effective. When properly handled and applied, behavior modification represents one of the best systems for dealing with many behaviors in the classroom. Nevertheless, like all intervention procedures and systems, it has its limits and problems. It also has potentials which have not been adequately explored; it could, for example, be used in systematic analysis of complex human behaviors such as love, affection, and teaching, which most psychologists and educators recognize as learned behaviors. Hopefully, some day we will be able to utilize the tools of the behavioral sciences such as behavior modification to provide the circumstances in which the most creative loving and teaching behaviors can be developed by all teachers.

17. SOME GUIDELINES FOR THE SCHOOL PSYCHOLOGIST IN HIS ATTEMPTS TO INTIMIDATE THE TEACHER DURING A CONFERENCE

Norman E. Bowers

Teachers are becoming increasingly vocal in various functions and aspects of the educational programs in the public schools. This is well and good when they demand increased salaries and other fringe benefits. However, an increasing number of classroom teachers have criticized or questioned diagnoses and recommendations of the school psychologist during a conference. In fact, there are documented instances in which the teacher actually proposed an alternative diagnosis and/or recommendation. These instances are occurring at such an alarming rate that they are beginning to pose a serious threat to school psychologists. It is the wise and forewarned psychologist who takes quick and definitive steps to head off such insubordination.

This article concerns itself with the development of guidelines for the psychologist in combating this problem. Listed and briefly described are 12 principles.

Principle of the Paternalistic "Put Down"

This should be employed at the beginning of each teacher conference in order to immediately put the teacher in a lesser, passive role. The psychologist should begin by stating that he knows the teacher has done the best she can with the child but that sometimes "our best is not good enough." This engenders a definite feeling of failure in the teacher and should deter any resistance or questioning during the remainder of the conference.

Source. Norman E. Bowers, "Some Guidelines for the School Psychologist in has Attempts to Intimidate the Teacher During a Conference." *Journal of School Psychology*, 1971, Vol. 9–3, 347–360.

Principle of Pseudoequivalence

Here the psychologist appears to be willing to put the teacher at his level and to discuss the child on a "colleague-to-colleague" basis, but in reality he is setting up a situation wherein the teacher will again feel inferior and unknowledgeable. The techniques go something like, "Well, I'm sure you are aware of the latest research in this particular area." Most of the time, the teacher will say "no" or shake her head, at which point the psychologist gives her a quizzical or incredulous look. One danger here is that occasionally you will find a teacher who is aware of the research in that particular area. An effective means of getting out of such a situation is to say, "Yes, but have you heard of the *latest* research?" and then refer to an unpublished study or some research in progress.

Principle of Multivariate Causation

Some teachers will press for clear statements of diagnosis and insist that the psychologist be concise and definite in his descriptions of the child. This principle involves the notion that the evidence gathered by the psychologist shows several trends or suggestions, but that no one single factor predominates. At this point, he suggests that the problem is probably a combination of several small factors, none of which in itself accounts for the problem, but in total combination cause the child to behave in certain ways.

Principle of "Great Psychologists" Explanations

When the psychologist is hard-pressed to pacify the teacher who insists on specific and meaningful information, he can refer to a famous psychologist. He need not have accurate knowledge of that psychologist's viewpoint. One possible danger is that some eager teachers might also know something about the psychologist you are discussing; therefore, it is best to choose one who is somewhat lesser known, such as Edwin Guthrie or Emil Kraepelin.

Principle of Platitudinous Jargonistic Terminology

Here the idea is to overwhelm the teacher with numerous, polysyllabic, highly psychological terms. They should be said rapidly, preferably several in succession. For example: "It seems clear to me that the problem here is a case of unresolved oedipal conflict with an underlying pseudo-passive dependency with an overindulgent, inconsistent, and seductive maternal figure, resulting in prepsychotic behavioral manifestations of occasional delusional thinking and sado-masochistic preoccupations."

Principle of "If-Then" Displacement

When the teacher begins to press for specific recommendations, the psychologist can put this principle into action. The idea is to stress what the child ideally needs, fully realizing that the ideal is totally unattainable. When the teacher counters with "But what can we do now?" the psychologist can dismiss the issue by suggesting that the teacher experiment and simply do what works, and/or be critical of the administration for not providing the necessary programs and personnel.

Principle of Hydraulic Remediation

One of the most irritating things for a psychologist is, after making a recommendation to a teacher, for her to say that she has already tried that and it doesn't work. The first response for the psychologist is to query, "But have you been consistent?" Most teachers will admit to occasional lapses, at which point the psychologist can give a short lecture on the merits of consistency in the handling of children. Once again, the onus is on the teacher. If by chance the teacher says she has been consistent, the psychologist can point out that the child's problem has been a long time in developing and that we should not expect changes in behavior in a short period of time. An understanding and supportive "Keep trying" is usually effective.

Principle of Bibliographic Directionality

When the psychologist suggests some type of intervention by the teacher, such as behavior modification techniques, the teacher will often want some specific instructions. At this point, the psychologist can say, "Well, it's pretty difficult to explain in just the few moments we have here today; let me refer you to a couple of books which should be of help to you." This has three positive effects. First, it gets the teacher off your back. Second, it shortens the conference. Third, it prevents the teacher from discovering that you don't know much about behavior modification techniques yourself.

Principle of the Interrogatory Reversal

Here the psychologist avoids a sticky or embarrassing question by returning it to the teacher. For example, the teacher asks, "Just what is a perceptual problem?" The psychologist can say, "Well, what is your notion of a perceptual problem?" Hopefully, the teacher will attempt to answer the question, and the psychologist can then criticize her definition. If by chance the teacher gives a good description of a perceptual problem, the psychologist can simply say, "Yes, that's pretty good, you've got the general idea." Then he can make a mental note of it for his own use. If the teacher will not accept this reversal technique and insist on an answer, the best approach is to suggest that she is not being cooperative and allude to the possibility that she does not have the best interests of the child in mind.

Principle of Discrepant Identification

When the teacher's view of the child's behavior is different from the psychologist's he can appear very surprised and say something like, "Are you sure we are talking about the same child?" This can be done in a smiling, facetious way, but it will hopefully make the teacher assume that the child's problems are exhibited only in her classroom, and that therefore she is to blame.

Principle of Massive Annihilation

This principle should be utilized as a last resort. At times a teacher is extremely aggressive and critical and none of the above techniques have worked very well. At this point, the psychologist can stand up, appear quite angry, and indicate that he is the school psychologist and that he is the school's authority on child behavior. If necessary, the psychologist can suggest that the teacher simply doesn't understand the situation and cannot appreciate the complexity of the total situation. This usually terminates the conference. If the teacher stalks out, there is little problem. However, many teachers will begin to cry. At this point, the psychologist can return to the *Principle of the paternalistic "put down"* and indicate that he knows she has done her best. He can then excuse himself, saying that he has another conference in a school across town in ten minutes.

Principle of Existential Support

Except in situations like the one just mentioned, the psychologist should use this principle in terminating conferences. He can say something like, "Well, this has been a good conference, and I'm sure if you do the things I mentioned, you'll be having no more problems with this child." Another specific technique is to say laughingly, "It could be a lot worse. I've seen some dandies in my time." If the teacher continues seeking support, the psychologist can, although this is not highly recommended, indicate that she should feel free to call on him in the future if the situation does not improve.

If school psychologists can utilize these guidelines effectively, I am certain that they should have little trouble with teachers in the future. However, I've seen some real characters as teachers in my time. So if you find that these guidelines are not very effective, please feel free to contact me at any time. You can call my unlisted phone number.

18. BEHAVIORAL COUNSELING IN THE ELEMENTARY SCHOOL

John D. Krumboltz and Raymond E. Hosford

"Same ol' run-around again," said Miss Ford as she returned from her conference with the school counselor.

"What's the problem?" asked Joe Peterson, a fellow teacher.

"You remember that I referred Don to the counselor because he would go into a terrible rage and kick and scream whenever he didn't get his own way. Everyone was afraid of him. I didn't know what to do. I had tried everything from sending him to the principal to standing him in a corner. Nothing seemed to work."

"Well, what did the counselor suggest?"

"Nothing, really. That's the trouble. The counselor said that Don's responses on the various tests indicate he is a very anxious and aggressive child who has a low self-concept. So what? I already know all that."

"Didn't the counselor have any ideas of what to do?" insisted Mr. Peterson.

"The only real suggestion I got was that Don needs to learn how to get along with others. But that is precisely why I referred him—I want to help him learn to get along with the other boys and girls, but I don't know how. I guess I was hoping for something more from the counselor," said Miss Ford with more sadness than anger.

"I know what you mean," Joe said. "Early in the year I referred Mickey, you know, the shy little girl who clams up whenever she is asked to give a report in front of the class. The counselor told me that she has an inferiority complex as the result of a fixation at a premature level of development. If knowing those words does any good, it sure doesn't show. Mickey, poor scared kid, is just as mousy as ever. I wish I knew how to help her."

"Maybe the counselor would like to be more helpful but doesn't know how either," suggested Miss Ford thoughtfully.

"Maybe so. But just once I'd like to see the counselor produce some results."

Source. John D. Krumboltz and Ray E. Hosford, "Behavioral Counseling in the Elementary School." *Elementary School Guidance and Counseling*, 1967, Vol. 1-1, 27–40. Copyright 1967 by the American Personnel and Guidance Association and reproduced by permission.

DIAGNOSIS VERSUS BEHAVIOR CHANGE

The complaints of these two teachers certainly do not apply to all counselors. But they do have one important implication: *A counselor's success is judged by the degree to which he can help pupils engage in more appropriate types of behavior.* When a teacher refers Don to a counselor because of his frequent temper tantrums, she hopes in some way that Don will decrease the frequency of these tantrums. She is not asking the counselor to improve Don's self-concept or to reconstruct his personality. If a teacher wants to help shy, withdrawn Mickey to learn how to participate in class, he eventually expects Mickey to talk more in class. He is not asking for the counselor's opinion about the origin of the problem or for a hypothesis about the inner state of the child's mind. The success of the counselor's work, regardless of the intervening processes used, will necessarily be judged by the observed improvement in the child's behavior.

In this article we propose that a behavioral approach to elementary school guidance offers counselors an effective way to specify and accomplish the purposes of counseling. We will first show how a behavioral counselor would handle the problems of Don and Mickey by applying some principles of learning. We will then consider some broader implications and problems of behavioral approaches to counseling.

APPLYING SOME LEARNING PRINCIPLES

The two problems described here are based on actual cases referred to an elementary school counselor who applied learning principles to resolve them. Though names and identifying data have been changed, these cases will be used to illustrate how actual behavior problems can be solved through systematic attention to the reinforcing consequences associated with different kinds of behavior.

Positive Reinforcement of Successive Approximations

Mickey, a bright sixth-grade girl, was referred to the counselor because she became extremely anxious when asked to give an oral book report before the class. Because Mickey had sometimes participated in class discussions, the teacher was surprised to see her become too nervous to continue. He quickly suggested that she give her presentation another time.

In talking with the counselor, Mickey explained that she wanted very much to talk in front of the class but had never been able to do so. Her cumulative record showed that her former teachers seldom asked her to give oral reports because of anxiety she developed when speaking before a group. The counselor thought the best approach would be to help her learn gradually the behaviors necessary in giving a report. Thus a program of counseling activities was formulated to accomplish this goal.

A combination of procedures was used by the counselor in helping Mickey learn the behaviors necessary to solve her problem. In the counseling setting, Mickey met with the counselor once a week for six weeks and practiced getting out of her seat, coming to the front of the room, and saying a few words. The counselor suggested she begin with brief reports and gradually build up to longer presentations. Mickey was always free to stop and sit down whenever she felt anxious about talking. During each session the counselor smiled, said "very good, Mickey," and gave other types of reinforcement as Mickey successfully role-played the part of giving a report.

The counselor also worked closely with Mickey's teacher in setting up a program for gradually increasing Mickey's ability to speak before a group. The teacher agreed to progressively include Mickey in a social studies committee which was giving oral presentations on various countries. At first Mickey was asked to help only by pointing on a large map to the city, river, or area that was being discussed by other members of the committee. Members of the group, at the suggestion of the teacher, gradually involved Mickey more in the discussions. Each week Mickey was asked to tell a little more about the location and terrain of a country while the other members of the committee covered the political, social, and economic aspects. At the end of the two and one-half months, Mickey's presentation was about the same length as that of other members of the committee.

Mickey was often thanked for helping out and was given praise and approval by the teacher and members of the committee each time she participated in the panel. The two co-chairmen of the committee were also encouraged to tell Mickey she did very well as she increased her participation, thus providing for peer reinforcement. Mickey gradually became more comfortable while in front of the class and eventually was able to give reports on her own. She was also among the students who volunteered to give an oral presentation at the end of the year when a few parents attended the culmination of the social studies unit.

The role-playing allowed Mickey to practice the behavior under low-stress conditions. When an individual role-plays a behavior enough times, the role becomes part of his repertoire of behavior. He is then better able to perform the behavior in other situations. In this case, the role-playing also gave the counselor an excellent opportunity to reinforce and encourage Mickey as she made increasingly better approximations to the desired behavior.

The counselor helped to arrange a program of systematic positive reinforcement in the classroom as well as in his office to help Mickey learn how to talk before a group. Behavior that is reinforced or rewarded is more likely to occur again (Skinner, 1953). Thus, to increase the occurrence of a particular behavior (in this case, Mickey's oral reports) it is often only necessary to insure that reinforcement be given soon after the behavior occurs.

A grades, approving gestures, and verbal remarks such as "very good" and "well done" are a few of the reinforcing stimuli effective for encouraging most school children in our society. The important aspect in Mickey's case was that reinforcement was given for any *improvement* in speaking before a group. She did not need to make a polished speech before receiving the approval and attention of her teacher, counselor, and peers. Each gradual step toward improvement was reinforced.

Several studies in counseling (Johnson, 1964; Krumboltz & Schroeder, 1965; Krumboltz & Thoresen, 1964) have shown that reinforcement procedures can be used very effectively in school counseling to promote or change a particular behavior. The annotated bibliography contains references that may suggest other principles and examples as well as theoretical formulations derived from research in learning.

Absence of Reinforcement after Undesired Behavior

An effective technique for eliminating undesired behavior is "extinction"— arranging for *no* reinforcement to follow the inappropriate behavior. The use of this procedure can be seen in the case of Don. Don was a third-grade boy who often gave rather violent displays of temper on the playground whenever he did not get his way. Since he was relatively new to the school, his teacher, Miss Ford, thought the tantrums would decrease as Don adjusted to the school situation. Rather than decrease, Don's tantrums became more frequent.

After talking with Miss Ford and the boy's mother, the counselor arranged to be on the playground to observe Don. He noticed that when Don began to scream and pick fights with others, the teacher would quickly respond and attempt to quiet him down. Don usually calmed down when Miss Ford sat on the playground bench with her arm around him. Miss Ford said that she felt Don needed a feeling of security since he responded very quickly to words of reassurance from her.

The next day when Miss Ford came to see the counselor, she asked what was causing the tantrums and what she should do about them. The counselor felt that in this case the increase in the tantrums resulted from the reinforcement Don received from Miss Ford whenever he kicked, screamed, or picked a fight. In effect, Don had more tantrums because he had learned that such behavior usually gave him the undivided attention of the teacher. The tantrum behavior apparently had been learned at home and generalized to the school situation.

The counselor explained to the teacher that behavior previously learned through reinforcement can often be eliminated by permitting it to recur without any reinforcement. Thus, a program for the extinction of the behavior was formulated with the specific goal of decreasing the number of Don's tantrums. In this case the principal of the school and the child's mother were included in the process. It was agreed that when Don began a display of bad temper on the playground, Miss Ford would busy herself with the others and in general ignore his behavior. The same procedure was used in the classroom. In those instances when the class was disturbed too much, Miss Ford would quietly escort Don to the hallway, and the principal would take him to the nurse's room where he would remain until he calmed down.

The conference with Don's mother revealed that the same type of behavior was manifested at home. After considerable effort on the part of the counselor, Don's mother also agreed not to provide him with reinforcement for the tantrum behavior. It was agreed that Don would be left in his room to "cry it out" each time he resorted to displays of temper. In a very short time Don stopped having tantrums both at home and in school—the tantrum behavior was extinguished.

By providing for no reinforcement after the tantrums, Don's counselor, teacher, and parents were able to eliminate the undesirable behavior. Extinction procedures as used here as well as other procedures (e.g., Wolpe, 1958) have been shown to be effective counseling techniques for weakening or eliminating deviant behaviors. It is possible that other methods could have helped Don learn to control his temper. However, a warm understanding approach would not only be ineffective in this case but, as used here, was actually partly responsible for maintaining and promoting the undesirable behavior.

Variety of Techniques

The behavioral counselor does not rely on any one set of counseling procedures but instead tailors specific techniques for specific problems. The techniques the counselor uses are employed to aid the student in learning those behaviors necessary to the solution of his problem. If the underachiever, for example, is referred for counseling, the behavioral counselor would not devote his time and energy trying to determine what is "abnormal" about the individual's personality by administering various personality tests. Rather, he would attempt to devise techniques and procedures that would be effective in helping the individual to improve his achievement. He would seek ways of providing more encouragement for constructive efforts at improving his school work.

Specific techniques for specific problems are not readily available but must be devised by the counselor to fit each individual problem. Procedures described in various research studies may be suggestive, however. The use of systematic positive reinforcement (Krumboltz & Schroeder, 1965; Johnson, 1964), tape recordings of students modeling a desired behavior (Krumboltz & Thoresen, 1964; Bandura, 1965), programmed instruction (Bruner, 1965), video-taped presentations and films (Krumboltz, Varenhorst, & Thoresen, in press), "behavior contracts" and role-playing (Keirsey, 1965), and systematic desensitization of anxieties (Wolpe, 1958; Lazarus, 1961) are some examples of procedures counselors might try to help students learn the behaviors necessary for the solution of their particular problems.

THE PURPOSES OF COUNSELING

The central purpose of counseling and the main reason for its existence is to assist each student, teacher, or parent with the specific problem for which he is seeking help. The main task then for counselors is to assist the individual in *learning* those behaviors which will result in a solution to his problem.

From a behavioral approach, all relevant goals and objectives of counseling must be focused on behavior. Thus, the counselor would state his counseling goals in terms of observable behavior rather than of some abstract inner personality process (Krumboltz, 1966). Since students' problems are different from each other, the goals of counseling would be stated differently for each individual. Broad general goals for all individuals, e.g., self-understanding or increased ego strength, are deemed by the behavioral counselor as too abstract to be useful in specifying the purposes to be accomplished.

The goals of the behavioral counselor may be organized into three categories: (1) altering maladaptive behavior, (2) learning the decision-making process, and (3) preventing problems. In each category the objectives of the counselor are specific changes in behavior sought by or for the student and agreed to by the counselor.

Altering Maladaptive Behavior

The situations of Mickey and Don provide good examples of goals that the behavioral counselor would use in instances of maladaptive behavior. For Mickey the goal of counseling was an increase in the skills necessary for giving oral reports before the class. For Don, the counselor's goal was to decrease the number of tantrums he was displaying at school. For both problems, observable changes in behavior were the explicit objectives of the counseling process.

The advantages of this approach can be easily seen. By avoiding ambiguous abstract terms, e.g., to increase Mickey's ego strength, the counselor was able to communicate with the teacher and Mickey as to what they were trying to accomplish. Thus, the counselor, teacher, and Mickey had a clear understanding of the goals of the counseling; all were able to take active roles in the process; and all could see progress being made toward the goal.

Learning the Decision-Making Process

A second major category of objectives in behavioral counseling is aiding students in learning how to make good decisions. Many personal and educational problems can often be solved when individuals know how to go about making a decision. Counselors can be effective in helping elementary school children to learn how to (1) construct alternative behaviors, (2) seek relevant information about each alternative, (3) weigh the possible outcomes and values of each alternative, and (4) formulate tentative plans of action.

Consider Frankie and Brian. Frankie blurts out incorrect answers without taking sufficient time to think through a problem. Brian, on the other hand, vacillates from one side of the question to the other and can never make up his mind. Both boys could benefit from some systematic help in learning how to make decisions wisely.

Research studies have shown that presenting information on probable outcomes (Gelatt, 1964) and reinforcing either deliberation or decision-type responses (Ryan & Krumboltz, 1964) influences the decision-making process. By aiding students to learn how to use the steps involved in the decision-making process, counselors and teachers are in effect providing students with problem-solving skills and attitudes which will aid them in meeting new problems in the future.

Preventing Problems

The third type of goal for counseling is that of preventing problems. By setting up educational programs that help students learn the behaviors necessary in the decision-making process, counselors can be effective in assisting students to solve some of their future personal, educational, and vocational decisions. But counselors must also be concerned about other educational practices.

Students who are discouraged because of harsh punishment for low grades or feel inadequate because of a constantly dissatisfied teacher or parent are all too often seen by a counselor after the damage is done. By asking for and taking an active role in the curricular and extracurricular programs of the school, counselors can help prevent educational practices which stifle the desire for learning and create serious emotional maladjustment.

STUDENT PROBLEMS SEEN AS PROBLEMS IN LEARNING

The way we conceptualize a student's problem will determine our goals and procedures in counseling. It is important then that school counselors conceptualize student problems in ways that suggest steps for solving them. As we have seen in the cases of Mickey and Don, the behavioral counselor does not view deviant student behaviors as symptoms of pathology but as inappropriate behaviors that have been learned in the same way that any other behavior is learned. The counseling process is a learning situation in which the counselor aids the counselee in learning those behaviors necessary to the solution of his problem. How behavior is learned and how it may be unlearned or altered become central issues for the behavioral counselor.

Since most learning is a function of environmental consequences, effective procedures for producing behavior change depend on the arrangement of the student's environment. In reality, environmental modification is the only channel open to counselors for influencing human behavior. The behavioral counselor thus looks at the student's environment to see what is maintaining the behavior and what changes in the environment would significantly aid the individual to learn those behaviors necessary for solving his problem.

Conceptualizing the problem as one of learning guides the counselor in the goals that must be accomplished and allows him to monitor progress objectively. Since counseling is seen as a learning process, the counselor becomes an integral part of the educational system and joins with teachers, administrators, and parents in helping children learn how to lead fuller, richer lives.

SUMMARY

A behavioral approach to counseling offers elementary school counselors an effective means for helping students with specific problems. This approach has several unique characteristics:

> *1.* Since most human behavior is learned, it treats the counseling process as a learning process.

2. It assumes that effective procedures for producing desired behavioral change lie in arranging the student's environment to promote the desired learning rather than in manipulating hypothetical processes or entities within the individual.
3. The outcomes and goals of counseling are stated and assessed as specific changes in behavior shown by the student.
4. The counseling interview itself is only a small part of the total process of helping the student learn to solve his problems. Teachers, parents, and peers are all seen as important persons in providing an environment conducive to new learning.
5. Counseling procedures vary for different individuals and are specifically designed for the particular problem of each individual.
6. Counseling procedures and techniques are derived from scientifically based knowledge of the learning process.

Some counselors have said that the behavioral approach is just good common sense. Parents, counselors, and teachers frequently use effective learning principles without realizing the application they are making. However, it is important for the counselor to know why certain procedures are used, when to apply them and for what types of students and which specific problems, and to accomplish which goals. The counselor can thus become an integral part of the educational process.

Annotated Bibliography

Bandura, Albert. Psychotherapy as a learning process. *Psychological Bulletin*, 1961, *58*, 143–159. Surveys many experimental and clinical studies using behavioristic psychotherapy. Relates that many types of deviant behavior have been treated successfully by direct focusing on the behavior itself.

Krumboltz, John D. Behavioral counseling: rationale and research. *Personnel and Guidance Journal*, 1965, *44*, 383–387. Asserts that the goals of counseling must be in terms of some end condition and not the means to achieve that end. Rationale for the behavioral approach, counselor limitations, and useful counselor activities are discussed.

Krumboltz, John D. Parable of a good counselor. *Personnel and Guidance Journal*, 1964, *43*, 118–123. This article provides a comparison of behavioral and client-centered approaches to a counseling problem. The similarities and differences in the assumptions and procedures of the two approaches are discussed.

Krumboltz, John D. (Ed.) *Revolution in counseling: implications of behavioral science.* Boston: Houghton Mifflin, 1966. Chapters by Krumboltz, Bijou, Shoben, McDaniel, and Wrenn explore the possibilities and problems arising from application of learning principles to counseling.

Krasner, Leonard, & Ullmann, Leonard P. (Eds.) *Research in behavior modification.* New York: Holt, Rinehart & Winston, 1965. Fifteen articles of research in personality, child, clinical, social, general, and experimental psychology are presented. Such areas as learning principles, the interview, vicarious reinforcement, verbal conditioning, modeling, small groups, and hypnosis are covered.

Magoon, Thomas. Innovations in counseling. *Journal of Counseling Psychology*, 1964, *11*, 343–347. Magoon presents possibilities in using audio-visual materials in career counseling.

Michael, Jack, & Meyerson, Lee. A behavioral approach to counseling and guidance. *Harvard Educational Review*, 1962, *32*, 382–402. A behavioristic model for counseling is presented as an approach for the development of a scientific approach to guidance. The phenomena of conditioning are discussed in terms of the experimental learning psychologist.

Ullmann, Leonard P., & Krasner, Leonard. (Eds.) *Case studies in behavior modification*. New York: Holt, Rinehart & Winston, 1965. The writers present a variety of behavioral problems in which psychotherapeutic procedures derived from social learning theory are applied. Cases are drawn from a wide variety of clinical and non-clinical settings.

References

Bandura, A. Behavioral modifications through modeling procedures. In L. Krasner & L. P. Ullman (Eds.), *Research in behavior modification*. New York: Holt, Rinehart & Winston, 1965.

Bruner, Fern. The effect of programmed instruction on information-seeking behavior in tenth-grade students. Unpublished doctoral dissertation, Stanford Univ., 1965.

Gelatt, H. B. The influence of outcome probability data on college choice. Unpublished doctoral dissertation, Stanford Univ., 1964.

Johnson, C. J. The transfer effect of treatment group composition on pupils' classroom participation. Unpublished doctoral dissertation, Stanford Univ., 1964.

Keirsey, D. W. Transactional casework: a technology for inducing behavior change. Paper read at California Assn. of School Psychologists and Psychometrists, San Francisco, 1965.

Krumboltz, J. D. *Stating the goals of counseling*. Monograph No. 1, California Counseling and Guidance Assn., 1966.

Krumboltz, J. D., & Schroeder, W. W. Promoting career exploration through reinforcement. *Personnel and Guidance Journal*, 1965, *44*, 19–26.

Krumboltz, J. D., & Thoresen, C. E. The effect of behavioral counseling in group and individual settings on information-seeking behavior. *Journal of Counseling Psychology*, 1964, *11*, 324–333.

Krumboltz, J. D., Varenhorst, Barbara B., & Thoresen, C. E. Nonverbal factors in the effectiveness of models in counseling. *Journal of Counseling Psychology*, in press.

Lazarus, A. A. Group therapy of phobic disorders by systematic desensitization. *Journal of Abnormal and Social Psychology*, 1961, *63*, 504–510.

Ryan, T. Antoinette, & Krumboltz, J. D. Effect of planned reinforcement counseling on client decision-making behavior. *Journal of Counseling Psychology*, 1964, *11*, 315–323.

Skinner, B. F. *Science and human behavior*. New York: Macmillan, 1953.

Wolpe, J. *Psychotherapy by reciprocal inhibition*. Stanford, Calif.: Stanford University Press, 1958.

19.   MEDIATION IN THE CLASSROOM

Barbara G. Peterson

Counselors and school psychologists frequently become aware of situations where a classroom group and a teacher are in conflict with each other. For the most part, when this occurs the class and teacher must somehow manage to live together for the rest of the school year. When the conflict exists for a prolonged period, the teaching-learning atmosphere becomes unproductive. The teachers and students may become so involved in a negative interactional process that they display considerable resistance to learning.

Various approaches to the problem have been used by pupil personnel staff members. One type of approach involves working with individuals or small groups of students referred by the teacher to try to effect attitudinal or behavior change. A second method has been to offer the teacher a chance to air his feelings about the situation and to explore alternatives.

A more active role on the part of the consultant has involved his presence in the classroom as an observer. On the basis of his observations of the interactional process, the psychologist or counselor later discusses with the teacher possible modifications of behavior which could result in an improved learning situation. The teacher is helped to realize that through his responses he may be reinforcing behaviors he wishes to extinguish. In some cases the counselor or psychologist becomes actively involved in the process of changing the patterns of reinforcement for individual students in the classroom.

Another style of participative consultation can involve the pupil personnel worker and the teacher in active confrontation and discussion of the problem with the class. William Glasser (1969, p. 123) points out that "responsibility for learning and for behaving so that learning is fostered is shared among the entire class. By discussing group and individual problems, the students and teacher can usually solve their problems within the classroom." In cases where the teacher is not skilled in the processes of conducting classroom meetings or where class behavior has deteriorated to a level where discussion is scarcely possible, the intervention of a member of the pupil personnel staff trained in group procedures may be required.

Source. Barbara G. Peterson, "Mediation in the Classroom." *Personnel and Guidance Journal*, 1971, Vol. 49(7), 558–561. Copyright 1971 by the American Personnel and Guidance Association and reproduced by permission.

THE TET PROGRAM

One training program, specifically designed to develop communication skills which facilitate democratic problem-solving (Gordon, 1968), teaches "active listening" (Rogerian reflection of feelings) and "clear sending" (direct formulation and expression of one's own feelings). The communication skills taught by Gordon in this Teacher Effectiveness Training (TET) program make it possible to resolve conflicts so nobody "loses." Together the class and teacher search for mutually acceptable solutions.

As soon as the learning climate begins to break down, teachers trained in this approach utilize the communication skills they have learned to confront the class effectively with their feelings about what is happening. Then they move into the process of listening to the concerns and feelings of the students. Tensions are more quickly dissolved when they are brought out in the open and discussed; once these conflicts are resolved, the class and teacher can refocus their attention on learning subject matter. Counselors and school psychologists who have undergone communication skills training may serve as mediators in classroom problem-solving sessions.

THE COUNSELOR AS MEDIATOR

When the counselor is serving as mediator, he may initially structure the situation by explaining that he has been asked to participate in a discussion with the students and teacher because comments from one or both seem to indicate that they are having a difficult time working together effectively as a group. He asks the group how they see the situation, and he listens non-evaluatively to the students and the teacher as they express their opinions about why the situation has deteriorated.

At first, many negative feelings are likely to emerge. Antagonisms between individual students or groups are brought into the open. Critical comments about the teacher's methods, his relationships with students, the curriculum, and teaching materials are usually brought out. Students will complain that "the class is boring," that they "aren't learning anything." Teachers needs to be prepared to face this initial barrage of negativism, and the mediator needs to be skilled in group procedures to deal with the interactions that occur.

For serious conflicts usually a class period each day for three to five days must be dedicated to the classroom problem-solving process. Less serious conflicts take less time. After the initial negative and critical comments, students begin to accept more responsibility for their own behavior and commitment to learning. In the beginning they may insist that the teacher must act more like a policeman in order to control them. After a few hours of discussion, some students begin to propose that they are capable of more self-control and self-direction than they have been demonstrating.

Gradually constructive solutions emerge from the group. Students analyze carefully the problems in classroom control and suggest ways of remedying the situation. Often they list classroom rules and regulations that would lead to improved behavior. There is usually initial disagreement among group members about what rules should be enforced and how they should be enforced. Meanwhile, the counselor makes no judgments, listening to all proposals and helping them move gradually toward defining some limits to which all can agree.

The class sometimes proposes consequences which should follow if individual students disregard the limits set. They may propose punishments such as five minutes of detention or temporary removal from the group or lowering grades or being sent to the principal. They discuss the effectiveness of various consequences and eventually propose a system that is workable and fair in their opinion and acceptable to the teacher.

Some groups arrive at a basic ground rule which may be stated something like this: "No student in this class has the right to prevent others from learning, although he himself may decide to fail by refusing to do his own work." Behaviors that disturb others are spelled out.

The class also may propose classroom activities which they would find rewarding. The teacher begins to see ways of modifying his approach to the curriculum. The types of activities which students recommend vary with the class; different proposals may emerge from various subgroups within the class. For example, in one ninth grade social studies class, one group of students wished to pursue the study of medieval plays and music, another wanted to focus on current events, while a third group wanted to be thoroughly familiar with the historical background material covered by the textbook. The teacher arranged for one day a week when groups of students could pursue these different interests. The first group shared their learning experience with the remainder of the class by presenting a medieval play with background music. Each week several members of the current events study group presented reports to the class.

In most classes, engaging in rewarding activities has been made contingent upon the successful completion of certain prescribed tasks and upon the maintenance of good behavior. Thus, classes may "earn time" for a spelling bee or playing educational games on Friday or at the end of the period by being cooperative and achieving certain educational goals. When the classroom group decides they want to earn certain rewarding activities, group members are more careful to behave in a way that will enable their friends to participate in those activities. Students are more likely to encourage one another to respond in productive ways.

When a class has previously had a particularly difficult time working together or when the solutions proposed are especially complex, it may be wise to draw up a written contractual agreement. Once the contract has been worked out to the point where all aspects are mutually agreeable, both students and teacher sign it. With each new classroom group, the contractual agreement is different in nature depending upon the subject area and the limitations and desires of the teacher and class. If the teacher or student feel that aspects of the contract are being violated, they are encouraged to confront one another directly. After a few weeks, a class period is taken to evaluate how things are going.

EVALUATION OF CLASSROOM PROBLEM-SOLVING

In one case where a contract was signed, six weeks after the problem-solving sessions the counselor returned to the class to ask the students to evaluate what had occurred since the discussions. The outcomes of the questionnaire were as follows:

1. Ninety-five percent of the students felt that the classroom atmosphere was either improved or greatly improved.
2. There was an increase in positive feelings toward the teacher and fellow students.
3. Seventy-six percent felt the class had accomplished more work since the problem-solving discussions, while 24 percent felt that they had done about the same amount of work, and no one felt they had done less work.

When asked to describe the problems of the class prior to the intervention program, one student described it as "total chaos." Another wrote, "No one had any respect for the teacher or classmates. There was always noise and confusion. And there was never anything accomplished."

Asked to indicate if there was any change following the discussions, one student wrote, "We have settled down and learned our limits. Now we know how far the teacher will let himself be pushed before he blows. We didn't know before, and we always tried to find out." Another student indicated that "the kids listen to the teacher more now. We seem to be moving along much faster now. It's more interesting." The description in general was of a more cooperative and respectful atmosphere.

The students felt that the problem-solving discussions helped because they brought the problem out in the open and people got their feelings out while hearing other people's feelings. They felt that once it was established that most people in the class wanted to learn, those who were making noise exercised more self-control.

In the group discussion that followed the written evaluations, the students indicated that one girl was still pushing the limits. They felt that there was so much antagonism between her and the teacher that it would benefit her and the class if she were transferred to another history class. One student indicated that the same girl acted much better in an English class they shared. The girl and teacher agreed that a transfer would probably be mutually helpful, and the recommendation was made and carried out.

A further attempt was made to evaluate objectively the effects of the group problem-solving process. An outside observer was asked to sit in an eighth grade English class to tabulate the rate of disturbing behaviors before and after the problem-solving. Disturbing behaviors were defined as (a) inappropriate talking to one's neighbor, (b) noise-making, (c) getting out of one's seat without permission at a time when it disturbs the class, and (d) physically bothering another student.

Because these behaviors were occurring at an extremely high rate, the teacher requested that the counselor come into the classroom to discuss the difficulty. Comments by students in the class and observation prior to the intervention confirmed the high rate of occurrence. Students agreed to a contract that stated that a student who was disturbing others would receive one warning followed by assignment of five minutes of noon-hour detention for each offense.

Following the six days of problem-solving during which a contract was drawn up, there was an extreme drop in the number of disturbing behaviors. The first day the teacher issued one warning; the second day she gave three warnings. There was a slight increase in disturbing behavior for two days until on the third day she kept four students for five minutes after class. On four out of the next seven school days, she kept several students for five minutes. There was a considerable drop in rate of disturbing behaviors as the students became convinced that she was going to follow through with the consequences.

CONCLUSION

Active intervention by pupil personnel specialists can be helpful in improving classroom learning environments where conflicts build up between teacher and pupils. The counselor or psychologist becomes the facilitator in a problem-solving process where the teacher and students confront their difficulties and work toward a mutually agreeable solution. This approach is worth further exploration in the present social atmosphere where confrontation in education is rapidly moving from the college to the high school and junior high school levels.

References

Glasser, W. *Schools without failure.* New York: Harper and Row, 1969.
Gordon, T. *Teacher effectiveness training.* Pasadena, Calif.: Effectiveness Training Associates, 1968.

20. ASSISTING TEACHERS WITH MANAGING CLASSROOM BEHAVIORAL PROBLEMS

•●•

Beth Sulzer Azaroff, G. Roy Mayer, and John J. Cody

PREPARING TO DEAL WITH BEHAVIORAL PROBLEMS

Elementary school counselors and other guidance personnel are often called upon to assist teachers with classroom behavioral problems. However, guidance personnel have, at times, found themselves ill-prepared to be of assistance due to a lack of information concerning various behavioral management procedures. Krumboltz and Hosford (1967, p. 38) have indicated that ". . . it is important for the counselor to know why certain procedures are used, when to apply them, for what types of students, for what specific problems, and to accomplish which goals." The intent of this article is to present, for the consideration of elementary school guidance personnel, several procedures for reducing undesirable student behaviors.

PUNISHMENT

The use of punishment in modifying student behaviors has been extensively discussed by the authors elsewhere (Mayer, Sulzer, & Cody, 1968). The following paragraph is a brief resumé of that paper.

Punishment has been defined (Azrin & Holz, 1966) as *a process by which an immediate presentation of a stimulus following an act reduces the probability of the occurrence of that act.* It is a procedure which, if employed properly, is informative and serves to reduce the occurrence of a specific behavior quickly and for a long period of time. It also decreases the probability that an observer will perform the punished behavior. However, punishment may have some undesirable side effects, such as escape and aggression. These reactions are socially disruptive and interfere with the educational process. Thus, alternative procedures for reducing student behaviors should also be considered.

EXTINCTION

Extinction, the removal of the reinforcement for a particular response, is currently being employed in counseling and guidance activities (Krumboltz, 1966; Krumboltz & Hosford, 1967) and has been effectively used by parents and teachers throughout history. The mother who never responds to the whining child eventually eliminates whining. The teacher who ignores the request, "Can I get a drink of water?" will eventually eliminate this as a request. The student who fails to achieve a higher grade because he copies incorrect answers will eventually stop copying. If reinforcement for a particular behavior is permanently removed, the behavior will be eliminated. Few papers, however, have pointed out the problems associated with the use of extinction, and guidance personnel need to be aware of these.

Problems with Extinction

(1) *Extinction takes time.* The whining child will continue to whine for a period of time before that behavior disappears. The request to go to the water fountain may be made several more times before it is eliminated. Sometimes it is impractical to wait for the behavior to subside gradually. We cannot wait for running-out-into-traffic or for swinging-a-cat-by-her-tail behavior to decrease gradually.

(2) *The rate of extinction is strongly related to the schedule under which the behavior has been reinforced in the past* (Ferster & Skinner, 1957). If the behavior has been intermittently reinforced it extinguishes much more slowly. If the mother had occasionally given the child what he wanted when he whined, whining would continue for a much longer period of time after reinforcement was permanently removed. On the other hand, had she always "given in" when the child whined, permanent removal of that reinforcer would result in a more rapid reduction in whining.

(3) *Sometimes it is not possible to remove the reinforcing stimulus.* Perhaps the act of swinging-a-cat-by-the-tail was being reinforced by the cat's meows and howls. Other than removing the cat (stimulus change) it would be impossible to stop reinforcement. In other situations, the individual attempting to reduce the behavior may not have the reinforcers under his control. The teacher may want to stop a pupil from stealing, but stealing may be reinforced by the attainment of material objects or by

admiration from the youngster's peer group. "Masochistic behavior" such as the head banging of the autistic child may be based on strongly conditioned reinforcement. Originally head banging may have been accompanied by the intermittent attention of parents, teachers, aides, or nurses. This pairing of the two events could have been responsible for what becomes an apparently "self-reinforcing" behavior (Azrin & Holz, 1966; Lovaas, 1966).

(4) *Identification of reinforcing stimuli is often difficult.* Does Sam respond rudely in class because his peers approve, because the teacher becomes angry, or because it gives him an opportunity to discharge aggression? Is it because his parents say "you show him he can't push you around," or because his parents give him negative attention for the behavior or what? What is reinforcing to one individual may not be reinforcing to another (Sulzer, 1966). Candy might strengthen the behavior of one individual but not that of another. Cigarettes make some people sick, while others will work for long periods of time to receive them (Lindsley, 1956). A definition of what is reinforcing to an individual becomes an empirical issue. Therefore, determination of an appropriate reinforcer must be based upon an objective observation of each individual's behavior.

(5) *Increase in response rate immediately following the removal of reinforcement delivery has been a consistently observed phenomenon among both animals and humans.* The crying baby cries louder before the crying subsides when ignored by its mother. The child who wants to get a drink may ask much more frequently for a few minutes before giving up. Though the increase in rate is a transitory one, in practice it can have some negative side effects. Mother and teacher may conclude too rapidly that their technique of ignoring the child is not effective, give up, and again reinforce the child. This situation sets the occasion for intermittent reinforcement. Its effect, increased resistance to extinction, has already been noted. In the long run the behavior then may actually become strengthened. When a mother or teacher complains, "I've tried everything and nothing works," they have probably been trapped into this bind.

(6) *The anger or rage which often occurs during the early phases of extinction* (Skinner, 1953) *is another problem.* Kicking or banging the vending machine when it fails to deliver its goods is an example of human extinction-induced aggression. The good student who cries in exasperation when he receives a poor grade on an exam also exemplifies his phenomenon.

Extinction Can Be Made More Effective When an Acceptable Alternative Behavior Which Will Yield Positive Reinforcement Is Available

For example, in an effort to obtain the teacher's attention or affection a student may withdraw and sulk in a corner. Such behavior could be ignored (the withdrawal of reinforcement, i.e., extinction), and whenever the student attempted to interact with other classmates the teacher could reinforce this behavior by giving him attention and praise. Or, when Johnny's verbal answer to a math question is incorrect, it may be ignored and the correct answer given by the teacher or classmate (model). When he later responds correctly, this response would be reinforced. The response the teacher reinforces is usually the response she is trying to teach or deems desirable.

Conditions Necessary for Extinction

Extinction can be an effective technique for reducing behavior provided that several conditions can be met in a particular school setting: (1) time for the behavior to subside gradually; (2) identification and control of the reinforcing stimuli; (3) access to acceptable alternative behaviors; and (4) the patience to ride out the storm of the transitory aggression and temporary increase in response rate.

TIME-OUT

"Time-out" is a procedure by which the opportunity or likelihood that an individual will receive reinforcement for his actions is removed for a brief period of time (usually about 10 minutes). While extinction removes the reinforcement for a specific behavior, time-out removes the opportunity for the student to receive essentially any reinforcement. A school example should serve to illustrate this technique. Mary has been disrupting the class by speaking out loud about matters unrelated to the class discussion. The counselor and teacher might decide that each time Mary speaks out she should be removed from the classroom and placed in a location where no one will respond to her. Eventually Mary's "speaking out" behavior should be reduced. Of additional value is the fact that the class is not disrupted as a result of Mary during her absence.

Several cases of the effective use of time-out have been reported. Wolf, Risley, and Mees (1964) reported using a time-out procedure with an autistic boy. For a few moments beyond the duration of the tantrum each time one occurred, they placed the child in a room isolated from his peers and aids. His temper tantrums were virtually eliminated. Unable to control the disruptive behavior of delinquent boys around a pool table with other techniques, Tyler and Brown (1967) reported that a brief confinement in a "time-out" room was a useful procedure in reducing their misbehavior.

Besides being employed as a technique for reducing undesirable behavior, time-out can be used to assist a student in regaining self control. When a student is too disruptive in a class and fails to respond to verbal controls, it sometimes becomes necessary to remove him. In such a situation "antiseptic bouncing" (Long & Newman, 1961) might be employed successfully. For example, if a student gets the giggles, it might be recommended that, before the giggling spreads to others, the teacher give the student a task to do such as taking a note to the office for her. Upon returning, the student would hopefully have regained control over her behavior and things would be back to normal. However, such a method should be used seldomly and cautiously. Some students may find that causing a disturbance is a good means of being excused from class. Thus, in the latter instance the teacher would be inadvertently reinforcing their disruptive behavior. Counselors can help teachers by assisting them in becoming constantly aware of the effect that their behavior is having on their students' behavior. When the teacher's behavior appears to be having a negative effect on a child's behavior, the teacher must be helped to recognize this quickly and to change her behavior to meet the demands of the situation.

SATIATION

Satiation is a method which temporarily reduces behavior through the *presentation* of reinforcement. A person who is no longer hungry will stop operating a food vending machine. When an individual has just consumed a large banquet meal he might say, "I'll never eat again." When behavior is satiated by physiological reinforcers (i.e., food, liquid, sex) the effects of satiation wear off fairly rapidly. Satiation has a longer lasting effect upon behaviors which are not strong in the repertoire of the individual (Azrin & Holz, 1966). If a youngster who is trying his first cigarette is made to smoke a whole pack, he will probably not want another one for a long time. The child who is instructed to say a dirty word hundreds of times will probably hesitate to say the world in the future. Though rarely permanent in its effects, satiation will sometimes diminish a behavior relatively quickly. This temporary reduction of the undesirable behavior provides an opportunity for the strengthening of desirable behavior.

One should be aware of the fact that a student can be satiated unintentionally. For example, suppose praise from the teacher is reinforcing to Jim. Jim does not successfully complete his math assignments but does well on all of his other subjects. The counselor observes that Jim's teacher gives him lavish praise for the well done subject matter. The counselor might conclude that Jim is satiated. He would then suggest to the teacher that she stop, or reduce, the amount of praise she gives Jim for his performances on subject matter other than math, and that the praise given to math assignments be contingent on their successful completion. Hopefully, Jim would do better in math in order to receive the teacher's praise.

USE OF MODELS

Praising the desired behavior of a classmate seated near a violator is a useful technique for handling minor infractions. In so doing, the intent is to provide a model demonstrating a positive behavior which others may imitate. The violator hopefully will observe and imitate the desired behavior. When he does, the teacher can then praise him for his "good work habits." Research has indicated that this opportunity is advantageous since praise from the teacher is likely to elicit and strengthen desired behaviors and to enhance the student's self-esteem and attitudes toward school (Staines, 1958; Davidson & Lang, 1960; Brehn & Cohen, 1962; Bandura & Walters, 1963; Bandura, 1965; Flanders, 1965; and Bandura, Grusec & Menlove, 1967).

Teachers must be warned to take care, however, not to use the same student as a model consistently. If a few individuals get all the praise, they may be perceived by their classmates as being "teacher's pets" and thus will not be imitated. Furthermore, the use of too much praise may satiate the student. Ideally, then, the praise should be spread to all students, but used discriminately so that the student emitting the desired behavior at the time is praised or used as a model.

REINFORCING INCOMPATIBLE BEHAVIORS

Reinforcing an incompatible behavior is a reductive method which teachers and guidance personnel use often since it is constructive, utilizes positive reinforcement, and avoids the negative side effects of some of the other techniques. In essence, this technique consists of the strengthening of a behavior which cannot coexist with the undesirable behavior. When a student is erasing the board or working diligently on a class assignment, he cannot be gabbing with his buddy in the back of the room. In order to strengthen incompatible behaviors, the teacher should praise the student when he does a good job of board erasing or is working diligently. Gradually the undesirable behaviors will be eliminated. Because strengthening of incompatible behaviors through reinforcement is a gradual process, this technique would be ineffective when immediate behavioral reduction is necessary.

STIMULUS CHANGE

All behavior occurs within a complex set of stimuli. When it is observed that a specific response tends to occur under a well-defined set of stimuli (discriminative stimuli) and does not occur under other sets of stimuli, it becomes possible to eliminate the behavior by changing the stimulus conditions (stimulus change). Suppose Johnny has a habit of poking Tommy whenever close enough to do so. Johnny does not poke any other children in the class. Changing the stimulus, Tommy, by separating the two boys would lead to the elimination of the poking behavior. Suppose that the verbal stimulus "don't cheat" is invariably followed by an increase in peeking at a neighbor's paper while the words "I know you all can be trusted to do your best and work by yourselves" are followed by independent work. Replacement of the words "Don't cheat" with "I know you can be trusted to do your best and work by yourselves," will result in the latter statement being paired with the desired behavior of independent work.

Though stimulus change has an immediate effect, a return to the original stimulus conditions often results in the rapid recovery of the eliminated response (Azrin & Holz, 1966). Seat Johnny within reach of Tommy and poking may well resume. Were a new proctor to come and say "Don't cheat," peeking would probably increase. Stimulus change, then, would be useful when an immediate reduction in behavior is desired. Permanence of the behavioral change is relative to the duration of the altered stimulus conditions.

Implicit in this discussion is that the use of stimulus change as well as all other procedures for eliminating behavior should be founded on empirical observation. While Johnny's change of location led to an elimination of poking it might not have worked with Susie. The discriminative stimulus for her might be boys or children. The words "I know you can all be trusted . . ." could have led to increased peeking by a different group. Stimuli which have been paired with reinforcement differ among individuals and sometimes from group to group. Thus, it is highly important for the counselor to observe the student's classroom behavior if this or one of the other procedures for reducing behavior were to be considered for use.

DISCUSSION AND CONCLUSIONS

Several methods of reducing undesirable behavior were presented for consideration by elementary school guidance personnel. The foregoing discussion suggests that there is no one best procedure for reducing or eliminating undesirable behaviors. The decision to use punishment or another method to reduce undesirable classroom behaviors must be founded on empirical observation. Elementary school counselors can assist teachers in selecting an appropriate procedure for reducing undesirable classroom behaviors through classroom observations, informal conferences, and in-service training programs. Such a selection must depend upon a variety of considerations. The seriousness of the misbehavior, frequency of its occurrence, time factors, control of the consequences, the public nature of the act, patience, ethics, and practicality are all important for the counselor and teacher to consider before final selection.

References

Azrin, N. H., & Holz, W. C. Punishment. In W. K. Honig (Ed.) *Operant behavior: Areas of research and application.* N.Y.: Appleton-Century-Crofts, 1966.

Bandura, A. Behavioral modifications through modeling procedures. In L. Kramer and L. P. Ullman (Eds.), *Research in behavior modification.* N.Y.: Holt, Rinehart and Winston, 1965.

Bandura, A., Grusec, J., & Menlove, F. Some social determinants of self-monitoring reinforcement systems. *Journal of Personality and Social Psychology,* 1967, *5,* 449–455.

Bandura, A., & Walters, R. *Social learning and personality development.* N.Y.: Holt, Rinehart and Winston, 1963.

Brehm, J. W., & Cohen, A. E. *Explorations in cognitive dissonance.* N.Y.: Wiley, 1962.

Davidson, H. H., & Lang, G. Children's perception of their teachers' feelings toward them related to self-perception, school achievement and behavior. *Journal of Experimental Education,* 1960, *29,* 107–118.

Ferster, C. B., & Skinner, B. F. *Schedules of reinforcement.* N.Y.: Appleton-Century-Crofts, 1957.

Flanders, N. A. Teacher influence, pupil attitudes, and achievement. *Cooperative research monograph no. 12,* Washington, D.C.: U. S. Department of Health, Education, and Welfare, Office of Education, 1965.

Krumboltz, J. D. *Revolution in counseling.* N.Y.: Houghton Mifflin Co., 1966.

Krumboltz, J. D., & Hosford, R. E. Behavioral counseling in the elementary school. *Elementary School Guidance and Counseling,* 1967, *1,* 27–40.

Lindsley, O. R. Operant conditioning methods applied to research in chronic schizophrenia. *Psychiatric Research Report,* 1956, *5,* 140–153.

Long, N. J., & Newman, R. G. A differential approach to the management of surface behavior of children in school. *Teachers' Handling of Children in Conflict,* 1961, *37,* 47–61.

Lovaas, O. I. Learning theory approach to the treatment of childhood schizophrenia. Paper delivered at American Orthopsychiatric Association, San Francisco, April, 1966.

Mayer, G. R., Sulzer, B., & Cody, J. J. The use of punishment in modifying student behaviors. *Journal of Special Education,* in press.

Skinner, B. F. *Science and Human Behavior.* N.Y.: Macmillan, 1953.

Staines, J. W. The self picture as a factor in the classroom. *British Journal of Educational Psychology,* 1958, *28,* 97–111.

Sulzer, B. W. Match to sample performance by normals and institutionalized retardates under different reinforcing conditions. Unpublished doctoral dissertation, University of Minnesota, 1966.

Tyler, V. O., & Brown, D. G. The use of swift, brief isolation as a group control device for institutionalized delinquents. *Behavior Research and Therapy,* 1967, *5,* 1–9.

Wolf, M. M., Risley, T. R., & Mees, H. L. Application of operant conditioning procedures to the behavior problems of an autistic child. *Behavioral Research and Therapy,* 1964, *1,* 305–312.

21. FUNCTIONAL USE OF ADLERIAN PSYCHOLOGY IN THE PUBLIC SCHOOLS

Theodore E. Grubbe and Marie E. Grubbe

INTRODUCTION

In working with children having behavior and conduct problems in the schools, the "Individual Psychologist"[1] finds the *Adlerian technique* simple and amazingly effective. Problem children have relatively simple patterns, and to those who can read and interpret the signs, the remedies are almost immediately apparent. With very young children, the problem can often be resolved by the removal of discouraging factors by the parents and psychologist. In older children, the need for training toward courage, independence, and the acquisition of social feeling is evident. "Individual Psychology" does not claim to cure all cases of problem behavior in children; however, even the most difficult cases respond positively when parents and teachers can be taught to cooperate intelligently with the approach.

In recent years, psychiatric formulations of human dynamics have made an impact on education. Within the last few decades the instinctual-biological theories of Freud[2] and his psychoanalytic school have become well-known in the American scene. *With Freud*, came new insights into human motivation and behavior available to the educator. However, the average parent or teacher would find it difficult to utilize these concepts for developing an understanding of a given child. For example, if the educator assumed that the student's hostility and aggressive behavior were based upon his Oedipus Complex, a repressed sexual desire for his mother, or that his shyness or lack of positive aggression stemmed from a castration fear, there is little the teacher could do, even if she did understand the concept and were able to investigate her assumptions.

In contrast, Adlerian Psychology implies movement. Every action of a child has a purpose. His misbehavior or behavior is his way of working toward a goal. Theoretically, the goal of a so-called normal person would be that of a complete human being, compensating for his personal weak-

Source. Theodore E. Grubbe and Marie E. Grubbe, "Functional Use of Adlerian Psychology in the Public Schools." Unpublished, March 1963.
[1] Alfred Adler refers to his concepts as individual psychology. The Individual Psychologist is an Adlerian Psychologist.
[2] Sigmund Freud, *New Introductory Lectures on Psychoanalysis*, New York: W. W. Norton & Company, 1933.

nesses and the experiences of childhood by some socially valuable, productive work. "Such a human being would develop the traits of honesty, sincerity, and responsibility. As he grew older, his social connections would become more extended, his usefulness wider, his poise better, and his cause greater. He would be independent in action and judgment and service, but his activities would be dominated by the social need of the time . . ."[3] It is apparent that very few humans make such concepts their goal in life. The goals often become more self-centered: a struggle for happiness with the least expenditure of energy—to dominate the environment, etc. The more inferior or inadequate the child feels himself in the beginning, the higher his goal of compensatory superiority becomes.

A misbehaving child is an unhappy and discouraged child. He feels inferior to the social situation. His goal becomes that of a striving for superiority, usually in a negative or misbehaving way. When the goal of the child is understood in terms of purposive behavior, then the psychologist, teacher, and parent are in a position to help the child redirect his goals toward a more useful function.

To be able to understand the goal of the child, understanding of the *total child* is necessary.

BASIC CONSIDERATIONS OF ADLERIAN (INDIVIDUAL) PSYCHOLOGY

The *concept of unity* of the human personality is the foundation of Individual Psychology. The second great principle of Adler's psychology is that the unit organism is a dynamic whole, moving through a definite life pattern toward a definite goal. "Viewed objectively and dispassionately we see that every human organism strives for a measure of security and totality which makes continued existence possible. The goal of the human race is maintenance of the human race."[4]

Inferiority feeling is the one dynamic force behind all human activity. This inferiority feeling is not necessarily a handicap; rather, it has proved itself to be the most cogent stimulus for the development of the human race. Our great inventions (the telescope, radio, television et al.) show the need for man to better his communication devices based upon his inferiority in this area. "The human baby is the only living animal that experiences his own inadequacy because his mind develops faster than his body. . . ." The young infant feels inferior because he cannot yet walk and thus his inferiority becomes the motivation for him to learn to walk.

[3] Alfred Adler, *The Pattern of Life*, Edited by W. Beran Wolfe, M.D. New York: Cosmopolitan Book Corporation, 1930.
[4] Ibid., Adler, p. 1.

However, there are many factors that work against the optimum compensation of the inferiority feeling—if in addition to the infant's normal inferiority (which through courage can be compensated for) there are physical weaknesses, the infant's struggle for social significance becomes far more difficult. These biological factors, or organ inferiorities as Adler refers to them, can intensify the inferiority feelings to such an extent that they may become inferiority complexes. The organ inferiority may be an actual physical defect of body, or a medically unimportant physical anomaly such as a birthmark, a mole, or a wart, red hair, or something similar. All of these factors can contribute to the development of an inferiority complex. It is well to point out that the inferiority complex is fully felt by the individual and openly exhibited through his behavior. The inferiority feeling permits compensatory endeavors while the inferiority complex inhibits progress, whether real or imagined. The fact that a child is beautiful can lead to an inferiority complex in that the child learns to believe that his beauty is the only contribution which is required of him in the social order.

The socio-economic level of the child also is within the group of factors that can intensify the inferiority feeling. Members of minority groups whether social, religious or economic often suffer an increase in inferiority feelings because of the additional difficulties imposed upon them. Great wealth can also be disastrous because the incentive to work and to contribute positively is frequently lacking.

The family constellation is a third set of factors that can intensify the inferiority feeling. The only child derives his inferiority complex from his abnormal importance in the family. The oldest child, having been an only child for a given period of time, finds himself displaced by a younger sibling and could become so discouraged from his fall from power that he never musters enough courage and strength to cope with the problems of existence objectively. The second child has an older sibling which can become a person to exceed, and in his aggressive behavior to excel the older sibling, he may overshoot his mark and become an objective rebel. An additional problem with the second child is that he could become the middle child with a younger sibling pushing from below. The youngest child, or the baby of the family, may literally give up in his striving for social recognition in positive ways and resort to other ways. It is not uncommon for the youngest to become a "show off." Other situations can contribute to the increased inferiority feeling, such as the only boy or the only girl in the family.

Sex itself could be a factor that complicates the adjustment of a child. Although times are changing, we still live in a civilization dominated by the masculine ideal. This places the girl-child as an inferior being, that is "She's only a girl."

The series of above factors are presented to illustrate the possible origins of the development of an inferiority complex. It is very important to keep in mind that none have to be contributing factors. Even with every biological, socio-economic, sex-role, and position in the family considered unfavorable, a child can grow up with a sense of equality and real worth-whileness. The child perceives life as he has learned to perceive it. The reactions of the authorities, whether parents or educators, to the child's growth and behavior can either increase or decrease the child's sense of inferiority. Blindness can make a child so discouraged that his dependency upon others is so complete he cannot function positively to any degree, or blindness can be a specific inferiority that merely offers a challenge. Such a handicap can be overwhelming, depending upon whether it is a feeling of inferiority or whether it becomes an inferiority complex. A child who is blind has the choice of recognizing blindness as the final conclusion of hopelessness in either a limited area of his activity or the total social scene. The choice the child makes is directly related to the degree of his feeling of inferiority.

"Patterns of life are usually fixed by the time a child is five or six years old. That is to say, a definite set of situations, giving a specific and characteristically individual tinge to the inferiority situation of each child, expresses itself in a characteristic goal in life. . . . Unless the individual gains insight by *later education* or by an *abrupt change of conditions*, this pattern of conduct—between the first inferiority situation and the final crystallized goal of what seems security, totality, superiority—continues as an unchanging dynamic unified stream."[5]

"Individual Psychology has especially concerned itself with the psychology of children, both on its own account and for the light it sheds on adult traits and adult behavior. It is psychology which allows *no gap to exist between theory and practice*. It fastens upon the unity of personality and studies its dynamic struggle for development and expression. From such a point of view, scientific knowledge is already practical wisdom, for the knowledge is a knowledge of mistakes, and whoever has this knowledge—whether it be the psychologist, the parent, or the friend, or the individual—immediately sees its practical application in the guidance of the personality concerned."[6]

The illustrative case of Fred may shed light on the practical application of individual psychology in a school situation. Fred was brought to the attention of the school psychologist with the following described symptoms:

[5] Ibid., Adler, p. 1.
[6] Alfred Adler, *The Education of Children*, George Allen and Unwin Limited, Museum Street, London, 1930.

"Very defiant to the teacher; vicious to other children; work habits poor; uncooperative; sullen. He responds negatively and bitterly to any attempt by the teacher to help. Disliked by children and adults alike."

On the basis of the described symptoms, the psychologist could see that Fred was a very unhappy and discouraged 5th grade boy; however, quite ambitious. It was apparent that his goal was to dominate and maintain a type of status that was socially acceptable, but nevertheless evident. From all indications, he had been successful in his negative endeavors. A conference with the principal and teacher confirmed to some extent the original interpretation of the psychologist. The problem was of long standing, but was becoming increasingly more difficult. The boy had been suspended many times from school, up to two weeks at a given time. He had been spanked by the principal on occasions for his open defiance. The parents had cooperated with the school and had been called in many times. They were at a loss as to what to do with Fred. Financially, the family was well off—a good income, a large home in one of the better neighborhoods, both parents with a college education. The parents were considering psychiatric help, perhaps residential treatment for the boy, but wanted the psychologist's opinion. They agreed to follow anything he suggested.

The mother was quite attractive; appeared to be in her late thirties. It was interesting to note the absence of the father at the conference. According to the mother, Fred was the oldest; he had a young sister (around 2) who was described by the mother as very docile and sweet. The two did not get along at all and the mother was afraid to leave them alone together. The father had his own business and worked long hours. He often came home tired and irritable. He was impatient with his son; often lost his temper with him. The father on many occasions had taken the boy aside and had "father-son" talks about his behavior and school work. They had disciplined him with spankings and other forms of coercive methods. They had deprived him of many things. The father had tried to take him fishing or include him on specific activities alone, but this usually met with resistance or an argument. They had tried to ignore his behavior, but he only got worse. They had tried to help him with school work and even hired a tutor for a while. Nothing seemed to work.

Comment: Even though the psychologist had not seen the boy up to this point, the goal of this child was obvious. The original hypothesis was correct. The boy was literally running the home. He could also dominate the school authorities' emotions. For eight years he had been an only child. He had been alternately pampered and rejected. He was given love and a certain amount of companionship, but at the same time, his father's striving ambition had left its mark of discouragement. In his own mind, he could lot live up to his father's expectations. To be useful might mean rejection or failure so he turned his energy to developing a type of social status which could neither meet with failure nor be ignored. In a sense, he was in open warfare with the authorities. The birth of the younger sister further contributed to his problem. He now had a younger female rival to compete with and he quickly learned that the parents were quite protective of her so the sister became a pawn in his struggle for dominance. As any child would, Fred knew his parents' vulnerable points and used them to the utmost. As was pointed out to the mother, probably Fred knew his mother's and father's weak points better than they knew themselves. He knew how to look to get them annoyed. He knew and used everything that was necessary for him to attempt to control and dominate.

Shortly after the initial conference with the mother, Fred was seen by the psychologist. A WISC revealed an I.Q. in the 120's, with no significant variance between the subtests. The Rorschach showed a boy with tension, uneasiness, and much hostile aggression. His perception of reality was adequate, but he viewed it with much anger. His adult authority relationships were strained and uncomfortable. There were many strengths noted. The boy was cooperative during the testing but immediately following the test, he left the room and went screaming down the hall that he had been "seen by the headshrinker" and "was nuts," "ha, ha!" etc. Of course, this got a reaction from several teachers and the principal. The psychologist said nothing about this incident but met with the parents and school authorities during the week and outlined a program.

The first step was to help the parents see the goal of their son. As long as the father or mother continued to react the way they felt emotionally in a given situation, this would tend to increase Fred's successful misbehavior. Individual psychiatric help was not advised as Fred's behavior was a social reaction within the family and school milieu rather than predetermined uncontrollable behavior based upon so-called repressions and unconscious hostility. If any outside help would have been recommended, it would have been family counseling. Based upon the parents' reactions, the psychologist felt that they were able to cope with the situation. Their own goals were generally in keeping with the mean, however, some drastic changes on their part.

The psychologist saw Fred again shortly afterward. The psychologist was friendly and discussed openly the boy's problem with school, and with home. It was interpreted in terms of purposive behavior, that is, the certain amount of pleasure he got out of upsetting authorities. Fred pointed out that he hated school and all his teachers. The psychologist had the authority in this case to suggest to the boy that he did not have to go to school if he did not want to, however, he must remain in the home during school hours. (Because of the severity of the boy's problem, the psychologist had brought this matter up with the authorities prior to meeting the student and received full cooperation. Unless there was improvement noted in behavior, the administrators were considering permanent expulsion for Fred.) Fred felt this would be wonderful and such a program was immediately started. (The psychologist sent Fred home right after the conference.) Also, it had been worked out with the parents that they were to do nothing when Fred was home but make certain that he stayed in the home during school hours. He could look at TV, listen to the radio; in fact, do anything he wanted to except leave the home during school hours. The parents were to be nice to him, be friendly, say nothing about school other than respond noncommitally about his questions or comments. It was pointed out to Fred that if he ever wanted to come back to school, he or his mother should contact the psychologist and make arrangements.

Fred stayed home for over a week. According to his mother, he was much enthused at first. He would sit at a chair by the window in the mornings and loudly laugh at the children who had to go to school. Each day, however, his enthusiams decreased. At 3:30, he could go out and play, or do whatever he wanted to do. The parents, in the meantime, were not responding to any of Fred's misbehavior. If Fred got impudent about something, they would not respond at all, or respond to the way they felt like responding. Each night when the father came home from work, he would take a few minutes out to have fun with his son or do something that was purely for companionship. At first, as in the past, Fred would rebuff his father and become impudent or nasty. The father *now* did not react by showing hurt feelings or anger but, rather, accepted the behavior with little or no reaction but continued in trying to win his son over. Fred tried everything to anger his father but the father was able to maintain a friendly interest in the boy—so thus the boy's goal to dominate his father's emotions became fruitless; but still he had his father's attention in a more positive way. It was a little more difficult for the mother who was with the boy all day, but somehow she managed. To say the least, it was "rough." During the day, Fred did many things to upset her; trying to sneak outside; messing up the kitchen; teasing the sister; teasing the dog; messing up the living room; playing the TV at top volume. Because the mother was now aware, as the father, of Fred's goal, it was easier not to respond to the misbehavior.

Before two weeks were up, Fred wanted to go back to school. The psychologist readily agreed, and Fred started back to school the next day. His return was structured in such a way that Fred was no longer in a position to manipulate the school authorities. If he exceeded what would be considered normal misbehavior, he would be sent home for the remainder of the day with no comment—no lectures, no reprimands, no second chances—just sent home where he could do what he wanted during school hours at home. The mother was to say nothing—perhaps greet him in a friendly way and be nice, no matter how she felt.

Comment: One of the basic assumptions of Individual Psychology is that basically the child (also the adult) wants social recognition on the useful side and will operate on this level, providing he has the courage to do so, and that he finds success. Only the discouraged and unhappy child resorts to the negative measures as did Fred. The program outlined was in effect to minimize the success of his uncooperative goal and help him gain the courage to operate more effectively on the cooperative side.

The teacher was instructed to give Fred as many encouraging experiences as possible within the classroom situation. Because the teacher was no longer vulnerable to Fred's aggressive behavior and understood his goal in terms of purposive behavior, this was easy to do. No longer would she fight or coercively discipline Fred. If Fred did not meet the standards set up in the class or became disruptive and tried to involve the teacher in a power struggle, he was merely sent home. The responsibility of his behavior was up to him. Daily he had a choice, for he was only sent home for the remainder of the day. It was also pointed out to Fred that he had the responsibility of getting the work done that he had missed. But, again, no one was going to remind him or make him do it; it was pointed out to him that if he didn't, he would ultimately fail the grade. If he were sent home early in the morning, he was free to return after school to pick up his assignments if he so desired.

Upon Fred's first return to school, he never made it to the classroom because he jabbed the girl in front of him in line with a pencil, causing a certain amount of injury and much pain—not to mention the commotion. The second day he made it to the classroom, but within five minutes dropped a huge potato bug down the back of a student sitting in front of him. Needless to say, this incident was not in keeping with classroom standards. Within a few weeks, Fred was managing to last until noon. And within six weeks, Fred was back in school on a full-time basis. The day he made it for the full-time was rather eventful, at least for Fred. His mother called the psychologist and related the incident.

"It was just before lunch, and the children were lining up in front of the cafeteria. Fred had acquired a straight pin for the purpose of secretly sticking people with it. (No doubt it would be possible to attach special significance to his fetish for sticking people with things, however the sticking, from the Adlerian approach, was merely a tool to achieve his goal of control, based upon his own strong feelings of inferiority.) As Fred was standing in line, he gave serious thought to the consequences of his act. He related to his mother (and this is interesting, because previously he never talked to his mother about his behavior; he denied everything when questioned) that certainly the sticking would create a scene but all he would get out of it would be to be sent home. As he put it, 'I am getting awfully tired of going home—nothing ever happens there.' "

Fred at home was becoming more enjoyable to his parents and as Fred said at a later date to the psychologist, "You know, my parents aren't so bad after all."

Many years have gone by since the referral on Fred. The psychologist occasionally had reports of some minor difficulty Fred got himself into at the high school level, and Fred was never considered a model student. He never completely gave up his negative way of behaving, but the move toward the positive side was evident. He never failed academically, but at the same time he never made the honor roll. It was interesting to note that when the parents stopped getting involved in separating the children from fighting and let the children settle their own disputes, the children actually became close friends. The mother was a little perturbed that her model daughter lost some of her angelic qualities when Fred began to give up his negative aggressive behavior. As a side issue, the younger sister was maintaining her status by her model characteristics, and the worse Fred behaved, the better she behaved. This particular type of goal-directed behavior lost its importance as Fred changed, and the sister was forced to find more constructive ways and perhaps more realistic ways of behaving. Also, because of the parents no longer protecting her against her "mean" older brother, she had to learn to get along with him, and in the long run she was not difficult at all.

DISCUSSION AND CONCLUSION

Although outside professional help was not recommended in this case, there are instances where this is advisable; especially when the inferiority complex is so deeply engraved as a part of the life-style of the child and considerable education, encouragement and support is needed. In some cases, this can only be accomplished in a therapy situation. With the case of Fred, an abrupt change of conditions and education helped the boy redirect his goal. His useless behavior became unsuccessful because the parents and the teacher were able to understand and change their ways of working and dealing with the boy. With these changes, Fred's only alternative was to accept the conditions he basically wanted originally—to be a useful member in social scene.

The concepts of Adlerian Psychology are not new to people in other schools of thought.[7] Many Neo-Freudians are following the socio-teleological approach to human dynamics, as first developed by Alfred Adler. Karen Horney,[8] Eric Fromm,[9] Harry Stack Sullivan,[10] and, more recently, Franz Alexander,[11] and Thomas M. French,[12] are but a few. Many psychologists who claim to be eclectic in their approach to human behavior are noted for their general adherence to Adlerian principles, yet often are not aware of the origin of their ideas.

Combs[13] uses the term, "Self-actualizing persons" and the concept behind it is not too dissimilar from an Individual Psychology point of view.

Any referral that is brought to the attention of the school psychologist can be understood in terms of purposive or goal-directed behavior. Consider, for example, such symptoms as a goal toward keeping the authorities involved with a child, that is, attention-getting: bashfulness, anxiety and fear, eating difficulties, poor scholastic achievement, laziness; moral behavior, etc.—or the following as possible ways to gain power over the authorities: disobedience, stubbornness, temper tantrums, bad habits, untruthfulness, and so on—or the following as ways to get back at the adult authority: stealing, enuresis, violence, and brutality.[14]

Goals, if understood, can be redirected toward a more positive function. If teachers, parents and others working with children know and can inter-

---

[7] Rudolf Dreikurs, *Character Education and Spiritual Values In An Anxious Age*, Boston: Beacon Press, 1957.

[8] Karen Horney, *Our Inner Conflicts*, New York: W. W. Norton, 1945.

[9] Erich Fromm, *Man For Himself*, New York: Farrer and Rinehart, 1947.

[10] Harry Stack Sullivan, *Concepts of Modern Psychiatry*, New York.

[11] Franz Alexander, *Our Age of Unreason*, Philadelphia: J. B. Lippincott, 1942.

[12] Thomas M. French, *The Integration of Behavior*, Chicago: University of Chicago Press, 1952.

[13] Association for Supervision and Curriculum Development, *Perceiving, Behaving, Becoming*, A Perceptual View of the Adequate Personality, Arthur W. Combs (University of Florida), Washington, D.C., 1962.

[14] Rudolf Dreikurs, M.D., *The Challenge of Parenthood*, New York: Duell, Sloan and Pierce, 1958.

pret the signs, they can redirect the goals toward a more positive way of behavior.

In the school district where the psychologist works, many faculty meetings are devoted to helping teachers learn more about recognizing the symptoms. A continuous parent study group goes on, sponsored by one of the parent groups. Parents can discuss their children's behavior in terms of goals.

Adlerian psychology is a real promise in the direction of truly helping in the development of an understanding of children and adults. It is easy to understand and makes logical and realistic sense to all involved with it.

"Do not forget the most important fact that not heredity and not environment are determining factors. —Both are giving only the frame and the influences which are answered by the individual in regard to his styled creative power."

Adler

Bibliography

Adler, Alfred, *The Education of Children*, George Allen and Unwin Limited, Museum Street, London, 1930.
Adler, Alfred, *The Pattern of Life*, Edited by W. Beran Wolfe, M.D., New York: Cosmopolitan Book Corporation, 1930.
Alexander, Franz, *Our Age of Unreason*, Philadelphia: J. B. Lippincott, 1942.
Allen, George, and Unwin, *The Science of Living*, New York, London.
Association for Supervision and Curriculum Development, *Perceiving, Behaving, Becoming*. A Perceptual View of the Adequate Personality, Arthur W. Combs (University of Florida), Washington, D.C., 1962.
Dreikurs, Rudolf, M.D., *The Challenge of Parenthood*, New York: Duell, Sloan and Pierce, 1958.
Dreikurs, Rudolf, M.D., *Character Education and Spiritual Values In An Anxious Age*, Boston: Beacon Press, 1957.
French, Thomas, *The Integration of Behavior*, Chicago: University of Chicago Press, 1952.
Fromm, Erich, *Man For Himself*, New York: Farrer and Rinehart, 1947.
Horney, Karen, *Our Inner Conflicts*, New York: W. W. Norton, 1945.
International Journal of Individual Psychology (Quarterly) Menser, 6 North Michigan Avenue, Chicago, Illinois.
Kegan, Paul, *Problems in Neurosis*, London.
Social Interest: A Challenge to Mankind, London and New York.
Sullivan, Harry Stack, *Conceptions of Modern Psychiatry*, New York.

V *Staff Group Consulting*

In the process of establishing priorities for modifying and monitoring the school milieu, the consultant identifies the importance of direct and scheduled contact with teachers. This involvement with teachers is important because of the teacher's nucleus-like position in the school setting as well as the abundance of recent evidence supporting the teachers' need and readiness for help. The teacher group is a fundamental activity in the process of creating a humane learning environment. Working in groups is both more effective and more economical than individual teacher consulting (Dinkmeyer and Muro, 1971).

It is the consultant's responsibility to organize, schedule, and facilitate the group meetings. In these group meetings, teachers usually gather to do the following.

1. Share concerns about children, the learning process, and the learning environment.
2. Learn how to deal more effectively with the misbehavior of children.
3. Develop new procedures for facilitating the total growth (social, emotional, physical, spiritual, and academic) of all children.
4. Give and receive feedback on how they relate to others.
5. Provide an ongoing communication network.

Through this process, a service is provided on an ongoing basis that helps to meet the daily needs of the teachers. Assistance with problem children, classroom disturbances, and personal concerns is provided instead of written reports, test results, and other forms of impersonal contact. Help is available for what is important to the teachers. The group is a place in which it is OK to make mistakes, share failures, and receive help and support from colleagues.

Lippitt presents some guidelines for training school personnel in how to establish and maintain effective interpersonal relations. His particular approach to this task is the sensitivity training group or "T" group. He identifies the components of a high quality program and presents a variety of possible ways to implement this program.

Peterson describes the "Teacher Effectiveness Training" program of Dr. Thomas Gordon. The program is designed to help teachers develop effective basic communication skills. This approach uses a specific course content presented in a readily understandable way to help teachers provide more meaningful instruction.

Watson describes his pioneering work with principal groups. He gives some case material, a report of his research in this area, and a series of implications for practitioners.

Dinkmeyer provides a theory and rationale for a procedure called the "C" group, which seems to combine the best features of the other procedures in this section. This process blends the didactic elements described by Peterson with the more experiential ideas presented by Lippitt. The group is called a "C" group because the factors that tend to make the group most effective begin with the letter "c" (collaboration, consultation, clarification, confrontation, communication, concern and caring, confidentiality, and commitment). He presents the goals of the group and several necessary procedures, conditions, and premises for effective contacts. Of special importance is the chart entitled "Identifying the Goals of Children's Misbehavior." This provides the teacher with a clear and meaningful way to understand and modify human behavior.

As these articles are read, considering the following.

● What are possible areas of focus for the group? Who should determine what material wlil be the focus of study in the group?
● Should printed material, films, and other structured material be a regular part of the consulting group?
● What does the consultant do when the teachers who need help the most will not attend the group meetings? Would it help if the administration made attendance at these sessions mandatory?
● Is it necessary or desirable to involve the principal or administrators directly in the teacher group sessions?
● What kinds of experiences or provisions can be provided to help humanize or in other ways facilitate the growth of principals?
● Dinkmeyer stresses the necessity of establishing a psychological foundation for human behavior. Other authors do not deal with this in as a direct a fashion. How important is a common approach or vocabulary to understanding and discussing human behavior in a group setting?
● Discuss the advantages and disadvantages of consulting in Dinkmeyer's "C" group, which is holistic and involves the teachers' feelings, beliefs, values, and attitudes.
● Why have pupil personnel workers been hesitant to work with groups of

teachers? Would you be willing to conduct a teacher group? List the advantages and disadvantages of doing this in your school.

● In forming a group of teachers, what factors would be important for composition? Do you advocate homogeneous or heterogeneous grouping according to sex? Age? Experience? Grade level? Subject matter? Philosophical orientation? Openness?

● Should the consultant allow the group to deal directly with the feelings, beliefs, attitudes, and values of the teachers? Is it good policy to stick to pure cognitive material in task-oriented fashion?

REFERENCES

Dinkmeyer, D., and Muro, J. J. **Group counseling.** Itasca, Ill.: F. E. Peacock, 1971.

22. SENSITIVITY TRAINING: WHAT IS IT? HOW CAN IT HELP STUDENTS, TEACHERS, ADMINISTRATORS?

Ronald Lippitt

Daily life in any classroom, school building or school system is sprinkled with difficulties of communication. Efforts to collaborate often face blockage as the result of "insensitivities" with regard to interpersonal relationships.

The following episodes are typical:

STUDENT I (to Student II): "Are you going to do any of those special projects she suggested?"

STUDENT II (to self): "He'd really kid me if I said 'yes.' (to Student I)— Naw, you won't catch me falling for her line. I've too many better things to do."

STUDENT I (to self): "Bet that's the way most of the kids feel. I'd be out of my mind to act like a teacher's pet. (to Student II)—Me too. Who cares about grades, anyway?"

And so ends Student I's thought about asking II to join him in a tempting joint project—in which Student II may well have had real interest.

TEACHER I (to Teacher II): "If only they didn't have parents, I think we could teach them. Actually, the kids are more intelligent every year."

ADMINISTRATOR I (to Administrator II): "The teachers just aren't committed to education any more. Look how they ignore faculty meetings and refuse to volunteer for any of the new programs we've suggested.

Source. Ronald Lippitt, "Sensitivity Training: What Is It? How Can It Help Students, Teachers, Administrators? *Childhood Education*, 1970, Vol. 46–6, 311–313. Reprinted by permission of Ronald Lippitt and the Association for Childhood Education International, 3615 Wisconsin Avenue, N.W., Washington, D.C. Copyright © 1970 by the Association.

And these days how many are willing to work with students after school?"

TEACHER (to Administrator): "About those three students who won't co-operate with me: okay if they sit in another room during my class period?"

Hundreds of such episodes could be cited of ways productive interaction is hampered in schools everyday. Participants in the drama of teaching and learning need to deal directly with such *affective* group-dynamics issues if teaching performance and learning quality are to be improved. Process learning or "sensitivity training" has begun to make important contributions toward these vital ends.

HISTORICAL BACKGROUND

What is this sensitivity training that Carl Rogers has called "perhaps the most significant social invention of this century"? How did it get started?

Today's sensitivity training group (T-group) was formed one summer night in 1946 at a teachers' college in Connecticut. A number of educators, community leaders from labor and industry, and members of diverse religious, racial and ethnic groups—who were meeting with the leadership of the State Interracial Commission—expressed the need to put the study of human relations fully on their agenda as means of improving awareness of issues of race relations and community conflict. To move beyond just talking about problems of human relations "back in the community" and continuing to avoid insight, involvement and commitment, a new ingredient was added to the discussions in the form of young scientists who, trained as group process observers, reported back what they saw happening in the study groups. Their analyses recounted what blocks to listening appeared to be operative, how certain persons dominated and thereby reduced the flow of productive ideas, ways status-concerns contributed to communications difficulties. As the participants looked at their here-and-now processes of interaction and group development (their "hang-ups" in today's idiom), they showed themselves increasingly sensitive to each other's needs and resources and found themselves psychologically freed to pursue new patterns of confronting difficulties, of discovering creative compromise.

The following summer (1947) the National Training Laboratory Institute for Applied Behavioral Science set up its first human relations laboratory at Bethel, Maine. Since then the NTL has pioneered in developing many types of programs for the study and improvement of personal sensitivity, interpersonal communication, and organizational effectiveness. During the past ten years need and demand for such technical help have grown into a major national "movement," with the development of many varia-tions in sensitivity training—some very helpful and some quite inappro-priate and even harmful for the improvement of education. Besides the original T groups, a large number of marathons, "personal growth labs," encounter groups, and nonverbal exercises have proliferated.

Let's summarize briefly some characteristics of *high-quality* sensitivity training programs and some of the traps of poor quality programs. Then we shall try to spell out types of laboratory learning opportunities that can be particularly of use to administrators, teachers and students.

SOME GUIDELINES FOR HIGH-QUALITY
SENSITIVITY TRAINING [1]

1. A good design for learning includes a carefully planned sequence of activities, in which the T-group or sensitivity sessions are but one component.

In a well-planned program mix are sessions for:

Conceptualization, to further understanding of key concepts and themes needed to deepen one's study of self, interpersonal relations, and group processes

Value confrontation, spearheaded by value-inquiry exercises to clarify goals and commitments for change

Sensitivity learning, to help the group develop the norms and sensitivity to support the learning needs of each member

Skill practice, to convert goals, sensitivities, commitments into action-com-petence

Application-planning, to convert learning into concrete plans, with steps for use in the relevant back-home setting and relationships.

No sensitivity training group, then, is by itself an adequate educational design for learning human relations. Poorly designed training experiences frequently do not include help with analyzing problems, projecting plans, and developing skills of transferring one's learning.

2. A clear rationale helps determine which outcomes are particularly desired and who should be grouped together for training.

Is the aim to improve team work of a school department or staff, or of an administrative council? If so, working together as a training group can

---

[1] For further exploration of guidelines for high-quality sensitivity training labora-tories, see Max Birnbaum's provocative analysis, "Sense and Nonsense About Sensi-tivity Training," *Saturday Review*, Nov. 15, 1969, pp. 82–84. See also Richard Batchelder and James Hardy's *Using Sensitivity Training and the Laboratory Method* (New York: Association Press, 1968).

have great advantages. For objectives of problem-solving or increasing communication between faculty and students, parents and teachers, blacks and whites, different groupings will be required. For inner self-development of the individual, going away to a personal growth laboratory made up of strangers probably is preferable, though least likely to have pay-off for changes in behavior in the back-home situation. Increasingly the latter type of programs involves development of self-selected trios who provide opportunities for intensive, intimate learning opportunities. Challenges of individualizing instruction are being explored in personal meditation or guided self-inquiry periods.

3. Explicit focus is given to designs for help in the everyday life situation to which trainees return, by way of backhome teams, telephone and tape supports, and follow-up sessions.

One of the most serious mistakes of much sensitivity training is failure to provide such continued support at the very time the learner is facing his greatest risk and stress when trying to apply the new, different ideas he has acquired.

4. Perhaps most crucial of all, whether the training program be for adults, youth or children, is selection of adequately prepared trainers and consultants.

Too often the error is made of selecting a trainee without careful inquiry about his preparation and experience. The mere fact of participation in one or more laboratory programs does not qualify one for leadership; special programs are available for the preparation of trainees. Another common error is to make exclusive use of trainers from either within or outside the system. A more productive strategy for protecting quality but guaranteeing followup and commitment is for school systems to create outside-inside teams. Professional development opportunities are thereby provided for selected staff members.

GLIMPSES OF POTENTIALITY

A few examples follow of the ways schools are utilizing sensitivity training designs to help improve the quality of education:

• A weekend lab for the administrative council with two hour follow-up sessions every two weeks. Major focus is on openness of communication and effective decision-making.
• A weekend lab of student leaders, administrators, and key teachers. Theme: "What kind of a school do we want and how can we cooperate in achieving it?"
• An all-day lab for students on the strategies and techniques of utilizing teachers and other resources to "meet your needs for learning and growth."

• A weekly lab session of fifth- and sixth-graders on sensitivity to the needs of first- and second-graders and on skills of helping them through the Cross-Age Helper's Program.

• A one-week lab in August for the total building staff, including secretarial, custodial, and other support personnel. The emphasis is on opening up and working on issues of relationships between old-timers and newcomers, teachers and administrators, parents and teachers, students and faculty. Task forces get started that will work through the semester. Every two weeks an hour of faculty meeting is to be devoted to a sensitivity learning design.

• A two- and a-half-day lab for the administrator and two peer-nominated teachers from each building in a school system, designed to help them take leadership in their building in developing staff professional growth activities; e.g., designs for sharing successful teaching practices and using tools for getting feedback from students. These building teams meet from 4:00 to 8:30 every two weeks to share problems, get additional skills, and work with their trainer on professional development as inservice-training-leaders.

• Two periods a week given by a classroom teacher for her class to focus the study of human relations in the classroom. She is using curriculum materials developed to help students study themselves as a classroom group and to explore their own identities.

Even more than the industrial leaders and social leaders who have been utilizing sensitivity training laboratories so successfully, educators need this powerful tool for getting involvement in the educational processes and for breaking down the many barriers that separate human beings from each other.[2]

23.   TEACHER EFFECTIVENESS TRAINING

•–•

Barbara G. Peterson

Teaching is an uncomfortable profession these days. Student protest movements extend down even into junior high schools, and all aspects of the

Source. Barbara Peterson, "The Teacher Effectiveness Program." *Journal of the SPATE,* 1971, Vol. 9–3, 71–75. Copyright 1971 by the American Personnel and Guidance Association and reproduced by permission.

[2] To get further information on the professional resources in your area, write to the NTL Institute for Applied Behavioral Science, NEA Building, 1201 16th St., N.W., Washington, D.C. 20036.

educational process are being challenged. New demands are being placed on educators—pressures to maintain classroom discipline in the face of increasing student rebellion, demands for teaching course content relevantly, expectations that students with special learning problems be reached and helped. Most teachers have not been taught the skills necessary for meeting these increased expectations.

The old authoritarian adult-student relationships which have always existed in schools are being vigorously attacked by students on all levels and by many educators. Simply maintaining a quiet and relatively orderly classroom atmosphere is a challenging task in many schools. Teachers remember fondly the days when students generally followed orders without question, when adults were respected merely because they were older. New methods for dealing with conflicts in the classroom are now necessary.

Society is demanding that courses be taught in such a way that their relevance to the learner be constantly evident. This requires a radical shift in teaching approaches when compared with the old method of a logical presentation of course content with the assumption that what is presented will be accepted as valuable to the learner at some future point in time. Learning established curricular offerings as preparation for college or career used to be an unquestioned assumption. Now the emphasis has shifted to relating the materials to the current felt needs of the students. Most teachers find this a difficult assignment.

Technological advances in instructional methodologies and innovations in educational philosophy demand a radically new role for the teacher in his relationships with students. This new role departs from the traditional one of authoritative information-giver and instead requires the teacher to perform certain functions for which most teachers have not been adequately trained, such as facilitating self-centered discussions, and encouraging student problem-solving.

The pressure to educate all students to a fairly high level in basic skills and to keep students in school for an increasing number of years has focused concern on the "problem student" who in earlier years would have been a school dropout. Schools are now expected to meet the needs of these students, to get them involved in the learning process, and to prepare them for life in a highly complex and rapidly changing society. Teachers need communications skills that will enable them to establish emotional contact with youth who are tuned out or turned off. Most teachers have not been taught the skills required for bridging the gap between course content and the students' concerns, for solving conflicts with students who challenge, or for reaching reluctant learners.

AN ANSWER TO THE CHALLENGES

A promising new effort to help teachers meet these challenges is the Teacher Effectiveness Training program designed by Thomas Gordon, a Pasadena psychologist. This program has already been offered in 50 school districts and is expanding rapidly. It is currently available to almost any district in California because of the growing staff of qualified instructors trained by Gordon in various areas of the state. Recently it has expanded to 15 other states.

The enthusiastic reception of Teacher Effectiveness Training is a result of its focus on skills training and immediate on-the-job application of new methods of communication and problem-solving. The course is carefully structured to provide opportunity to practice these skills during the three-hour training sessions which run 10 weeks. The cost of the program is $50 for 30 hours, exclusive of costs for obtaining college credit. In most school districts teachers earn in-service training credits when the program is sponsored by the local district or county. There is an increasing trend toward incorporating the training into teacher education programs.

INCREASING COMMUNICATIONS SKILLS

The first communication skill taught during the course is that of "active listening" or responding to another person's feelings in a way that indicates he has been heard and understood. In the process of active listening, the listener reformulates and reflects in different words the feeling he heard expressed. Active listening involves an effort to enter the other's world and an attempt to perceive things through his eyes, a process which offers maximum possibility of increasing the openness of communication. By contrast, passive listening is only one-way communication and does not prove the listener has understood.

Teachers find immediate application of the skill of active listening in conducting content-centered classroom discussions. Students who were formerly timid in class discussion began to talk when the teacher listens in a nonevaluative way to class contributions.

Active listening also assists teachers in leading productive discussions about students' life problems or their difficulties in adjusting to adults and peers in the school. When an individual student is upset about a problem, teachers can move into a counseling role when they are skillful, active listeners. Through this process the problem learner can come to see the teacher as an adult who is genuinely concerned about his feelings—whether they be feelings of personal failure, inadequacy, or frustration. The teacher can begin to break through barriers of resistance, hostility, and fear which are standing in the way of the student's learning potential.

Teachers also need to learn effective confrontation: how to get students to modify student behavior that is interfering with the job the teacher has to do. Typically adults have used ineffective ways of approaching students in such situations. Teachers and administrators frequently use commands, warnings, threats, and criticisms when students are acting out or interfering with classroom instruction. Generally, these responses provoke antagonism and defensiveness on the part of the students or result in conforming behavior only briefly, if at all. In increasing numbers, students refuse to be intimidated into conforming.

The Teacher Effectiveness Training program teaches some new skills of effective confrontation. Gordon refers to the process as "clear sending" of one's own feelings. Teachers learn to send "I messages" which are direct expressions of their own feelings. This is a more effective confrontation technique than sending a command or a judgmental message which is apt to be in the form of "You messages."

For example, with a student who frequently turns in work after the date it is due, a "You message" and an "I message" might sound like the following:

YOU MESSAGE: "You are always turning your papers in late. You should be more organized so you won't get your grade lowered because of missing deadlines."

I MESSAGE: "I am concerned about all the late assignments I receive from you. I find it really hard to decide how to grade you fairly."

In a situation where students are acting up while a math teacher is trying to explain a new idea, the two types of messages are contrasted.

YOU MESSAGE: "You boys in the back of the room are disrupting the class. You never pay attention. No wonder you can't do your assignments."

I MESSAGE: "I find it very difficult to go on explaining tomorrow's math lesson when there's talking going on. I am getting impatient because I feel you'll have a hard time doing the assignment tonight unless you listen."

When children behave in unacceptable ways, they are almost invariably aware that their behavior must be annoying to their teacher. They expect a response. An honest expression of feeling on the part of the adult leaves the responsibility with the child for modifying his behavior. Also, when the teacher honestly expresses his own feelings, he is seen as a more real, more authentic human being.

MUTUALITY IN DECISION-MAKING

When rules and policies are set by the teachers and administration without student participation, students have relatively low motivation to carry them out; they are likely to test the limits and to rebel against the policies which are seen as imposed restrictions. On the other hand, mutual discussion and agreement on classroom rules and policies by teachers and students is a constructive and democratic way of attaining a cooperative school atmosphere. Frequently, limitations are imposed by higher authority in the area of policies and rules, but within each classroom there is a latitude or area of freedom within which teacher and students can mutually participate in developing behavior norms and classroom policies. The Teacher Effectiveness Training course shows teachers how to conduct such discussions, using the skills of active listening, clear sending, and arriving at mutually acceptable rules and norms.

CONFLICT RESOLUTION

Traditionally when conflicts have existed between students and teachers in school, educators have thought in terms of only two approaches to the problem—an authoritarian approach or a permissive approach. A person exercising his authority over another must have power over the other, or the ability to reward or punish the other. Teachers of young children can easily influence their students by using their power and authority. Children develop different mechanisms for coping with excessive use of authority, such as rebellion, withdrawal, submission. None of these responses leads to the development of a self-motivated, self-disciplined, responsible student. Permissiveness, on the other hand, tends to result in unmanageable classrooms and undisciplined students. At the junior high school level, teachers suddenly find themselves having relatively little power over their students. The threat of bad grades or disciplinary action is less influential with most adolescents than the approval or disapproval of their peers.

Conflicts will inevitably occur between teachers and students. Conflict is not necessarily bad; it can result in learning constructive ways of dealing with future problems in relationships. Teachers who have mastered the communications skills taught in Teacher Effectiveness Training (TET) can engage in a process of mutual problem-solving with a classroom group or with an individual student when conflict occurs. TET shows teachers how to get students to join them in a search for a solution to conflict which is acceptable to both the teacher and the students. When agreement is reached, a verbal or even a written contract may be drawn up clearly stating the proposed solutions. Making conflict resolution a participative process results in more genuinely cooperative and responsible behavior on the part of students.

CONCLUSION

At this time of crisis in our schools, it is painfully clear that the old authoritarian and permissive solutions to conflict are inadequate. Teacher Effectiveness Training makes the ideal of democratic problem-solving workable. In addition, Teacher Effectiveness Training offers teachers the opportunity to learn skills of communication which will increase their effectiveness in reaching problem learners, in leading relevant classroom discussions, and in resolving classroom management problems. It merits careful consideration and evaluation as an integral part of programs for the preparation of teachers.

24.   GROUP WORK WITH PRINCIPALS: IMPLICATIONS FOR ELEMENTARY COUNSELORS

Drage H. Watson

The principals wanted to be in a group so they started one. They chose a meeting place, selected a time, and asked me to lead them. They separated into two groups following the fourth meeting. They held one-and-a-half-hour sessions in a restaurant once a week for the school year. Interest was high. Attendance was perfect except for emergencies.

Each man was interviewed individually before the group started. These talks covered five topics: questions; commitment; role; data; and goals. Each member was asked if he had any questions and why he wanted to be

Source. Drage H. Watson, "Group Work With Principals: Implications for Elementary Counselors." *Elementary School Guidance and Counseling*, 1969, Vol. 3–4, 234–241. Copyright 1969 by the American Personnel and Guidance Association and reproduced by permission.

in a group. He was also asked what he thought about having me, an assistant superintendent, for a leader and if he would fill out written forms during the group meetings.

The men all wanted to know each other better and to learn more about themselves, to share problems and learn group techniques, and to be able to handle their fears of working with teachers and parents. They accepted the idea of filling out forms and encouraged me to lead the groups and set goals for them.

Seventeen of the 18 men were elementary principals. Ten of them had counselors. This article is about elementary principals, group work, and counselors.

THE ACTION

RALPH: "Listen, fellas, I don't know if this is what you want to talk about, but I've got this teacher and . . ."

MEL: "That's what we want."

RALPH: ". . . and I wish I had the courage to move this one little girl out of her room."

JOE: "Ralph, have you tried to. . . ."

The groups were problem-oriented and loosely structured at first. They talked about their problems. Structure started during the seventh session.

The first structured session was a repression demonstration. Then men were verbally given nine words, one at a time, and they wrote as many words as they could associate with each of the nine words during a one-minute period. They then made a chalk board chart that showed the individual word totals and average response numbers for each person. Finally they discussed how the members followed a pattern of repression on one word that had strong negative emotional tone. This discussion helped the groups loosen up and learn to work on a deeper level.

PETE: ". . . well, that's the problem. What should I do?"

JOE: "I find it helpful to. . . ."

Five other basic techniques were used. We began to establish behavioral contracts. The man who brought a problem to the group was expected to accept a behavioral contract at the end of the session. A contract consisted of three phases: The member accepted a tentative solution, agreed to try this solution between sessions, and finally reported back to the group during the next session.

MAC: "Wait a minute. We've been meeting for two months and I still don't know Bob. How can I say something I don't like about him?"

MEL: "You just did."

We moved away from the problem orientation. The behavioral contract was no longer appropriate. The men decided to get input on a structured basis. To do this, we set up the following procedure.

1. An extra chair was placed in the circle.
2. Each member in turn occupied the chair for as long as he wanted.
3. While a person was in the chair, he told the group one thing he liked about himself and one thing he did not like about himself.
4. Other members talked when they had questions or comments.
5. When the member in the chair decided to leave it, he either asked for a volunteer or selected the next member to occupy the chair.

We followed Input with the Feedback Chair. During these sessions this was the routine:

1. An extra chair was placed in the circle.
2. Each member in turn occupied this Feedback Chair, which by now was called the "Hot Seat."
3. All members, in turn, told the hot seat occupant one thing they liked about him and one thing they did not like about him.
4. One member at a time commented while the hot seat was occupied.
5. Members took the chair on a voluntary basis.
6. Discussion followed.

JOE: "Well, first of all, I've been finding out a lot about myself, and then I really learned some good techniques for working with groups of my own faculty more effectively. I can open them up."

PETE: "You want to use techniques to make your staff come to you. I wonder why you feel this need to have everyone open up to you on everything."

It was called PR-5. It developed as an outgrowth of Input and Feedback Chair. This is the way it worked.

1. One man in the group (Presenter) talked with another man (Reactor) for five minutes (5)—PR-5.
2. The reactor, chosen by the presenter, reacted in any way he wished.
3. The reactor became the presenter at the end of five minutes, and selected a new reactor.
4. They repeated the process until all members had participated.

Although we did not label them as such, the men used many sessions and parts of sessions for cognition. This involved responding to a question such as: "How have you changed during the last month or six weeks?"

THE IMPLICATIONS

JOE: "The other day I asked a teacher what I could do to help her and she said, 'You make me feel like I'm using the wrong fork.' "

The first implication became obvious during the sessions. Some principals who had counselors in their schools were taking such an active part in planning their guidance programs for the next year that their counselors began to think they were not needed. It was, for instance, threatening to some counselors to hear their principals talk about using a feedback chair when the counselors did not know what it meant.

RALPH: "Wayne, you better either transfer that teacher or learn to live with the situation."

The implications of the strength gained by these men will not be known for months. The expression of the strength came through in their reactions to several questions. The average for all members is plotted on the continuum for each question (Figure 1).

It is obvious that the principals:

1. Felt strongly that the experience was personally and professionally helpful to them.
2. Did not feel as strongly about the impact the group had on their work with teachers and students.
3. Would recommend group work for teachers and especially for other principals.
4. Were consistent in their answers to these questions and the one following.

The men were asked to answer in writing: What implications has participation in the group had for your work? The 18 members wrote 45 responses to this question. These responses fell into five categories dealing with interpersonal relations, intrapersonal relations, role, intellectualizing, and students. The distribution of responses by categories is presented in the graph (Figure 2) on page 202.

Group work for these principals had the most meaning in the area of interpersonal relations. The process of working with other men on an intensive level had the effect of causing these people to see group work as

1. *Do you feel the group discussions have been helpful to you personally?*

2. *Do you feel the group discussions have been helpful to you professionally?*

3. *Has your participation in the group had any impact on your work with teachers?*

4. *Has your participation in the group had any impact on your work with students?*

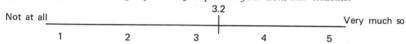

5. *To what extent would you recommend group participation to other principals?*

6. *To what extent would you recommend group participation to teachers?*

FIGURE 1

having the most implications for working with other people. Most of the men tried new techniques with and became much more sure of their faculties. They developed more confidence in themselves and more patience with their staffs.

RALPH: "I'm not as tense in faculty meetings as I used to be."

MAC: "I have more patience. I'm not the only one who tries and fails and not the only one who tries and succeeds."

JOE: "I listen better."

PETE: "The group has helped me better understand myself."

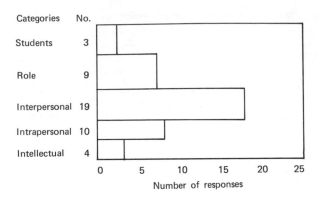

FIGURE 2

Elementary counselors working with these men must have some of the same confidence and patience. The counselor must also have something to say to a faculty. These principals will help build strong elementary guidance programs.

RALPH: "I think I'll just start myself a teacher group next year."
JAKE: "Wait a minute, Ralph, you've got a counselor. What about her?"
RALPH: "Well, I've got to get involved some way."

Ten of the 19 statements in the interpersonal section dealt with "knowing that there are others with whom I can talk." This area has been developed by many elementary counselors. It must be a cornerstone of elementary guidance. Principals need someone with whom they can talk. This person must have the patience and training for listening and the knowledge necessary to establish a helping relationship. Principals who have been involved in group work demand this.

PETE: "I came into the group to find out how to do things, but now it's different."
JAKE: "You've gone through some changes. I'd like to hear more about how you feel now."

The men listed exactly the same number (19) of comments under the combined intrapersonal and role categories that they did under the interpersonal heading. It is interesting to speculate whether the intrapersonal category grew as the groups shifted away from a problem orientation. A comment such as "It has made me aware of my position" dealt directly with role. Other comments, such as the following two, indicated that the shift from the problem orientation had an effect on responses.

1. Many of my ideas have been put to work because of this group influence.
2. This experience has given me the desire to try new projects.

In the intrapersonal category the men referred again to confidence and also to insight. Elementary counselors should find fertile ground for innovative programs under the direction of men who see themselves as more courageous and insightful. These men will also be less inhibited and more demanding than the typical principal.

HANK: ". . . and that's my theory on discipline."
BOB: "Who cares what your theory is? You're not getting the job done."

The men talked to each other. Intellectual chatter from associates did not impress them. Programs did. The elementary counselors who worked with these men had programs.

The men did not relate their group experience to their work with children. Many of the behavioral contracts dealt with students, but the men must have felt more intensely about their work with other adults. It seems, then, that they would seek one kind of help in their work with adults and another in their work with children.

For instance, these principals felt rather confident in their approach to a particular problem and how they dealt with the student involved. This confidence was reflected in the reference to student problems at the more superficial behavioral contract level of group work. These men will undoubtedly continue to use their counselors as sounding boards for action they contemplate in the resolution of student problems.

The group members, on the other hand, felt more deeply about their work with teachers, parents, and other principals. They expected their counselors to work toward the initiation of developmental programs designed to enhance the relationships of adults associated with school systems.

Several questions might be asked regarding further implications of this type of work with principals. The answers to most of the questions involve suggestions for developing a group program within a school setting.

What are some implications that come out of principal-counselor consultations?

To the extent that consulting implies talking over a subject with someone to decide points in doubt, the program just described is not consultation. A principal might consult an instructional consultant regarding a textbook series or even a guidance consultant about educational information, but to be effective the relationship between a principal and a counselor must be much deeper than discussion regarding points in doubt.

Principal-counselor consultation results in the solution of problems. A principal-counselor relationship exemplified by participation in group work results in a developmental program of working with adults that goes beyond either problem-solving or prevention.

It enables people to talk with each other without the fears and anxieties that traditionally cause lack of respect and inefficiency. It eventually enables adults to talk with each other and with children in a way that facilitates the greatest possible learning efficiency in the classroom.

Would it be advisable for the counselor to run such groups with his own principal in one of the groups?

The problem of power is merely a myth. Participation by both principal and counselor in the same group might, in fact, be one of the activities that separates *great* elementary guidance programs from *good* ones. The principal can participate in either counselor-led parent groups or teacher groups. I have had requests to have a counselor lead a principals' group and have known of principals who joined their own faculty groups. As a principal, I have joined faculty groups and led parent groups. As assistant superintendent I have led teacher, counselor, parent, administrative, and mixed groups. I urge all counselors to encourage their principals to participate in a group with them.

How would this be developed in another school setting where someone like me is not available to run the group?

There *is always* someone like me available if the school has a guidance program and the services of a counselor on at least a part-time basis. I suggest that the counselor begin either a teacher or a parent group as early in the year as possible with the principal in a participating role. The single most important criterion for choosing between a teacher or parent group is whichever one is needed first. This need should be decided cooperatively between the counselor and principal. A second criterion might be the relative ease with which a counselor feels he can institute work with one or the other of these groups. The principal is likely to be cautious about his participation in either group. It is of the utmost importance, therefore, that the planning and implementation be done with the principal and counselor working together.

The principal and counselor together should issue invitations, in writing, to a given group of parents, i.e., all first grade parents, all the parents in one room, or all parents who have expressed a specific interest. I recommend a faculty invitation from the counselor with principal endorsement.

Both of these invitations should be specific regarding the nature of the group and the duration of the sessions.

PETE: "I think every principal in the systems should be in a group, especially the new ones."

MAC: "Especially the old ones!"

RALPH: "I can hardly wait for September."

JOE: "Me too."

25. THE "C" GROUP: INTEGRATING KNOWLEDGE AND EXPERIENCE TO CHANGE BEHAVIOR: AN ADLERIAN APPROACH TO CONSULTATION

Don Dinkmeyer

The pupil personnel specialist has often considered the child to be his major concern, and has functioned as if direct work with children in diagnosis and counseling were the top priority. However, the history of guidance services has not been dramatically productive in the realm of changing behaviors and beliefs. It has become increasingly apparent that in many instances he is working with the wrong client. When the teacher has discussed a problem with a child, he has reacted as if the child were requesting the help. This has resulted in many referred clients who were unmotivated, unconcerned, and hence uninvolved in the process. Translation of counseling theories into effective procedures with children and adolescents has been a problem. Given the additional handicap of working with the wrong client, the counselor has little hope of being effective.

If the specialist is to be effective, he must become competent in procedures for working with adults. The original focus in consultation was in working with individual teachers. Individual consulting has been hampered by several considerations:

There is a tendency to counsel students, hearing feelings and helping them explore alternatives, but to advise staff members. Acting as answer man and producing simple solutions for complex problems has tended to put the guidance worker into the category of the "medicine man." Teachers

Source. Don Dinkmeyer, "The 'C' Group: Integrating Knowledge and Experience to Change Behavior: An Adlerian Approach to Consultation." *The Counseling Psychologist*, 1971, Vol. 3–1, 63–72. Copyright 1971 by Division 17 of the American Psychological Association and reproduced by permission.

expect miracles, refer as if the problem now belonged to the specialist, and often set the specialist up for defeat.

One cannot consult effectively unless he can get into the internal frame of reference of the consultee. It is basic to become aware of the consultee's perceptions and beliefs. One must become sensitive to the consultee's beliefs about persons, human relationships, and how to effect change in behavior (Combs, 1969).

In individual consulting the questions that might attempt to explore the teacher's feelings and attitudes often seem threatening and consequently produce defensiveness. The consultant's suggestions may be responded to with, "I've tried that. I have too many children in the room to do that. Nobody could do that and still teach," or other responses which block communication. Most significant, though, is the fact that the consultant is "stuck" with his limited resources—self. His education, experience, and perceptions can never embrace all the types of situations which teachers will present. However, as leader of a group of teachers, he has access to the experiences, insights, hypotheses, and possible procedures which can be developed by the group. In addition, he can observe how the teacher operates in this social field and develop awareness of her style of life and methods of relating.

RATIONALE

It is important to understanding the rationale for working with teachers in groups. Unless one is aware of the potential benefits in this didactic-experiential group, one will not be aware of the possibilities which exist in group meetings with teachers.

This group work takes on additional meaning when we recognize that man is best understood as an indivisible, social, decision-making being whose actions have a social purpose (Dreikurs and Sonstegard, 1968). This view of man as a social being develops new awareness and gives meaning to all of his verbal and nonverbal interactions and transactions.

Placing teachers in a group recognizes that basically most problems are interpersonal and social. The problem that the teacher presents originated in group interaction with the children. She needs to become aware of the necessity of understanding behavior in its social context. The problems with the child originated in the classroom group and they can often best be solved by the teacher participating in a teacher group. The group then has the opportunity to analyze the child's life style as it is expressed in his social transactions and psychological interaction with the teacher. His unique approach to the tasks of life will be consistent with his concept of self and his assumptions about life. More important, the consultant and the group have an opportunity to observe the teacher's life style and her characteristic pattern of response to children and members of the group.

The group setting, then, provides the leader, the consultant, and the members of the group with an extremely valuable social laboratory, a miniature society or microcommunity. As the teacher learns to function as a member of the group, she will begin to develop some insights about how children respond in the group. She will develop skills in working more effectively with children in a group. The group setting has both diagnostic and therapeutic values since certain behaviors can only be observed in the group setting. There is considerable difference between telling about how she relates to others and the child, and becoming involved in relating to others in a way which reveals her characteristic approach to life's problems.

There are also a number of therapeutic effects which can be best processed in the group setting. The group provides the opportunity for a unique type of acceptance. This is a setting in which the teachers can experience the empathy which comes from their peers. It also provides the opportunity to ventilate and express how they feel. In the group one can try out some behaviors and ideas and at the same time process the feedback from members of the group. This type of group also helps the teachers realize that their problems with children are universal. Recognizing that there are others with similar problems can bring cohesion to the group. It can stimulate altruism and the desire to help fellow professionals become more effective persons. Each member can be a therapeutic agent for every other member.

The group provides a special opportunity to hear about another's problem and develop some ideas about how to handle a situation which, to that point, the teacher had not even mentioned. Spectator therapy, learning from another's experience, is a major benefit.

It has been demonstrated that the group process helps its members become more aware that most of their concerns are social and interpersonal. These challenges are a product of interaction with the child and, in some instances, of failure to understand the child's goals and purposes. This unique setting provides the opportunity not only to talk and release one's feelings about the problem, but to investigate some new ways of handling it. There is a unique opportunity to get the kind of assistance from a colleague which is often not available in any other setting. Schools have not devised effective ways for teachers to share with each other effective procedures in the teaching process. The "C" group[1] is a channel for communication.

---

[1] Such a group is so named since, as discussed in a later section, its principal components begin with "C".

Because the significance of behavior always lies in its social consequences, one is able to both explain the transaction that occurred with the child and become more aware of her own investment in the interaction with the child. The teacher can become more aware of the traditional methods of responding to children who are difficult to teach.

The group setting provides a new way to see the life style, faulty assumptions, and mistaken ideas of both child and teacher. It is essentially a holistic approach in the sense that it takes into consideration not only the intellect, feelings, and behavior of the child, but of the teacher also. It creates an experience in which the teacher enters into a supporting, caring, accepting atmosphere. She has access to feedback about her behavior, feelings, and attitudes and through this develops a new perspective on human relationships and more effective procedures for working with children. The group also is of major benefit to teachers who do not have major difficulties with children, because it gives them an opportunity to contribute, feel needed, and accepted.

In order to understand group dynamics in children in groups, teachers must have an experience as a member of a group. Often teacher education has not given them the opportunity to have an experience either as a group member or a group leader. If teachers are going to deal with the whole child, it is apparent they must be engaged in situations in which they participate as "whole teachers." They must participate with their feelings, attitudes, purposes, and values. They must not only talk about the child, but also become aware of their feelings. As the teacher becomes able to recognize and verbalize "He makes me mad; I'd really like to get even but know I can't," she has access to diagnostic procedures and therapeutic resources which were formerly blocked in the strictly intellectual problem-solving approach.

THE COUNSELOR AND THE ADMINISTRATOR

The development of teacher groups requires that the leader spend considerable time in establishing the climate and setting for teacher groups. The original contact is made with the administrator. It is imperative that administrators understand how "C" groups can help them accomplish their objectives in staff and student development. The teacher group is a dynamic in-service procedure which combines the didactic presentation of concepts for relating more effectively with children while providing the members with an experience which helps them become aware of how their feelings, perceptions, and beliefs affect their interaction with children. It is apparent that in-service education which stays at the cognitive level and does not engage or involve the "whole teacher" cannot be efficacious in regard to practice. Teachers may come from such meetings with more ideas, but without any commitment to personal change. The administrator who is interested in affecting the learning climate of the school can accomplish this best through the teacher group. Through teacher groups the guidance worker and administrator can collaborate. The counselor can become a significant resource for administration, not merely an ancillary service.

It is the administrator who can supply the encouragement, space, and facilities necessary for group work. His enthusiastic public support of the concept and his efforts to develop schedules which make it convenient for teachers to participate are critical in the establishment of the program.

The consultant will make the teacher group program known to the staff through varied media. During an early faculty meeting or formal in-service session he can describe the program. He can also supply the teachers with printed material which clarifies the purposes, activities, and benefits of the program. As he engages in individual consulting and identifies teachers who are good candidates for a teacher group, he can encourage their participation in the development of a group.

GOALS

The goals of teacher groups include the following:

1. Developing an understanding of the practical application of the dynamics of human behavior. This will help teachers compherend how a social-psychological theory and practice of human behavior can help them relate more effectively with children.
2. Acquiring an understanding of self and developing awareness on the part of teachers of their role in the teacher-child conflict. The teacher develops not only an intellectual comprehension of why children function as they do, but gets into touch with her own motives and feelings and becomes aware of the way in which they influence her interaction with children.
3. Developing acquaintance with new concepts and procedures while integrating them with one's own value system. One thus derives the benefits which come from group thinking.

ORGANIZATIONAL DETAILS

The establishment of teacher groups, just like the establishment of group counseling with students, requires careful attention to a number of organizational details. The total staff must be oriented to the purposes and directions of the teacher group program. The first group of teachers will preferably be people who have social and professional power within the staff. They will be people who are valued and respected by the staff members. It is important to dispel any faulty assumptions that members may have about this being group psychotherapy, sensitivity training, or any other fantasy the staff chooses to place upon this activity. In some instances it will be valuable to use some faculty meeting time to demonstrate the way in which the group actually proceeds.

A basic problem involves developing appropriate meeting arrangements. These groups function best when they meet on a weekly basis, preferably for at least one hour. The teachers should make a commitment to continue this type of activity for a minimum of six to eight weeks. "C" groups have met at a variety of times and places in my experience with educational groups. In some instances the "C" group will meet before the school day, during the lunch hour or immediately after school. Where it is possible, a group of teachers may meet while other specialists in physical education, music, and art are responsible for their classes. Some school districts arrange to have parents supervise a study period while the "C" group is in session. In some instances teachers who felt the value of this type of procedure have made arrangements within the staff whereby they divide their class by five and send their class for a study period in each of five other teachers' rooms, thereby engaging five teachers in the supervision of their class while they engage in the "C" group. Of course the courtesy is exchanged.

The possibilities for effective ways to utilize the "C" group within the professional development of an educational staff are unlimited once administrators and consultants think creatively about the advantages. It is usually important to establish some ground rules about group membership. It is preferable to have the group a closed group, meaning that no one joins the group once it has started, and to begin new groups when you have additional teachers interested in the group process. This provides for better continuity and does not necessitate the continual process of reviewing the history of the group and past interactions.

The group should meet in a physically comfortable setting which permits them to sit in a circle. The arrangement should be such that the room is pleasantly furnished and creates a confidential atmosphere. In many instances this can be accomplished in some area of the counselor's office space.

GROUP COMPOSITION IS AN IMPORTANT CONSIDERATION

Experience dictates that it is important to have a heterogeneous type of group in the sense that the members represent experienced as well as inexperienced teachers, older as well as younger staff members, and people with different types of orientation to educational approaches. It is usually best to work with staff members who are able to share some similar interests, i.e. the primary grade teachers or the junior high staff. Frequently a great discrepancy in the age level of the children being discussed will serve as a handicap in terms of the concerns of the teachers in attendance.

In developing the first group, consider obtaining for the group at least two experienced teachers who can contribute to the professional growth of the group as well as several young teachers who can bring their new ideas about educational procedures. Our focus is on developing an improved channel of communication and thus this type of diversity is necessary.

Experience indicates that teacher groups work best when they are restricted to five members plus the leader. This permits the leader to involve each member of the group at each meeting in some exploration of her concerns, in contrast to developing a case study approach which focuses strictly on one child or one teacher and her problems. The value in the process comes as members recognize that they all have problems and that they can benefit from the mutual opportunity to share and discuss ideas. The small size of the group ensures that everyone can become involved at each session.

Membership in the group is always voluntary, never by recommendation of others. Before becoming a member of the group, the leader will have a brief interview with each potential member to clarify goals of the group in general and to establish some concrete, individual goals which that teacher hopes to accomplish through participation. Members qualify for participation by having a concern that she wants to discuss, a willingness to discuss that concern, and a real interest in being helpful to other staff members. They must recognize that members are making a contract which involves their willingness to present their concerns as well as to be of assistance to others.

GETTING STARTED

Even though the leader will have clarified through verbal as well as written material the purposes of the group, and will have gone through an individual interview with each group member, the first session of the group is likely to produce a degree of anxiety and confusion both on the part of the leader and the group members. This is a new experience and there will be some preliminary attempts to clarify roles and purposes. It will be important to set the stage by restructuring the purpose of the group and by seeing to it that while the anxiety level of members is reduced, at the same time the leader is not diverted from the primary purposes of this group. Experience indicates that the group members should be well acquainted with each other. Sometimes this can be accomplished through a micro-lab experience in which members go through some communication exercises which enable people outside the group to observe how people inside the group are communicating, and vice versa. Exercises which facilitate an awareness of verbal and nonverbal communication are helpful. Some of the assignments that are productive involve having half of the group become concerned with a topic such as "Become a Group" or "Make Yourself Known to Each Other." The other half of the group observes how this procedure is processed and then gives specific feedback to group members about what they liked and did not like about what they saw in that individual's human interactions.

One of the most effective procedures for breaking down interpersonal estrangement is Dr. Herbert Otto's Depth-Unfoldment Experience (DUE) (1967). In this procedure the leader tells the group that the first task is to get to know each other better. Members are then given some possibilities of exploring various ways to get to know each other better. The leader then introduces the DUE Method, suggesting that it is an approach which requires a deeper sharing of self and courage. He suggests that while it may produce tension, the benefits are distinctly worthwhile. He only utilizes the approach if all members of the group are willing to cooperate. Each individual has a set period of time (5 or 6 minutes) to share himself, using the first part of the period to tell about key experiences in his life that he believes made him the person that he is. The final minute is used to describe the happiest moment of his life. If the group member doesn't use all of his time, the other participants may ask him questions. This method is always begun by the leader setting the tone and establishing the depth of the experience by sharing himself with the group.

PSYCHOLOGICAL FOUNDATIONS FOR "C" GROUPS

"C" groups operate most effectively when the leader understands and utilizes a socio-teleological approach to human behavior (see Figure 1). The following assumptions about human behavior provide direction for analysis of the interaction which occurs in teacher-student transactions and also in the interaction between members of the group:

1. Behavior is understood on a holistic basis and comprehended in terms of its unity and pattern.
2. The significance of behavior lies in its social consequences.
3. Man is understood as a social being whose behavior makes sense in terms of its social context.
4. Motivation is best comprehended by observing how the individual seeks to be known or become significant.

5. Behavior is goal-directed and purposive.
6. Belonging is a basic requisite for human development.
7. Behavior is always understood in terms of the internal frame of reference of the individual, his perceptual field.

The leader has some didactic material which he shares with the group so that they become acquainted with the socio-teleological approach.

COMMUNICATION PROCEDURES

It is now apparent that there is no single method of teaching which can clearly be shown to be associated with either good or poor teaching. Effectiveness is not based upon methodology, but upon the ability to communicate and motivate. Teaching is a unique profession in the sense that it requires that one respond immediately to a transaction and in an effective manner. For example, when teachers encounter misbehavior they cannot go back to a laboratory and do research, nor can they find a special way of computing or analyzing the data. In contrast, they must respond instantly and in an effective manner.

The teachers are taught through the "C" group experience to utilize four procedures for improving communication. The teacher must recognize that in most communication with children she is sending messages with emotional as well as intellectual content. Thus, the procedure in communication involves:

1. Indicating that the teacher understands their feelings. Through reflective listening clarify that she got the message. "You feel angry; you are very disappointed."
2. Indicating how their behavior and feelings are affecting the teacher. State her own feelings about how this comes over to her.
3. Utilizing conflict resolution to come to an agreement by reaching a solution that is agreeable to the teacher and the child, taking into account the thoughts, feelings, and behavior of both parties.
4. When agreement cannot be reached through the hearing and sharing of feelings and conflict resolution procedures, permit the child to experience the logical consequences. This is done in a friendly but firm fashion which does not interfere or contrive to make the teacher a winner (Dreikurs and Grey, 1968).

THE LEADERSHIP OF TEACHER GROUPS

The leadership of teacher groups obviously necessitates possessing the general skills required for group counseling leadership. In addition, beyond

FIGURE 1
Identifying the Goals of Children's Misbehavior

INCREASED SOCIAL INTEREST ←————→ DIMINISHED SOCIAL INTEREST

MINOR DISCOURAGEMENT ↕ DEEP DISCOURAGEMENT

USEFUL		USELESS		
Active Constructive	Passive Constructive	Active Destructive	Passive Destructive	Child's Action and Attitude The Message
"Success" Cute remarks Seeks praise and recognition Performs for attention Stunts Overambition Impression of excellence (may seem to be an "ideal" student, but goal is self-elevation not learning)	"Charm" Excess pleasantness and charm "Model" child Bright sayings, often not original Little initiative Exaggerated conscientiousness "Southern belle," (are often the "teacher's pets")	"Nuisance" Show off Clown Restless Talks out of turn "The brat" Makes minor mischief "Walking question mark" (questions not for information but for notoriety) Speech impediments Self-indulgence	"Laziness" Clumsiness, ineptness Lack of ability Lack of stamina Untidiness Fearfulness Bashfulness Anxiety Frivolity Performance and reading difficulties	"Nuisance" Show off Clown Lazy Puts others in his service, keeps teacher busy. I only count when I am being noticed or served.
A Criterion of Social-Emotional Maturing is "Social Interest" Respects the rights of others Is tolerant of others Is interested in others Co-operates with others Encourages others Is courageous Has a true sense of his own worth Has a feeling of belonging Has socially acceptable goals Puts forth genuine effort Meets the needs of the situation Is willing to share rather than "How much can I get?" Thinks of "We" rather than just "I"		"Rebel" Argues and contradicts Openly disobedient Refuses to do work Defies authority Continues forbidden acts Aggressive May be truant	"Stubborn" Extreme laziness Stubbornness Disobedience (passive) Forgetting	"Stubborn" Argues Temper tantrums Tells lies Disobedient Does opposite to instructions Does little or no work Says "If you don't let me do what I want you don't love me." I only count when I am dominating.

CORRECTIONS OF MISBEHAVIOR

Teacher's Reaction	The Child's Probable Goal And His "Faulty Logic"	Teacher's Corrective Procedures	Teacher's Interpretations Of Child's Goal To Him
To be kept busy by child. To help, remind, scold, coax and give child extra service. Is delighted by constructive AGM child. Is annoyed. "He occupies too much of my time." "I wish he would leave me alone."	GOAL I. (AGM) ATTENTION— GETTING Child seeks proof of his acceptance and approval. He puts others in his service, seeks help. "Only when people pay attention to me do I feel I have a place."	Give attention when child is not making a bid for it. Ignore the misbehaving child. Be firm. Realize that punishing, rewarding, coaxing, scolding and giving service are attention.	All questions must be asked in a friendly non-judgmental way and NOT at times of conflict. "Could it be that you want me to notice you?" "Could it be that you want me to do special things for you?" ". . . keep me busy with you?"
Feels leadership of the class is threatened. Feels defeated "Who is running this class? He or I?" "I won't let him get away with this."	GOAL II. POWER Wants to be the boss. "I only count if you do what I want." "If you don't let me do what I want you don't love me."	Withdraw from the conflict. "Take your sail out of his wind." Recognize and admit that the child has power. Appeal for child's help, enlist his cooperation, give him responsibility.	"Could it be that you want to show me that you can do what you want and no one can stop you? "Could it be that you want to be the boss?" ". . . get me to do what you want?"

FIGURE 1 *(continued)*
Identifying the Goals of Children's Misbehavior

INCREASED SOCIAL INTEREST◄────────►DIMINISHED SOCIAL INTEREST

	USEFUL		USELESS		
	Active Constructive	Passive Constructive	Active Destructive	Passive Destructive	Child's Action and Attitude The Message
			"Vicious" Violent Brutal Steals (Leader of juvenile delinquent gangs)	"Violent passivity" Sullen Defiant	"Vicious" Steals Sullen Defiant Will hurt animals, peers and adults Kicks, bites, scratches Sore loser Potential delinquent I can't be liked and I only count if I can hurt others.
			"Hopeless" Stupidity Indolence Inaptitude (Pseudo feeble-minded) (Inferiority complex)		"Feels hopeless" Stupid actions Inferiority complex Gives up Rarely participates Says "leave me alone, you can't do anything with me." I can't do anything right so I don't ever try. I am no good, and incapable.

(left margin, top to bottom) MINOR DISCOURAGEMENT ◄── ──► DEEP DISCOURAGEMENT

that basic level of skill, the leader must be effective in his relationships with professional peers. Members will often learn more from the model of the types of relationships he develops and the message he sends within the group than from what it is that he advises or suggests that they do. This specialist must understand human behavior, motivation, classroom proce-

CORRECTIONS OF MISBEHAVIOR

Teacher's Reaction	The Child's Probable Goal And His "Faulty Logic"	Teacher's Corrective Procedures	Teacher's Interpretations Of Child's Goal To Him
Dislikes the child. Feels deeply hurt. Is outraged by child. Wants to get even. "How can he be so mean?"	GOAL III. REVENGE Tries to hurt as he feels hurt by others. "My only hope is to get even with them."	Avoid punishment. Win the child. Try to convince him that he is liked. Do not become hurt. Enlist a "buddy" for him. Use group encouragement.	"Could it be that you want to hurt me and/or the children?" "Could it be that you want to get even?"
Feels helpless. Doesn't know what to do. "I can't do anything with him!" "I give up!"	GOAL IV. DISPLAY OF INADEQUACY Tries to be left alone. Feels hopeless. "I don't want anyone to know how stupid I am."	Avoid discouragement yourself. Don't give up. Show faith in child. Lots of encouragement. Use constructive approach.	"Could it be that you want to be left alone." ". . . you feel stupid and don't want people to know?"

Source. Presented by Dr. Don Dinkmeyer. Adapted from Edith A. Dewey, January, 1970. Adaptation of charts by Dr. Rudolf Dreikurs, M. L. Bullard and Pearl Cassel.

dures and group dynamics, and help the group to develop recommendations which idiographically fit each member.

Functions and responsibilities of the leader include:

1. Structuring the group from its inception so that both purpose and focus are clear. It should be apparent that this is not case study, child study, group therapy, or sensitivity training. Instead, there is a meshing and assembling of child problems and teacher attitudes to make the greatest progress to help the teacher to understand herself and how she can use her resources to facilitate the development of the child. Group members begin by examining the external unit (the child) but always consider at the same time the internal unit (their own feelings, beliefs, attitudes) and how the internal unit affects the transaction.

2. Being sensitive to feelings which are expressed and unexpressed. He must be aware of all of the messages, verbal and nonverbal, implicit and explicit. He observes the tone of voice, facial expression, and other forms of body language. He must be alert to deal with feelings that occur in the "here and now" of the group as well as to help teachers understand the feelings which occurred at the time that they were dealing with the child. When strong feelings are brought out in the group, the leader deals with these feelings in terms of their meaning for relating in the classroom.

3. Focusing on helping group members see how their ideas about human behavior are related. He makes them aware of the way in which they have similar ideas and the way in which they may have differences of opinion. This process helps to clarify their beliefs. The linking process also, while underlining similar problems, helps to universalize or bring a more cohesive group as the members begin to recognize how their problems are similar to those of others in the group.

4. Being a facilitator in the sense of being concerned about having all members participate in the group. This necessitates a patience which permits quiet members to participate through passive listening as well as through verbal participation. He has great faith in the mechanism of spectator therapy and the benefits that may come from hearing about how others approach problems. However, at the same time he anticipates that all group members will be willing to share and discuss the problems which they have mentioned to him privately and for which they contracted in terms of their membership in the group.

5. Being vitally interested in helping the group focus on the transactions that are occurring in the "here and now" between them. He deals with these interactions because they help to make the members aware of the potency of interpersonal relationships.

6. Basically, being an encourager. He is concerned with helping group members focus on the assets and strengths of participants in order to develop feelings of adequacy.

   Through both formal and informal procedures he helps each member acquire an asset inventory of his particular strengths in working with children. In some instances he utilizes special exercises such as Multiple Strength Perception (Dinkmeyer and Muro, 1971).

7. Helping the group clarify the basic problems, see the real issues, and find alternate solutions. His social psychological orientation, which makes

him aware of the pattern and purpose of behavior, is used to help him in generating tentative hypothesis.

8. Recognizing that he is a resource which can help teachers to realize that they will change children best as they make a personal commitment to changing their own pattern of interaction with children. He never encourages general talk which permits teachers to escape from a recognition of their own part in behavior problems which children are manifesting.

"C" GROUP COMPONENTS

The "C" group developed because of the mounting evidence that lectures, discussion, and telling would not help change the basic attitudes of teachers, parents, and students. The focus in these groups is on personal involvement and a growth experience which provides an opportunity in the group setting to exchange and test ideas. The setting permits the concepts to be evaluated and eventually internalized and enables the teachers to become aware of their own strengths and capabilities. It is a unique experience in the sense that it is holistic insofar as the leader has access to the feelings, ideas, concepts, and behaviors of the participants. Thus, it involves the affective, cognitive, and actional domain. The teacher's feelings, beliefs and behaviors are always openly revealed and considered.

The group is called a "C" group because the factors that tend to make the group most effective begin with a "c."

1. *Collaboration* The group works together on mutual concerns as equals. There is no superior-inferior relationship. They are consultants to each other.
2. *Consultation* The group consults by providing and receiving ideas about the specific application of new approaches to relationships with children.
3. *Clarification* The group clarifies for each member what it is she really believes and how congruent or incongruent her behavior is with what she believes. Through the clarification of these beliefs, systems, and feelings it is possible to become aware of the congruency or incongruency between behavior, belief, and feelings. Participants come to learn how their beliefs and faulty assumptions keep them from functioning more effectively.
4. *Confrontation* The group expects each individual to see herself, her purposes and her attitudes and to be willing to confront other members of the group.
5. *Communication* The group is a new channel insofar as it communicates in a holistic sense not only content but feelings. Teachers are now available to each other as "whole persons."
6. *Concern and Caring* The group shows that it is involved both with its members and children.

7. *Confidential* Discussions are not repeated outside the group.
8. *Commitment* The group develops a commitment to change. Participants are concerned with recognizing they can really change only themselves. They are expected to develop a specific commitment which involves an action to change their approach to a problem, to be taken before the next "C" group (Dinkmeyer, 1971).

SUMMARY

The pupil personnel specialist client is often the teacher. Traditional approaches in working with teachers have not been highly effectual. The "C" group combines a didactic and experiential set of procedures while recognizing teacher and child interaction in the light of socio-teleological premises. A number of essential details in organizational procedures with administration and group members are set forth. Group composition is especially important, as are procedures of getting started. The groups operate on the basis of social-psychological principles and within the framework of the specific components of the "C" group.

References

Combs, A. W. et al. Florida studies in the helping professions. University of Florida Monographs, Social Sciences No. 37. Gainesville, Florida: University of Florida Press, 1969.

Dinkmeyer, D. The C-Group: Focus on self as instrument. *Phi Delta Kappan*, 1971, *52*, 617–619.

Dinkmeyer, D., & Muro, J. *Group counseling: Theory and practice.* Itasca, Illinois: Peacock Publishers, 1971.

Dreikurs, R., & Grey, L. *Logical consequences.* New York: Meredith Press, 1968.

Dreikurs, R., & Sonstegard, M. Rationale of Group Counseling. In D. Dinkmeyer (Ed.), *Guidance and counseling in the elementary school: Readings in theory and practice.* New York: Holt, Rinehart & Winston, 1968, p. 280.

Otto, H. *Group methods designed to actualize human potential: A handbook.* Chicago: Stone Brandel Center, 1967.

Parent and Family
VI Group Counseling and Consultation

Few would deny the significance of the influence of the family on the development of the individual. Family life is the milieu in which the culture and values of the society are transmitted to the individual. Within the family atmosphere the child develops his original identity as a person. His understanding of emotional and social relationships come from those he observes and experiences. Children are excellent observers, and although they may misinterpret parental intentions, it is in this milieu that the self-concept and feelings of adequacy originate. It is within the family that the needs for love, security, belonging, recognition and approval, and independence are either met or thwarted. The child's position in the family siblingship also influences his orientation toward persons. His interpretation of his position as the oldest, second, youngest, middle, or only child influences how he feels about himself and how he relates to others.

An awareness of the significance of the family's influence on the child's development suggests that educators, psychologists, counselors, and others who are concerned with human development should put intensive efforts into the training of parents in more effective parenting procedures. Actually, parent education and parent groups until recently, have received only sporadic attention from educators. There has been an awareness of the importance of the parents role, but training has not been understood or accepted as a school personnel responsibility.

Several factors have brought increased acceptance of that responsibility for parent education. The focus of pupil personnel specialists training has moved from remediation to prevention and developmental services. Students in training have been exposed to the Family Education Center, Parent "C" Group, Family Group Consultation, and Parent Effectiveness Training processes in their program. Equipped with skills in family counseling and consultation, they have been able to implement more effective programs.

The democratic revolution has also made parents more aware of their rights so that they are less willing to accept ineffectual specialists who appear only to elicit information and assign blame. Instead, they are asking for assistance in relating more effectively with their children. This demand has come from parent groups outside the schools such as the Family Education Centers, based on Adlerian principles, and from parents who have had access to educational experiences that have alerted them to more effective procedures.

We must face the major societal problem that parents seldom have adequate training to function effectively with their children, despite the fact that they play such a significant and continuous role in the development of their children and thereby of our society. It is within the family that the child first understands human relationships and the culture. In the family he develops his unique approach to the social and work tasks of life, while acquiring basic social and relationship skills. Failure to provide educational experiences for parents not only neglects a highly significant clientele (it might even be observed the clientele that financially supports the schools and indirectly, via the school board, engages in decision making about service needs), but also through this neglect fosters poor academic achievement and immature social and emotional development. The broad goals of education can only be achieved through effective contacts with parents and the family.

It has been observed that parents of elementary school children are usually eager and receptive to school supported services that provide assistance in raising children. They have come to expert little practical assistance, but innovative parent programs not only can educate parents and benefit children but, as a concomitant, can develop support for pupil personnel programs. As parents have frequently stated to the specialist running such programs, "I never thought I could get any practical help from the schools." While that may be a general evaluation of their own school experience, it also points to the need for improved public relations, through providing helpful programs.

The articles in the section that follows present a variety of family counseling and consultation models that indicate the potential of these processes.

Christensen essentially portrays his model as an educational endeavor. He believes that lack of knowledge and experience on the part of parents brings about maladaptive behavior. This assumption is that if people are provided with new and pertinent information they will be capable of bringing about change. Excerpts from a counseling session with parents and their children clearly illustrate the process of obtaining the subjective report of the parents' perceptions of their interaction with the children. A children's interview clarifies how the counselor validates his hypotheses.

The interviews demonstrate how the counselor systematically investigates typical incidents and through the process of determining from the parents "And what did you do about it?" develops hypotheses about the purposes of the behavior.

The family education model is always done in a public session in order to spread the educational effect. Audiences have included as many as 300 in sessions conducted by Christensen. Training in this model is available at the University of Arizona with Christensen and from a number of other institutions with educators who have an Adlerian orientation. The process is also taught at a number of the Alfred Adler Institutes throughout the nation.

Dinkmeyer's parent "C" group model presents knowledge about human behavior in the format of group interaction. The "C" group not only provides information but helps the parent to understand how their beliefs and attitudes affect the relationship with the child. It has been demonstrated that the feedback from peers and the benefits of group thinking provide an added therapeutic or growth element. Often parents will accept ideas from other parents but not from the professional, and they are always influenced and encouraged when results are reported by other parents. The commitment to change made publicly in the group and the mutual encouragement between members are dynamic forces that aid parents.

Dinkmeyer's article acquaints the leader with the significance of the group mechanisms for producing interaction. Specific "C" group components are detailed, and a brief excerpt from a "C" group illustrates the process.

Carlson's article is an excellent supplement to the article by Dinkmeyer because it provides insight into the progress of a group of five mothers who met for a series of four sessions. The samples of group interaction make known the typical concerns and the progress made over several sessions. The processes of universalization, focusing on specific incidents, and the benefits of group thinking are clearly portrayed. The final session suggests that leaders may want to stimulate capable and sensitive parents to help other parents by forming additional groups. It is crucial that parents who lead parent "C" groups have some training in understanding human behavior and group leadership skills, as well as some supervision from a specialist while leading groups. Parent leaders have immense potential to improve relationships by creating "C" groups and parent study groups. Additional insights into the "C" group can be obtained from special chapters in Dinkmeyer and Muro (1971), Dinkmeyer and Carlson (1973), and through special workshops on the process.[1]

Fullmer's Family Group Consultation operates on the premise that one needs to intervene in the family interaction process. He believes that behavior comes out of the interpersonal relationship and communication between two persons.

---

[1] For more information write to Communication and Motivation Training Institute, 11061 NW, 23rd Ct., Coral Springs, Florida 33065.

These relationships eventually represent the group, community, and larger social systems that he calls the culture. One person's changing his behavior necessitates that others change their response to him and this breaks up the redundant and nontherapeutic relationships. Thus, behavior is changed by redefining one's relationship with another.

In the Family Group Consultation process each person must speak for himself and no one speaks for anyone but himself. The emphasis is on here and now interaction because these interactions represent the same forces that operate when family members are away from the session. Initially, the family contracts for sessions by number, usually four. The approach utilizes ideas from Adlerian family counseling and behavior therapy. Focus is on conflict resolution, crisis management, and the improvement of communication by developing mutual meanings. The family members are taught to identify cues that trigger emotional outburst and to learn to control their behavior which controls the responses from others. Fullmer and Bernard (1968) supply more details on the Family Group Consultation process.

Satir is concerned with working with whole family units. She believes that this is where problems have been created and where they can best be treated. Before the work of Satir and her enlightened colleagues, disturbed children or the "symptom bearers" were treated in isolation. Now consultants are working with the whole family as the treatment unit and are experiencing positive results. This article presents her approach, which is referred to as "conjoint family therapy."

Gordon's Parent Effectiveness Training is concerned with improving communication and conflict resolution procedures. He helps parents become aware of roadblocks to communication and new ways to conceptualize problem ownership. A detailed description of how to communicate more effectively in various parent-child interactions is included.

Sauber introduces us to Multiple Family Group Counseling, a process that has been explored most extensively with parents and adolescents. He presents an interesting list of Functional Family Concepts that serve as a baseline for evaluating dysfunctional processes. Clarke's concepts to stimulate awareness of the communication of positive feelings between parents and adults are also described. The MFGC is a time limited approach as are most of the systems described in this section.

In reading these articles, consider the following questions and suggestions:

● Is parent counseling and consultation a function of the school or does it more properly belong with the agencies? Develop a rationale for your position that considers the history of school and mental health services.
● What are some of the major factors that currently restrain pupil personnel specialists from functioning in this area? What are your feelings about using the processes described with parents? Discuss procedures you believe fit with

your rationale and also why you might not use some of the processes proposed.
● What are the similarities that you find in the work of Christensen, Dinkmeyer, and Carlson? Contrast the advantages and limitations of the Family Counseling or Parent "C" Group model. What do you think about the assumption that the person must accept the responsibility for changing his behavior?
● How much time do you believe should be spent by the school pupil personnel specialists in working with parents? Develop a hierarchy or priority of services that indicates the relative importance of this functon in contrast to other pupil personnel services.
● What are the specific intervention procedures suggested by Christensen and Fullmer? How comfortable do you feel in guessing and making tentative hypotheses about the purpose of behavior from hearing about interaction between parents and children.
● Which of the processes appear to be most economical and efficacious in the long run? Defend your rationale.
● Christensen focuses on incidents and "there and then" behavior. Fullmer is concerned more with "here and now" interaction, while the "C" group might include both dimensions. Discuss your ideas about the effectiveness of these diverse emphases.
● Gordon's P.E.T. appears to be more concerned with developing parenting skills than dealing with specific family problems. What do you believe are the advantages and limitations of such an approach?
● What is your position on Sauber's statement that children under nine are not included because they are not mature enough verbally and intellectually to undertake the communication expected in the group?
● How might you integrate these procedures into a pupil personnel program for a large urban district? For a suburban district? For a rural district? Would the procedures be more appropriate for certain populations and less appropriate for others?

REFERENCES

Dinkmeyer, D., and J. Carlson. **Consulting: Facilitating Human Potential and Change Processes.** Columbus, Ohio: Charles Merrill, 1973.
Dinkmeyer, D., and J. Muro. **Group Counseling: Theory and Practice.** Itasca, Ill.: Peacock, 1971.
Fullmer, D., and H. Bernard, **Family Consultation,** Boston: Houghton Mifflin, 1968.

26. FAMILY EDUCATION: A MODEL FOR CONSULTATION

Oscar C. Christensen

The earliest basic patterns of social behavior are learned within the family unit. Adler (1927), Preston (1966), Dreikurs (1968), and Dreikurs and Soltz (1964) are among those who placed an emphasis on the importance of the socialization process in the family setting and in addition stressed that behavioral problems are generated when the socialization process is defective or changed. They also concluded that fundamental defects in learned behavior patterns experienced in the basic family unit (even from early childhood) became an integral part of a faulty life style or personality of the individual. They also emphasized the significance of the study of personal interrelationships at home as the basis for understanding social problems in public education.

It is from this theoretical orientation that the consultant operates. The assumption that undergirds parent and family counseling in the school setting is that counseling is an educational endeavor rather than a medical pursuit.

"The model alluded to here is essentially an educational one, which makes the assumption that the lack of knowledge, information, or experience, rather than illness, is the basis of maladaptive behavior. While counselors, and indeed schools are poorly equipped to cure illness, they are well designed to provide information, experiences, or education. It is assumed that people, if provided new or pertinent information, are capable of applying the new information to their situation, making the corrections necessary to bring about change." (Christensen 1969, p. 13)

Whereas the curing of illness is the exclusive domain of medicine there is no question but that the eradication of ignorance is justifiably the domain

Source. Oscar C. Christensen, "Family Education: A Model for Consultation." *Elementary School Guidance and Counseling*, 1972, vol. 7–2, 121–129. Copyright 1972 by the American Personnel and Guidance Association and reproduced by permission.

of education. If one accepts this premise, then any means of instruction which permits learning to take place can justifiably be called counseling. If providing new information is the key to family counseling, then the quality and appropriateness of the information becomes paramount.

INTERVIEW WITH PARENTS

The counseling session typically begins with the subjective report of the parents. In the interview excerpts that follow, the counselor is working in front of an audience. The audience setting, or open center counseling, has the purpose of educating the audience as well as the parents being counseled. The first excerpt illustrates the gathering of subjective data.

COUNSELOR: "Ben and Betty are with us and just to get off the ground, why don't you tell us the names and ages of your children?"

MOTHER: "Don, age 8, third grade; Bill, age 7, in second grade. There is 14 months difference in their ages."

COUNSELOR: "Now, some of the speculation which I would have a trained audience do would be to describe these children to me. The purpose would be to sharpen their perception by making suggestions—not necessarily with the idea of being accurate, but understanding why they are wrong, if they are wrong. One would expect Don to be more outgoing, more interested in a variety of things, not just athletics but reading and books as well."

MOTHER: "Don is more competitive, very competitive."

FATHER: "Yes, Don is more competitive."

COUNSELOR: "What does that leave for Bill?"

FATHER: "Bill is more, if I may say so, a mama's boy."

COUNSELOR: "Comfortable?"

FATHER: "In a sense, lovable, cute, small for his age, less competitive, but more demanding in many ways."

In this example, the parents have described the children as they perceive them, and the subjective labels or descriptions have done little to clarify the situation. The counselor can begin to objectify the data by asking for descriptions of interaction between the parents and the children. Thus, subjective parental observations can be objectified by asking the parents to complete the interactive pattern or picture. Each time the parent describes a behavior, the counselor simply asks, "And what did you do about it?", thereby getting the parental response to the child's behavior and completing the interaction between the parent and the child. In the next excerpt, the counselor encourages the parent to describe typical moments in the course of the day. This procedure is designed to explore the interaction patterns between parent and child.

COUNSELOR: "One of the ways of getting at interaction in a second person way, other than observing it, is to have parents describe typical days and typical situations. One of the things that you'll note I'll be doing during the course of their description is interrupting a lot (which they learn to tolerate), but at the same time I'll be focusing on specifics. Mother, would you take us through a typical morning at your house?"

MOTHER: "Many times they get up together, but usually Bill is the first one up. Don will usually get his clothes on immediately. He is ready to eat breakfast and he is ready to go to school at the time he is supposed to go."

COUNSELOR: "What does old Bill do?"

MOTHER: "Bill is fooling around, anything he can think of to get out of getting dressed. It is not that he doesn't like school. He seems to like school at this point, but he'd rather stay home and do things he prefers to do, like draw, or read, if he happens to want to read. But it usually takes a bit of pushing to get him to his clothes—not every morning though."

COUNSELOR: "What do you do about the fact that he's dawdling?"

MOTHER: "I get very angry first."

COUNSELOR: "Tell us how you do that. What is your procedure?"

MOTHER: "Well, you know, it's the prodding every five minutes until it gets to be 16 minutes before it is time to go to school."

COUNSELOR: "At what point does he move? When does he know you mean it?"

MOTHER: "Sometimes at the 15-minute mark and sometimes it is this helpless thing of 'Well you have to help me.' "

COUNSELOR: "And what do you do about it?"

MOTHER: "I feel that I shouldn't have to help him, of course."

COUNSELOR: "But what do you do?"

MOTHER: "Sometimes I do have to help him, because we are at that frustrating stage that all mothers go through, 'Well, I've gotta get him going, so I'll help him.' "

In this example, guesses that were made during the first insert are becoming objectified. Bill's demanding is more clearly defined as a means of keeping mother busy by occupying mother's time, and asserting his place in the family as the helpless child. However, further validation is required. A shift to a different time period, during which the interaction pattern can again be observed through the mother's report, provides such an opportunity.

COUNSELOR: "What happens after school? Let's take that time span now."

MOTHER: "Well, I really can't say too much about that because I work full time."

COUNSELOR: "Good! Has anybody ever told you that you shouldn't work?"

MOTHER: "No."

COUNSELOR: "Do you ever feel guilty about it?"

MOTHER: "I'm beginning not to. Now last year I was not working when they came home from school. But this year, if you want to know about right now, I'm not sure what happens other than from phone calls I get."

COUNSELOR: "Who is calling?"

MOTHER: "They are calling me—the boys. I have a neighbor who watches them, but they generally call me when they get home."

COUNSELOR: "All right, and what are they calling you about?"

MOTHER: "Sometimes to say hello and sometimes to say school is great. At other times Bill is calling and is upset, because Don kicked him because Bill wouldn't change his shoes—that kind of thing."

COUNSELOR: "And what do you do about it when Bill calls and tells you Don kicked him because he wouldn't change his shoes?"

MOTHER: "Well, actually, in that instance, I didn't talk to Bill; I talked to Don. He was the one that called and told me what had happened. Bill had called and couldn't get me—that sort of thing."

COUNSELOR: "So Don called."

MOTHER: "So Don called to report on himself; yeah, he really did."

COUNSELOR: "And what did you do about it?"

MOTHER: "Well, over the phone I said that I didn't think this was very nice. He was not to take it upon himself to enforce something that I had asked Bill to do."

COUNSELOR: [To audience] "Are you beginning to see something of the universality of motherhood? On the drop of a dime, in this instance, we can always get a lecture. The same thing is true of 'mothers' of both sexes who go into teaching—become teachers. We talk too much. What do you suppose would have been a better response to Don's fighting with Bill?"

MOTHER: " 'Thank you for telling me,' probably would have been a better response."

COUNSELOR: "Or, 'I'm sure he can handle it,' and hang up. The only way I'm comfortable in making that kind of guess is that I am beginning to get some glimmer of the purpose of Don's calling. You see, Don and Bill have to cooperate, even in something like fighting, in order for one guy to be the good guy and one guy to be the bad guy. It really makes very little difference as to which one starts the fight, the outcome is predictable. In the typical fight Don, in some fashion, wins until Bill cries so that mother 'bawls out' Don. Both children are thus paid off. Is fighting one of the things that they do well together?"

MOTHER: "Oh, beautifully!"

COUNSELOR: "How does dinner go?"

MOTHER: "Dinner doesn't go too great! Some nights Bill is very picky. Maybe I should say he is a discriminating eater."

COUNSELOR: "With the exception of eggplant, I'd suggest probably, he's picky!"

MOTHER: "He's very picky; he really is! He does not, what I feel as a mother, eat nearly enough. Some nights he has chocolate milk for dinner, and that's all. He doesn't touch a thing."

COUNSELOR: "And what do you do about it when he is not touching a thing?"

MOTHER: "Prod a little bit, you know. I keep getting from my husband: 'Don't force him to eat; this won't do any good.' I know objectively it won't do any good, but I still have to say, 'Please, Bill, come on try it, it's very good.' "

COUNSELOR: "And how do you feel when Bill turns up his nose at his three favorite vegetables that you have cooked especially" . . .

MOTHER: "He doesn't like any vegetables; that's never happened. I guess, as a mother, I feel a little upset, because I've cooked his favorite food, and he's not eating it."

COUNSELOR: "Do you feel hurt by it?"

MOTHER: "Not really hurt, no. I get a little angry, because I've spent this time after I come home from work, you know, fixing dinner and darn it, he's not eating it! In 20 minutes after dinner he's going to be asking for a cookie or something like that, and I'm going to have to go through the saying, 'No you can't have it because you didn't eat supper,' or give in and let him have it and feel he isn't getting enough proper kinds of food to eat."

COUNSELOR: "And when you give in and let him have the cookie, what do you feel like then?"

MOTHER: "Relieved in some ways that it is all over, you know."

COUNSELOR: "Do you also feel defeated?"

MOTHER: "Yeah, I guess I feel defeated a little bit, because I don't know how to handle it any better."

COUNSELOR: "All right, now let's just demonstrate another microcosmic kind of technique. I am interrupting, to point out what's going on. In attempting to understand purposive behavior one has to see the complete interaction to understand. To know only what the child did, is like reading a play with all the parts cut out except one. But as soon as I ask a mother, 'And what did you do about it?' I get both sides of the interaction. When I ask a mother how she felt in her specific situation, I begin to get a glimmer of insight into the purpose for which the child used the interaction.

"The non-eating, in this family I'm guessing, is a technique that Bill has developed for showing his mother who is boss. And the fact that she feels defeated by it (for example, she says, 'You can't have a cookie,' knowing full well the kid is going to get one somehow), is further proof of the youngster's power.

"My initial hypothesis of attention-getting as the child's goal is now changing to power, and I've semi-validated it with mother's feeling in terms of a specific behavior; and while the hypothesis is only tentative, at least I'm guessing in the right direction. This permits me to make some recommendations about at least two of the kinds of experiences that mother is having. The thing that we have discovered in this kind of counseling, which I think is kind of refreshing, is that when I make the recommendation for mother in one area she comes back two weeks later and has taken that recommendation and translated it into about six or a dozen other similar areas. That is what happens when we are working with very intelligent people who are capable of making use of information without always having to assume a therapeutic kind of counseling relationship. Instead of this very direct kind of approach creating a dependency, I really find that it creates an independency. As mother becomes educated to use some of these techniques, she doesn't need me, and I'm discarded rather rapidly."

The focusing on mother's feelings about the child's misbehavior stems from a theoretical bias concerning purposive behavior. If one accepts the premise that behavior has purpose and that purpose is interpersonal by nature, then the behavior of the child should elicit some kind of response in mother. The feeling of anger or defeat experienced by mother would be interpreted from the Adlerian frame of reference as mother's response to an expression of power on the part of the child. This zeroing in on the purpose of Bill's behavior permits the counselor to begin thinking in terms of remediation.

The role of the "good" brother was not overlooked in the counseling session and was attended to for the benefit of the parents and the participating audience as follows:

COUNSELOR: "The other role that we've not clearly defined, and I suspect that if I didn't consciously work at remembering I would have forgotten, is the role of Don. We haven't heard anything particularly negative about Don, and my guess is that he's spending a portion of his time reminding mother of all the things Bill has done wrong. In a sense this is a way of Don demonstrating his discouragement. Don is telling us: 'I really don't think I'm much, but by George, Bill is even worse.' I am much more concerned that we help Don find some ways of being of value, of being a whole person, without having to be perfect as a means of attaining this kind of recognition."

By this time we begin to see Don as the good brother—capable and achieving—and Bill as the underachieving, incapable, helpless baby brother. The hypothesis is that the boys are both ambitious and highly competitive, and each has found a role from which he can dominate the family. Both are also hypothesized as discouraged children in that they have interpreted being "good enough" as needing to be powerful or superior (either positively or negatively) as a prerequisite to being acceptable. One has selected being powerful in a dominant way, the other has selected being powerful in a negative way, the helpless way.

Having made these hypotheses, the counselor interviews the children with the parents absent. The children's interview is to validate hypotheses, not to check on the parents' accuracy or veracity.

INTERVIEW WITH THE CHILDREN

COUNSELOR: "Hi boys!" [boys enter]

DON: "Hi!"

COUNSELOR: "Thanks for coming. Do you know why you're here?"

DON: "Yes."

BILL: "No."

COUNSELOR: "Yes and no! Pull your chairs up a little bit, and I'll pull yours [Bill] up a little bit. Trapped me! Did you see that? What did I do?" [Audience laughter]

DON: "What did you do?"

COUNSELOR: "Well, I gave your brother a little bit of help. Did he need help?"

DON: "No, he could do it himself."

COUNSELOR: "But very frequently we find that he somehow gets more help than a lot of other people, Don. Did that ever happen at your house?"

DON: "Yes."

COUNSELOR: "Well first I've got to talk about why you are here, so that you'll know what's going on. This is a class of teachers and parents and counselors, and we're trying to learn more about how families work, and your mom and dad have been helping us. Now it is your turn to help us. We appreciate your coming. Mom tells me that in the morning, Bill, you find it very difficult to get ready for school—can't find your shoes and what else?"

DON: "He can find his shoes."

BILL: "I can find my shoes."

COUNSELOR: "But you can't tie them?"

BILL: "I can tie them."

COUNSELOR: "And does mom have to say, "Hurry up, hurry up, hurry up" a thousand times?"

BILL: "Yes."

COUNSELOR: "Why does she do that?"

BILL: "I don't know."

COUNSELOR: "Why do you suppose you spend so much time dawdling and taking time and having to be told to hurry up?"

BILL: "Because I am tired."

COUNSELOR: "Because you're tired, that's a possibility. Would you like to know what I think?"

BILL: "What?"

COUNSELOR: "I could be wrong, but could it be that when you take so much time in the morning getting ready for school, this is a way you have of keeping mother busy?"

BILL: "No."

COUNSELOR: "No? Could it be that when you take so much time in the morning getting ready for school, that this is a way of telling mother who is boss?"

BILL: "Yes."

COUNSELOR: [To audience] "I will not accept this verbalization alone. I can only accept the eyeball (twinkle-recognition)! I don't know how to describe this; we call it a recognition reflex, which is something like the 'hand in the cookie jar' look. I'm sure only a few people here could see it, but there was a glimmer—just a faint one, because I wasn't that accurate. It was in the right direction, but not precisely in his language.

"I guess maybe another way to say it, Bill, is that when you take so much time in the morning getting ready for school, it is a way you have of making mother help you."

DON: "He always wants someone to dress him."

BILL: "No I don't."

COUNSELOR: "Not really, do you?"

BILL: "No."

COUNSELOR: "Because, you see, when we dress you, we're really being disrespectful. We're acting like you can't really do it yourself and, frankly, I think you can."

BILL: "I know I can."

COUNSELOR: "Do you know what is going to happen tomorrow morning?"

BILL: "What?"

COUNSELOR: "What if I were to help mother by telling her not to help you dress, absolutely not help, what do you think would happen?"

BILL: "I'd dress myself."

COUNSELOR: "I'd expect you would."

DON: "And he'd be late!"

COUNSELOR: "Now I really have to call attention to why Don said that. After I said something very complimentary about Bill, that I thought he could dress himself, what did you immediately do?"

DON: "What?"

COUNSELOR: "What was your response when I told everybody here—all these people—that I really thought Bill was capable of dressing himself tomorrow? What did you do to Bill?"

DON: "I didn't do anything."

COUNSELOR: "Yeah, you said something about he'd probably be late. Why would you say that about him?"

DON: "Because he's too slow dressing, and he won't help."

COUNSELOR: "But could it also be that it is very important for you to be better than Bill?"

DON: "No." [Don laughed]

COUNSELOR: "See, what I think is going on at your house is that Don sometimes feels that he has to be perfect. How do you feel when you make mistakes?"

DON: "Pretty let down."

COUNSELOR: "But making mistakes is all right as long as you learn from them. And really you don't have to be perfect. I think people will like you just the way you are. You don't even have to be better than old Bill."

BILL: "I'm not old."

COUNSELOR: "Yeah, but you're 'good old Bill' to me."

BILL: " 'Good and young Bill.' "

COUNSELOR: "Bill doesn't have to always have people in his service before we can know that he's a pretty good guy."

An attempt was made in this portion of the interview to provide Bill with insight as to the purpose of his dawdling behavior, and also to provide Don with some insight into his apparent need to be perfect, which is interpreted in this instance to mean better than Bill. Both are mistaken perceptions by the children. Some validation of the hypothesis of power in Bill's case was made via the recognition reflex. Bill's conflict between his short term goal of being powerful through helplessness and the idealized goal of self-sufficiency was noted. The remainder of the interview with the children was employed to test the hypothesis of the power goal through one or two other illustrations.

INTERVIEW WITH PARENTS

The parents then returned for recommendations and termination of the interview. As far as it is possible, specific recommendations for parental behavior are desirable. One or two small changes in the parents' behavior are required in order to provide the children with the opportunity to change their behavior. In this instance the counselor is attempting to assist mother to withdraw from the telling or hurry-up role which she plays in the mornings with Bill. The counselor is also attempting to assist mother and father to accept Don without the requirement of being the perfect child, thereby assisting Don to accept himself.

COUNSELOR: "All right, Bill has developed a pretty good way of keeping mother occupied to the exclusion of Don in the morning. My recommendation is to give Bill some new opportunities to discover that he can do things without being prodded. Mother, could you just be quiet tomorrow morning? Could you do that?"

MOTHER: "Yeah, I'll try anything."

COUNSELOR: "No, you can't try. Either you do it or you don't do it. You can't try to keep quiet. Now I sense that this might be too difficult. Could I state it a different way? Will you interact with Bill on any topic other than 'hurry up'? If he comes wandering out with his shirt tail hanging out and he can't find his socks, say, 'Did you notice out the window there's a bird?' I don't care what you talk about, don't respond to the dawdling. I couldn't ask you to be quiet because you're a natural-born mother and they just don't know how to keep quiet. If you can't be quiet, leave.

"We have two things to go with in terms of both youngsters, don't we? The first order of business is to assist Bill in discovering that he too can be a good guy, however you define that. The second line of business is to help Don discover that he can be acceptable without being Mary Poppins —that he doesn't have to be perfect, that he doesn't have to put down Bill as a way of demonstrating his importance."

The final instructional area is an attempt to introduce the parents to the role of encouragement in changing the child's behavior.

COUNSELOR: "The other side of the coin is the process of encouragement. I would have to describe both of these boys as discouraged. The fact that Don does everything so perfectly, but for the wrong reason, in itself illustrates a sense of discouragement. Both boys, therefore, have to be supplied with some courage. We call that encouragement. The processes of encouragement are all of those things which imply 'I think you can make it.' The lack of sympathy, the providing of opportunities to succeed, the positive comment are methods used. I think that with these techniques we become very compatible with some of the behavioristic modality. I like the word recognition as opposed to praise, which I think is pretty artificial. Recognition of the youngster in all kinds of positive ways before he has to demand your time and attention can be developed. Specifically tomorrow can you withdraw from telling Bill to hurry up?"

MOTHER: "Yes."

COUNSELOR: "Okay. That is encouragement. If mother implies to Bill that she believes he can do this and that he can make it without her help, this is positive. I call it encouragement. He doesn't have to be praised for getting to school on time, but one ought to be able to comment on it positively as he is leaving the door. A happy swat on the fanny and a 'See you tonight!' is recognition."

Parents are also alerted to the fact that the modification of behavior patterns with one child in the family will have an influence on the behavior pattern of the other children in the family. For example, as the bad child becomes good there will be a characteristic deterioration of the good child's behavior. The parents are also alerted to the possibility that children may redouble their efforts at maladaptive behavior in order to retain the interaction pattern which they had perfected.

The entire counseling procedure may take 45 minutes to an hour and may be done in several different settings. While it does have value as an office practice, its greater value lies in the possibility of using the model in front of large groups of parents or teachers as a community mental health technique. There are several distinct advantages to the large group modality, not the least of which is its consistency with the educational model. Out of any given group it is estimated that about 80 to 90 percent of the parents can make direct use of the information that the family in focus receives.

If one views the monumental task of reeducating an entire generation of parents and teachers as being a legitimate part of the counselor role, we must encourage numbers of parents to become involved in a dialogue with teachers and counselors and to learn viable child-rearing, adult-child relationship techniques which will produce the kind of adults which can best survive in a democratic society.

References

Adler, A. *Understanding human nature*. Translated by W. Beran Wolfe. Garden City, N.Y.: Garden City Publishing Co., 1927.

Christensen, O. C. Education: A model for counseling in the elementary schools. *Elementary School Guidance and Counseling*, 1969, *4*, 12–19.

Dreikurs, R. *Psychology in the classroom*. (2d ed.) New York: Harper & Row, 1968.

Dreikurs, R., & Soltz, V. *Children: The challenge*. New York: Duell, Sloan & Pearce, 1964.

Preston, G. H. *The substance of mental health*. New York: Holt, Rinehart & Winston, 1966.

27. THE PARENT "C" GROUP

Don C. Dinkmeyer

It is generally accepted that parents and the family exert the original and perhaps most significant influence on the development of the individual. Until recently, however, school counselors have not developed programs to involve parents.

One of our most significant societal problems stems from the fact that parents seldom receive adequate training in relating effectively and in a growth promoting manner with children. School counselor-consultants need to be cognizant of the influence of parental behavior on the social, emotional, and intellectual growth of the student. Unfortunately, when educators do become aware of the importance of parent-student relationships, their good intentions are often hampered by their methods. The occasion for contact is often a "crisis," and the message parents hear leaves them feeling at fault or inadequate to cope with the problem. Seldom are parents provided with positive procedures to help them relate more effectively with their children.

The model that enables group members both to acquire knowledge and evaluate beliefs and attitudes is called the "C" group. This concept has been applied extensively with teacher groups (Dinkmeyer 1971; Dinkmeyer & Arciniega 1972; Dinkmeyer & Carlson 1973). The "C" group was developed to present knowledge about human behavior in a group setting. The group setting not only allows for the sharing of ideas and procedures but also helps members become more aware of the feelings, attitudes, and beliefs that affect their relationships with their children. One of the features of the "C" group is that it helps the parents understand how such beliefs as "I must be in control" or "Disobedience is a personal challenge and must be met with force" keep them from functioning most effectively with their children. In contrast to discussion groups that do not consider how parents' beliefs keep them from putting their knowledge into action, the "C" group deals with the affective, cognitive, and behavioral domains. It goes beyond involving "the whole child" to involving "the whole parent" in the session. Parents are helped to consider how their beliefs may be blocking more effective relationships with their children.

Source. Don C. Dinkmeyer, "The Parent 'C' Group." *Personnel and Guidance Journal,* 1973, 52–4, 252–256. Copyright 1973 by the American Personnel and Guidance Association and reproduced by permission.

THERAPEUTIC FORCES IN "C" GROUPS

The leader must create a climate and establish a pattern of interaction that facilitates both understanding of and change in behavior. The leader's knowledge of procedures for facilitating the therapeutic forces in groups is basic to the success of parent groups (Dinkmeyer & Muro 1971). The following group mechanisms or forces are particularly important in working with parent groups.

Acceptance. In this process respect and empathy develop among members of the group.

Feedback. In this process members share with each other their impressions of the impact of specific attitudes and behavior on the parent-child relationship. The feedback that members receive about their procedures enables them to develop self-awareness.

Universalization. In this process parents become aware that their concerns with their children are not unique but are held in common with other parents.

Altruism. In this process members are stimulated by the opportunity to help others.

Spectator Therapy. In this process members develop an understanding of their situation by hearing a similar situation presented by another member. This gives the group situation an added dimension over individual consulting.

"C" GROUP COMPONENTS

This approach has been titled the "C" group because the factors that make it effective begin with a *C*. Below are described the specific components of such a group.

1. *Collaboration* and working together on mutual concerns are emphasized. The leader has an equal position: There are no superior-inferior relationships between the leader and the group or among members of the group.

2. *Consultation* is both received and provided by the parents. The interaction that occurs within the group between the leader and the members helps group members to become aware of new approaches with children.

3. The group *clarifies* for all members their belief systems, their feelings, and the congruence or incongruence between their behavior, beliefs, and feelings. Clarification and congruence help parents understand how beliefs influence actions.

4. *Confrontation* adds an element of strength in that it produces more realistic and honest feedback. There is an expectation that each individual will see himself or herself, see his or her own purposes, attitudes, and beliefs, and be willing to confront other members with their belief systems.

5. The group is *concerned* and shows that it cares. This concern leads mem-

bers to collaborate, consult, clarify, and confront. The group confronts for purposes of helping and because members are truly involved with developing the human potential of children and group members.

6. The group is *confidential:* Whatever is discussed within the group stays within the group.
7. The group helps individuals develop a *commitment* to change. Participants in the group become involved in helping members recognize that they can really change only themselves. They may come to the group expecting to change children, but they soon learn that *they* must develop a specific commitment involving an action they will take before the next "C" group meeting in order to change their approach to a problem (Dinkmeyer & Carlson 1973).

ADMINISTRATIVE DETAIL

To gain benefits from "C" groups with parents, the leader must pay close attention to organizational details. It is important to secure the support of the central administration of the school system and the local building principal. Support can usually be obtained when administrators are made aware that this process is preventive and broadens the scope of services. Effective parent "C" groups have positive public relations value and tend to create community support. In some instances it is the most effective procedure for making the counseling service visible, accessible, and accountable. It is important to present the concept to the parent organization of the school, since homeroom parents can be of assistance in generating enthusiasm, making contacts, and handling details. The idea of parent "C" groups should be presented at an open meeting so that the community is made aware of the new service.

It is advantageous, however, to restrict the first group to a specific grade level. Experience indicates that parents of first grade children are generally receptive to this kind of group. Once the target grade and classroom are selected, notices are mailed to all parents. Follow-up calls are made until the first group is enrolled. The group should have a minimum of five parents but no more than eight, so that all members can become involved at each meeting. It is important to have a brief individual interview with each parent to clarify the structure and purpose of the group and to elicit specific concerns and a willingness to share and to be of assistance to one another.

The meeting should be held in a comfortable setting where members can be seated in a circular fashion. It is preferable to conduct meetings for mothers during the school day. The members are expected to make a commitment to meet for a minimum of six to eight weeks, each meeting being restricted to an hour and a half.

THE PARENT "C" GROUP IN ACTION

At the first meeting the leader introduces himself or herself and asks the members to introduce themselves briefly, telling the names and ages of their children, starting with the oldest. They are also asked to describe briefly and specifically their concerns with a specific child. After all the members of the group have introduced themselves, the leader talks briefly about general principles, but the meeting focuses mainly on specific concerns with children.

After this brief presentation and discussion, which should be restricted to 10 minutes, the leader selects a parent who has a concern that is common and that represents an area in which this parent can achieve success. The parent is asked to present a specific behavioral incident and to share the feelings he or she experienced when the child misbehaved. The leader and the members help this parent to consider the purpose of the behavior and possible alternative procedures. The following brief excerpt from a parent group will illustrate how the counselor guides the early diagnostic phase of the discussion.

PARENT A: "Jack is so lazy and uncooperative. I just don't know what to do."

COUNSELOR: "You are discouraged. Tell us about a specific time when this happened." [The counselor actively listens and elicits specific events.]

PARENT A: "Monday I had to get off to work, and he still was not dressed for school."

COUNSELOR: "What did you do?" [The counselor determines parental response.]

PARENT A: "I scolded him. He must know better. I've told him countless times."

COUNSELOR: "How did you feel?" [The counselor explores feelings to consider the purpose of the child's action and to examine the parent's belief system.]

PARENT A: "I was very angry and upset."

COUNSELOR: (to members of the group) "Have any of you ever had this happen to you? What do you think is the purpose of this behavior?" [The counselor attempts to universalize and explore the child's purpose.]

PARENT B: "I know how she feels. It seems to me Jack wants to control."

PARENT C: "Yes, it's a familiar scene. I guess some children are just that way."

COUNSELOR: (to Parent A) "What do you think about the idea that Jack gets power and control over you by this behavior?" [The counselor explores a tentative hypothesis.]

The discussion continues to develop understanding of the child's purpose, to explore the belief system of Parent A that hooks her into the power struggle, and to consider alternative procedures. As the group members become better acquainted, they consider what beliefs and attitures on the parent's part prevent the relationship from becoming more effective. The groups operate on the fundamental premise that parents can change a child's behavior only if they are willing to change their own first.

If examination of the specific incidents does not provide ideas that clarify the child's purpose and suggest new procedures, the parent is asked to provide some further details. When did the complaint begin? How are the siblings different in personality traits? How does the child function in such situations as getting up, dressing, taking care of his or her room, eating, obeying and cooperating, taking care of personal property, doing chores, getting to bed at bedtime, relating to peers and siblings, relating to school-work and teacher, etc.?

Members of the group develop and share tentative hypotheses about the purpose of the behavior. They examine the beliefs about parental behaviors that may be affecting the relationship. Parents are helped to understand how their beliefs hinder progress, and they are helped to refine the alternatives that fit their personalities and their specific concerns.

It is important that the leader have maximum involvement and participation in the problem solving. The leader avoids the role of the "expert" and encourages the contributions of members by asking, "What do you think about that?" While leaders do contribute their expertise in human relationships, they seek to stimulate the members to use the resources of the group.

It is crucial that the time be divided so that all parents have an opportunity to present and benefit from the discussion of concerns they have with their children. Parent "C" group meetings will not be effective if the time is spent focusing on one or two parents. All members should be involved in the process of presenting a concern.

The meeting is usually closed by the leader's asking each parent to clarify the specific commitment he or she has made in terms of changing an attitude, belief, or procedure. The following meeting begins by the leader's asking, "How did things go with your new procedure last week?" Excuses for failing to function are not accepted. Parents who provide such an excuse are asked if they believe the plan is appropriate or if they want to change it. This second meeting is spent in clarifying procedures and, if time permits, in considering new problems.

PREPARING COUNSELORS TO LEAD "C" GROUPS

The parent "C" group process is taught to counselors after they have developed group process and communication competencies. The consulting module acquaints the student with a theory of human behavior and then provides a series of parent group demonstrations. Students learn the specific skills of: (a) systematically exploring specific parent-child interactions; (b) utilizing the therapeutic forces of the group to promote the development of members; (c) understanding the meaning of behavior; (d) clarifying, confronting, and obtaining commitments from parents; and (e) encouraging parents to become aware of their strengths and to utilize the strengths of their children. Students are expected to successfully lead parent "C" group sessions during the course.

Experience indicates that graduates of programs offering such training are successfully leading "C" groups and, furthermore, are broadening the base of support for their programs.

The parent "C" group provides a unique opportunity for the counselor to work in a preventive or developmental sense and affect a significant but often overlooked client: the parent. Through this procedure counselors are able to help more students as well as parents of the students. In this age of accountability, this process helps make counseling more visible, accessible, and relevant.

References

Dinkmeyer, D. The "C" group: Integrating knowledge and experience to change behavior. *Counseling Psychologist*, 1971, *3*, 63–72.

Dinkmeyer, D., & Arciniega, M. Affecting the learning climate through "C" groups with teachers. *School Counselor*, 1972, *19*, 249–253.

Dinkmeyer, D., & Carlson, J. *Consulting: Facilitating human potential and change processes*. Columbus, Ohio: Charles E. Merrill, 1973.

Dinkmeyer, D., & Muro, J. *Group counseling: Theory and practice*. Itasca, Ill.: F. E. Peacock, 1971.

28. CASE ANALYSIS: PARENT GROUP CONSULTATION

•••

Jon Carlson

Until recently, most school districts have assumed little responsibility for parent education. There has been little opportunity for groups of parents to come together to discuss and obtain guidance for their problems relating to childrearing (Hill & Luckey, 1969, p. 309). By consulting with parents, we are essentially affecting the child by communicating with significant adults in his life. It is the parents who provide guidance for the child's growth, development, and behavior, and it is from them that he observes the nature of human relationships. By directly helping the parents, we are therefore providing indirect service to the child.

In the following example, the primary objective is to make the relationship between the parents (in this case, mothers) and their children more effective and growth-promoting. It is believed that mothers need more education in childrearing. A woman can become a mother without any prerequisite training in child management. If problems occur, the woman usually does just what her own mother did or, if she had an unhappy childhood, just the opposite. This particular project developed from the planning of the consultant and the school counselor.

The counselor decided to establish groups of mothers to talk over some of the normal concerns they may have about their children. The parents were grouped either by their children's age or grade level. In the case at hand, all mothers had children either in the fifth or sixth grade. The mothers were contacted when the counselor had grade-level meetings to inform parents about the guidance program in the elementary grades at their school. The counselor at this time asked for volunteers to meet for one hour per week during the afternoon for a period of six weeks, and a large number agreed to join child-study groups.

The model that was used was developed by Dinkmeyer and Caldwell (1970) and is essentially as follows:

1. Keep the group small enough (five to nine) so all can participate actively.
2. Clarify with the parents that the group will be dealing with *normal*

Source. Jon Carlson, Case Analysis: Parent Group Consultation *Elementary School Guidance and Counseling,* 1969, Vol. 4–2, 136–141. Copyright 1969 by The American Personnel and Guidance Association and reproduced by permission.

problems of *normal* children. Give examples of typical eating, sleeping, and disciplinary problems that might be considered. Develop an awareness of the phenomenon of universalization—that all parents have similar problems.

3. Introduce the members to each other by having them give their names and the ages of their children. This enables them to develop some fellowship and an awareness of their individual situations.

4. Get someone to begin by discussing a problem that she has. Be sure she describes the problem in specific terms and indicates what the child does, how she responds, and the child's reaction.

5. Begin to work with problems of common concern in order to use the mechanics of universalization. Members of the group are encouraged to provide each other with ideas. The counselor is considered as an additional resource as well as leader of the group dynamics. The counselor should try to focus on attempting to consider some concern for each participant.

6. Ask the group members to summarize what they have learned. It is very important to have the members say what they are going to do with their new information. This forms a public commitment and increases the chance of a behavioral change (Mayer & Cody, 1968). This also is a time for the counselor to correct faulty impressions and to receive other feedback about the group's progress.

The following case demonstrates this process: Five mothers of fifth and sixth grade children met with the counselors (the author and Don Dinkmeyer) during the first session. After a short introduction about the purpose of parent groups, the mothers introduced themselves and gave the names and ages of their children. The counselors then asked who would like to begin. After a specific incident was related by one of the mothers, the counselor inserted the following statement in an attempt to universalize the problem. "How many of you other mothers have this same or a similar problem?" This tended to increase the active involvement of the group.

From here, the group moved from incident after incident on topics such as waking children in the morning, children not wanting to eat their breakfast, not wanting to brush their teeth, not doing their chores, or not coming to dinner when called. During the summary session, the counselor helped each member of the group to develop new approaches to work with before the next session. At this time, he also gave each participant a copy of *The ABC's of Guiding the Child* (Dreikurs & Goldman, 1964). They were asked to read it and consider some of the ideas that are presented.

The next session began as follows:

C: What did you get from our meeting last week? (General discussion and identification of new concepts by the group.)

M_1: Well, she is still Sally.

C: But are you still Mother? Did *you* do anything different? (The emphasis in this consultation is on recognizing that mothers can only change their behavior and hope that this will change the interaction of their children.)

After a short discussion the mother reported that she had not tried anything different. Another mother asked if she would try some of the things that were suggested to her last week and she replied that she was not sure how to go about it.

C: What would you like to change? Take one specific thing.
M_1: Mmmm, her attitude in general.
C: We need something more specific and tangible.
M_1: How about when I try to wake her in the morning. I say it is time to get up and she says try and make me.

The power contest between the mother and daughter was by this time evident to the group. After a short discussion, they recommended that she buy her daughter an alarm clock and let her be responsible for her own awakening. Thus, the mother would be extricating herself from the conflict and leaving her daughter without an opponent. Another mother volunteered.

M_2: I already had success using what you said. My daughter tried to get my attention by playing the same song on the piano over and over. I used to rush in and tell her to stop it and then the battle would start. This time, I shut the door to the kitchen and turned up the radio and went about my housework. She soon stopped and began to play another song.
C: Very good. In other words, you removed the wind from your daughter's sail. Did anyone else have any other results this past week? (One mother began to talk about the difficulty that she was having with her son swearing and the other mothers voiced similar dilemmas.) What could you do about something like this?
M_3: You could ignore it.
M_5: Ignore it; depending on the word, I might tell him that he is not very nice.
C: What about the logical consequences of the situation? (Dreikurs & Grey, 1968).
M_1: Well, if they swear, I won't take them someplace that they want to go.
C: Wouldn't that be more of a punishment?
M_4: Yes, I guess it would.
M_1: What about if I tell him that if he can't talk properly outside with people, he will have to come inside to his room where there are no people to hear him, until he feels that he can talk to others without swearing. (The entire group felt that this would be a very good way to handle this situation.)

At this time the discussion was shifted to *The ABC's of Guiding the Child*. The group talked about the principles set forth in this pamphlet and discussed similar topics. The members were depending more upon other members of the group for aid and solicited less and less assistance from the counselor. During the third session, the counselor passed out a copy of "Child's Mistaken Goals" (see Table 1). This helped clarify the previous materials and accelerated the progress of the group.

The final session opened with:

C: Did anybody try anything different this past week?
      I've been trying things and I have become less critical of myself. I've

TABLE 1
Child's Mistaken Goals [1]

Goal of Misbehavior	What Child Is Saying	How Parent Feels	Child's Reaction to Reprimand	Some Corrective Measures
Attention	I only count when I am being noticed or served	Annoyed Wants to remind, coax Delighted with "good" child	Temporarily stops disturbing action when given attention	Ignore Answer or do the unexpected Give attention at pleasant times
Power	I only count when I am dominating, when you do what I want you to	Prevoked Generally wants power challenged "I'll make him do it." "You can't get away with it."	Intensifies action when reprimanded Child wants to win, be boss	Extricate self Act, not talk Be friendly Establish equality Redirect child's efforts into constructive channels
Revenge	I can't be liked, I don't have power, but I'll count if I can hurt others as I feel hurt by life	Hurt, mad "How could he do this to me?"	Wants to get even Makes self disliked	Extricate self Win child Maintain order with minimum restraint avoid retaliations take time and effort to help child
Inadequacy	I can't do anything right so I won't try to do anything at all; I am no good	Despair "I give up"	No reprimand, therefore, no reaction Feels there is no use to try Passive	Encouragement (may take long) Faith in child's ability

[1] By Nancy Pearcy, Parent Study Groups, Corvallis, Oregon 97330.

been changing and now the entire house is running smoother. I really can understand how 'good mothers are America's tragedy' (Dreikurs & Goldman, 1964).

M_2: Children can do a lot more than we let them do. We do too much for them. As I have realized lately, children are quite capable of taking care of themselves. They really are very capable.

C: Could it be that you are saying that we don't give children enough responsibility? (Carlson & Mayer, 1969). (All the mothers agreed.)

When mothers can realize this fact and begin to do something about it, they have come a long way. With this in mind, the following was presented:

C: I feel that you are in a position to take this procedure and these concepts and meet with other mothers, some of your neighbors maybe, over a cup of coffee, and talk about some of these same things that we have discussed. Concern yourself with the normal problems that they might be having with their children. It is time for you to help other parents understand the dynamics of their child's behavior while recognizing that their problems are much like the problems of other parents. (This idea is taken from Christensen, Merten, & Mead, 1966, and the work they did in Oregon.)

M_1: The mothers who need this kind of help won't come to the school for a group of this kind.

C: Might they come to your house for an informal meeting?

M_2: Yes. We can work on a different population than you work on at school.

M_3: Maybe we can help each other because our kids play together and we can encourage them for the changes that they make.

Thus, a core group has been established that will help take the burden of parent education off the counselor's already overloaded work schedule. A group of mothers who have been exposed to new ideas can be leaders in the parent-educational program of the community. Under the supervision of the counselor, who started out as five mothers, might become twenty-five (five x five new group members), and so on.

References

Carlson, J., & Mayer, G. R. Fading: A behavioral procedure to increase independent behavior. *The School Counselor*, 1971, 18(3), 193–197.

Christensen, O. C., Merten, F. T., & Mead, D. E. *A guide to parents.* Eugene, Ore.: School of Education, Division of School Psychological Services, University of Oregon, 1966.

Dinkmeyer, D., & Caldwell, E. *Developmental counseling and guidance in the elementary school.* N.Y.: McGraw-Hill, 1970.

Dreikurs, R., & Goldman, M. *The ABC's of guiding the child.* Chicago: North Side Unit of Community Child Guidance Centers, 1964.

Dreikurs, R., & Grey, L. *Logical consequences: A new approach to discipline.* New York: The Meredith Press, 1968.

Hill, G. E., & Luckey, E. B. *Guidance for all children in the elementary school.* New York: Appleton-Century-Crofts, 1969.

Mayer, G. R., & Cody, J. J. Festinger's theory of cognitive dissonance applied to school counseling. *Personnel and Guidance Journal,* 1968, *47*, 233–239.

29. FAMILY GROUP CONSULTATION

Daniel W. Fullmer

The purpose of this article is to help orient the practicing counselor to the method and applications of Family Group Consultation (FGC) and the Family Bond Inventory (FBI). The FBI is a recent development in FGC that has led to the possibility of identifying interpersonal conflicts within a family. This instrument could be used by professional practitioners to measure change in the relationships within the family during treatment. Adlerian family counseling, behavior therapy, group psychotherapy or any method involving significant portions of a family group could use the measuring techniques as there is a cultural baseline for human behavior. This concept is similar to Skinner's (1971) idea of the culture as a set of reinforcement schedules.

London (1969) talks about behavior control by information, psychotherapy, hypnosis, conditioning, electronic tools, coercion, assault (punishment), drugs and surgery. As counselors, we have an aversion to coercion as a controlling device. However, we embrace information and the means to influence by our "preferred method" of intervention. FGC works because the forces operating in the consulting session are the same forces operating in the family group when they are away from the session. The primary force in family interpersonal relationships is the control exerted by one person's behavior over another person's behavior in the interaction process. If one person changes his behavior, other people need to change their

Source.   Daniel W. Fullmer, Family Group Consultation. *Elementary School Guidance and Counseling,* 1972, Vol. 7–2, 130–136. Copyright 1972 by the American Personnel and Guidance Association and reproduced by permission.

response to him. However, if one person continues his usual behavior, every other person can continue to respond in the same fashion and a redundant patterning of family group behavior continues (Fullmer & Bernard, 1972).

FAMILY GROUP CONSULTATION (FGC)

The theory basic to the method of FGC states simply that behavior comes out of the relationship. The relationship is interpersonal, involving communication between two persons (dyad), the dyad is part of a group, the group is part of a community, the community is part of a larger social system that I call a culture. To change behavior in A, one must redefine the relationship with B (Hall, 1959). This is accomplished by exposing the control system used in a relationship to verbal interaction techniques and the FBI.

SON: "What is this all about? Why are we here?"

MOTHER: "I don't think it is safe to talk about our troubles in front of him (son)."

FATHER: (looked impotent in the social stress being pushed by the son and mother)

COUNSELOR: "Are you (family) always this stressed emotionally?"

MOTHER AND
SON
TOGETHER: "What do you mean?"

COUNSELOR: "You seem so upset that I pick up an emotionally tight climate, very distressed. Are you always like" . . .

SON: "Usually."

MOTHER: "We didn't want to come. Doesn't the idea of telling it all to each other seem to be destructive?"

COUNSELOR: "Oh, how so?"

MOTHER: "Giving up the secrets—I don't like it."

SON: "What secrets? Now I'm curious. I want to be here."

Behaviorists would expose the control system by focusing on the changed reinforcement schedules in the environment between B and A (Fullmer, 1971). Adlerians would say that person B followed the direction in the prescription given by the counselor and logical or natural consequences followed (Fullmer, 1971). Each of these is correct, to a degree, no matter what method is used. The important variable is that information is *selectively managed* by the method of intervention. FGC uses the familiar verbal model for managing the selection of information in counseling. Family members gather together for one to two hours and talk. The counselor (usually two counselors) tells the family or families that each person will speak for himself. *No one will speak for anyone except himself,* is the major guideline for exposing the information-behavior control system.

MOTHER: "This thing is not working. I think the whole business has just upset our family."

SON: "Things have really improved. I can see how to interrupt the fighting."

FATHER: "We have a long way to go."

MOTHER: "I don't care what you say, things are not good. You haven't helped."

Sessions are contracted by number. Initially there are four sessions; however, more sessions may be added if participants wish.[1] Long-term or short-term, FGC is only one of several intervention methods used. Frequently the range of clinical, educational and social resources managed include the full scope of mental health services (Hart, 1971; Blum, 1972).

The formula used to monitor and guide the verbal interaction in each session consists of the "speak only for yourself guideline" and, in reference to time and place, an emphasis on the here-and-now rather than the then-and-there. However, references to past events are not uncommon and future references are frequent in plans to try out new behavior and to change schedules of reinforcement. FGC is not mutually exclusive. Ideas from other approaches such as child-rearing ideas from Adlerian family counseling or behavior therapy strategies to change a specific habit or behavior are frequently used. The counselor is responsible for the management of the type of behavior interventions used in FGC.

Conflict resolution and crisis management are major goals of FGC. If two persons communicate, harmony and/or conflict may result. When their meanings match we find more harmony than conflict. Conflict is usually present at some level in all interaction. The FGC method teaches techniques to resolve the conflicts as it is unrealistic to attempt to avoid conflict in human relationships.

---

[1] Additional detailed discussions of the method may be found in Fullmer & Bernard (1968) and Fullmer (1971).

SON: "I don't see how our being here will help us. You (counselor) have not told us anything. We talk and you observe—is that all you do?"

COUNSELOR: "What would you like to have me do?"

MOTHER: "I'm against being here. What do we need to do?"

COUNSELOR: "Why not begin by describing an incident. Tell what happened before, during and following the incident. Any incident will do."

SON: "Like the one we had this afternoon before coming here?"

MOTHER: "I don't remember any incident."

SON: "My schoolwork."

MOTHER: (cut in) "He is flunking two subjects in the last quarter of his senior year. He won't graduate. He was called in by the Principal." (son did graduate)

SON: "Only a little time was spent on the schoolwork. Mostly, it was a school politics issue."

MOTHER: "You are going to fail."

SON: "I can redo the 12th grade."

The family members continued to expound and challenge each other and the counselor. The session ran over the one and one-half hours by 30 minutes because the family could not decide if they should return. They were told to go home and take with them the task of deciding. The counselor indicated that he was disinterested in working with people of such low motivation.

COUNSELOR: "After all, it is difficult work to meet with people like you. It is not difficult to see why you have problems with each other."

The family had a task. They left with directions to phone the center and leave the decision with the secretary. The following day a message was received. They would continue and complete the initial four sessions. *Second Session*: the family arrived on time. The first task was to complete the family bond inventory, a projective inventory of family relationships. When each member completed the task the counselor asked for any reactions each person had during the exercise.

MOTHER: "I thought it was silly."

SON: "The emotional thing kept coming up."

FATHER: "Yes, did you find it that way too?"

COUNSELOR: "Anything else?"

MOTHER: "Emotional content? What do you mean?"

SON: "Well, you can't place yourself in relation to another person without thinking about whether you're angry or not."

COUNSELOR: (to mother) "What do you think everyone else will do when placing symbols? Do you think your son will place them like you did?"

MOTHER: "Yes."

COUNSELOR: "Tell us about it. How do you think he did it?"

MOTHER: "He (son) would place himself between his father and me."

The FBI seems to be an integral part of FGC and the remainder of the article will be devoted to it's usage in FGC.

THE FAMILY BOND INVENTORY (FBI)

Purpose. The Inventory (FBI) will reveal each individual's perception of the key relationships in his or her family. The conflicts between family members can then be discovered. The findings can also be used to help one learn how to resolve conflicts. The primary bonds or alliances between family members will be revealed through the placement of symbols that represent each family member.

Directions. Given a blank sheet of paper, place symbols representing your family member (F father) (M mother) (♂ son) (♀ daughter) (X any significant other person who has regular contact with the family).

Several life situations may be suggested. Be sure to include: (1) How you see your family members now; (2) How you wish they were, if different from how they are; and (3) any situation where an issue of disagreement may exist.

Number each sibling position, for example: Boy ① oldest child; girl ♀② second oldest child. Explain the X as a grandmother, aunt, etc. Draw a circle around your symbol ♀②

Some suggested situations follow. (a) Place the symbols in *any manner you wish* to show how you see your family. (b) At a mealtime (indicate which meal); (c) Show how your family is arranged for sleeping, (sleeping pattern); (d) Show how your family is arranged between 4 and 6 P.M., the reintegration period (explain your choice). Add other situations as needed. When each person in the family group has finished, permit each other member to see each set of results. Exposure will not invalidate the results or future use of the inventory. The reason for sharing the placements is to discover each family member's reaction to each other's placement of himself. It is helpful to tape record this activity so reruns can be made during further discussion.

Each person should look for differences and similarities between his placement of symbols and the placements of each other person. The reason is that differences in placement of symbols are concrete representations of possible conflicts. The counselor should verify this by asking each member to make his own statement about what he thinks the different placement means. The counselor may also interpret the results.

Interpretation of the FBI

In a cross-cultural study of personal space within the family group, Cade (1972) found that through the placement of figures representing individual family members, the basic organization principles within the family could be discovered. The structure of organization in families in each culture studied, Japanese, Filipino, and American, show a hierarchy with parents highest in status and power and children ranking from oldest to youngest. The relative placement of each person in the family reflects the structure and defines the function each person can perform. Any violation of the cultural pattern signals a conflict between the persons in regard to their respective functions within the family structure. The relative status structure defines the relationships within the family. The relationship definition tells each person what to do and what not to do. Each person places himself as he sees and defines his relationship with others in the family. Other persons may disagree with one member's placement of himself, but two things remain significant, the *pattern* of placements and the *personal distance* between family members.

The normal family pattern and symbol placement for American families is from male to female and parent to child as is shown in Figure 1.

The examples above are typical sample placements for families with normal or healthy interpersonal relationships. Deviations from these typical patterns usually signal a conflict-producing relationship. Deviations are represented by placements which exceed the norm for the American family.

The normal circle symbols are ½-inch in diameter. Each symbol is normal when separated by 1½ to 3 inches distances measured from center to center. Deviations of more than 3 inches represent potential conflicts. Four inches and more give results that may safely be representing major conflicts. Some examples of deviation patterns and personal distance pro-

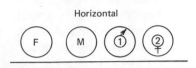

Horizontal

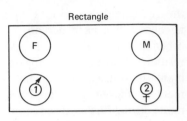

Rectangle

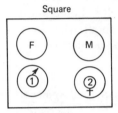

Square

(Give each person a blank sheet of paper)
(Each example is placed on an 8½ by 11 in. page)

FIGURE 1

duced by families in the initial sessions of consultation are shown in Figures 2 to 4.

The subject of each conflict is then explored through verbal interaction in the family consultation session. The beginning of each discussion comes when placement patterns are first shared among family members. *Important*: When family members have arguments, the FBI will tell the counselor whether the interpersonal relationships within the family are normal or not. If the relationships are normal, conflicts can be resolved by the verbal interaction in family consultation. If the relationships are deviant, the definition of the relationships in question must be changed before conflicts will subside. The FBI may also be used to redefine relationships and may be given over and over again without hazard.

How To Use the Results

The counselor may give oral reports to the family immediately.

COUNSELOR: "Let's look. Here, take each one and pass them among yourselves. See if you all placed them alike."

SON: "Why did you put yours like this, Mom?"

(Paper 8½ by 11 in.)

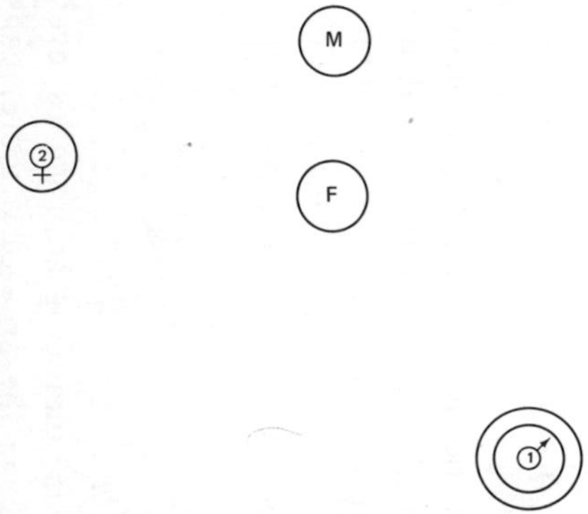

(Drawing made by male child age eleven)

FIGURE 2
Family A.

(Paper 8½ by 11 in.)

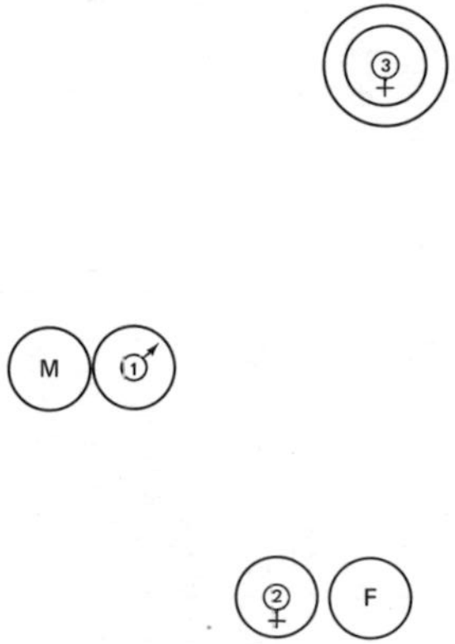

(Drawing by girl child ③ ♀ age nine)

FIGURE 3
Family B.

(Paper 8½ by 11 in.)

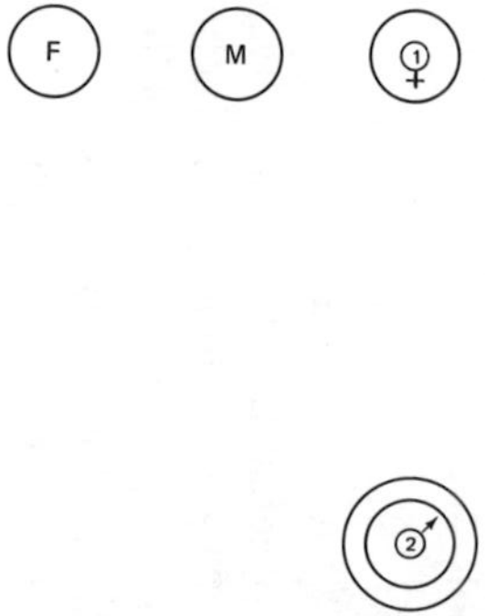

(Drawing by boy child ② ♂ age eleven)

FIGURE 4
Family C.

MOTHER: (greatly surprised) "What do you mean? I was just putting the symbols down the way it is."   .

SON: "Sleeping in a row?"

The mother had tried to defeat the instrument by giving what she thought were bland responses. The directions given included the statement that anyone could rig the responses but the person doing it would know it if she or he lied. The pattern of placements would not look (or feel) correct. There was no attempt to confront the mother with what she had done. She was aware that the others knew what she had done.

The second session was a sharp contrast to the initial session. The son remarked about it. He wondered how two sessions could be so completely different. All interaction had been in relation to the instrument.

Near the close of the second session a task was assigned. The family was to begin by appointing one member each morning, on a rotation basis, to have the duty. The duty was to interrupt any escalating interaction by simply asking, "Hey, what's happening now?" The principle participants are to discuss what has just taken place. If the discussion begins to escalate in a similar manner, then the process is repeated. Following detailed discussion of the directions, the family went home.

The FBI revealed the existence of powerful normal relationships between family members. (Father-Mother, Father-Son, Mother-Son) We learned from the instrument that the mother is not a reliable informant on family issues. But she knows everybody knows and the potentially destructive interaction to confirm it was avoided. During the second and third sessions, the mother gave evidence of conscious effort to be more reliable.

The counselor must avoid "head trips" with the family about their behavior and stick with the description of one incident at a time. The sequence again: what happened, what happened just before, just after, and during the incident? What response did you make? What happened then? Etc.

The next stage involves helping each member of the family understand how to control his own behavior. Each family member learns to identify the sequence of cues which trigger emotional outbursts and loss of control. The individual can learn to manipulate his own input in interactions which in turn controls responses from others. This is the only concrete source of control anyone has in an exchange of messages during an interaction with another individual.

SUMMARY

In FGC, like other group counseling approaches, everyone improves at his own rate. The gains are in the area of a more realistic evaluation of the functioning of each family member and the family as a whole. The family may then try to practice new behavior in the FGC sessions or at home.

The FBI helps to discover the emotional relationships that each person feels toward each other family member. The counselor may use results from the FBI to validate or invalidate his subjective perceptions of the family's interpersonal relationships. The results may also be useful as a measure of behavior change in an individual family member or to help the family change behavior.

References

Blum, R. H. and Associates. *Horatio Alger's children*: (Role of the family in origin and prevention of drug risk). San Francisco: Jossey-Boss, Inc., Publishers, 1972.

Cade, T. A cross-cultural study of personal space in the family. (Unpublished doctoral dissertation), University of Hawaii, Honolulu, 1972.

Hall, E. T. *The silent language*. New York: Doubleday & Co. (Premier Book, Paper), 1959.

Hart, Patricia. Interpersonal distance in selected social and personal relationships as a measure of alienation among young middle class drug users. (Unpublished doctoral dissertation), University of Hawaii, Honolulu, 1971.

Fullmer, D. W. *Counseling: Group theory and system*. Scranton, Pa.: Intext Educational Publishers, 1971.

Fullmer, D. W., & Bernard, H. W. *Family consultation*. Boston: Houghton Mifflin Co. (Guidance Monograph Series II Counseling), 1968.

Fullmer, D. W., & Bernard, H. W. *The school counselor-consultant*. Boston: Houghton Mifflin Co., 1972.

London, P. *Behavior control*. New York: Harper & Row, 1969.

Skinner, B. F. *Beyond freedom and dignity*. New York: Alfred A. Knopf, 1971.

30. CONJOINT FAMILY THERAPY: AN APPROACH TO THE TREATMENT OF A DISTURBED FAMILY

Virginia Satir

Conjoint family therapy appears to be a promising method of treating individual symptomatology through using the whole family unit. The name,

Source. Virginia Satir, "Conjoint Family Therapy: An Approach to the Treatment of a Disturbed Family." *Forest Hospital Publications*, 1966, pp. 60–64.

conjoint family therapy, can be defined as follows: "joint"—having all family members together at one time in one place with the same therapist, and "con"—treating all the member's as contributors to a single system of which each member is also a receiver instead of treating one in the service of the other. The symptom bearer primarily signals the presence of dysfunction in the system.

Family therapy theory is based on the idea that the family members operate as a system, and therefore each member is an essential part of maintaining, shaping, reshaping, and perpetuating the system as it moves through time and inevitable change. Logically, from this frame of reference, it follows that there is no one significant member. Everyone is significant. To understand the behavior of one member, one must understand the behavior of all.

A system requires component parts which can be described as entities in themselves, but are essential to each other in the achievement of a joint outcome to which the parts of the system are committed. Each system appears to have rules for the operation of each part, mostly related to time and particular function. The component parts of a family system are: (1) human beings, which include adults, male and female, who wear three labels: self, marital partner, and parent; and children, male and female, who wear labels of son and/or daughter to a mother and to a father, and brother and sister to each other: (2) context, which is time and place and situation.

The joint outcomes are: (1) that the children shall come out as powerful, independent, sexually delineated, productive adults, (2) that the male and female adults are sexually validated and personally enhanced and (3) that the whole family contribute to the work of and progress of the society in which they live.

The means of accomplishing this is through the communication that has been developed. If the ways of communicating are indirect, incomplete, unclear or incongruent, the accomplishment of the joint outcomes are in jeopardy. When the lack of accomplishment is grossly obvious, the persons manifesting it are labelled symptomatic.

This theory obviously rests on an *interactional* basis of behavior. For me, this concept is made up of three parts: (1) internal perception of self, (2) external manifestation of self, and (3) response to feedback from another. Each of these parts can be examined and studied separately. However, behavior requires the interaction and interdependence of all these parts. The *process* by which any self does this seems to be a primary determining factor in the appropriateness or fittingness of his ensuing behavior.

Perhaps too briefly stated, the family system is derived from the processes that each of the two individual adults who begin a family, developed to integrate internal perception, external manifestations, and response to feedback; how the processes of one adult were integrated with those of the other; and what each child used out of what was there for his own perceptions, manifestations, and response to feedback.

That is, each person has an *internal perception*, which I call the self concept which encompasses both his cognitive and affective parts; each person has a *manifestation* which is obvious to any other, but usually not in the same way or as completely to himself, that is how he looks and sounds, and what he says and does through words, voice tone and pace, facial expression and body movement and tonus. Each person has a way of dealing with *feedback*, that is response to others. One cannot not react.

Communication, the ways of giving, receiving, and checking out meaning, becomes the means of maintaining, shaping, reshaping, and perpetuating the system. In turn, it maintains, extends, or corrects each member's perceptions which influences the individual behavior of all of the members. The ways of matching internal perception with external manifestation and feedback to and from others by each member becomes the picture of *communication* of a family system.

Conjoint family therapy as a treatment modality is the application of the previously described principles to the literal family group. The goal is to change the system, which means changing the processes of coping which in turn changes behavior.

These principles can be modified to apply to individual and group therapy. The family group differs from any other group in that its members have a long shared culture, specific shared experiences, a specific set of idiosyncratic norms and values, and literal life-death significance relationships. For me, working with the literal family is a richer resource for the accomplishment of my therapeutic task, namely to enable change in behavior of all family members which means changes in the processes for coping.

> *George Coyle, a husband and father, age 40, arrives at his home at 6:00 P.M. on Tuesday, June 4, 1964, after a day's work. Following an interval of fifteen or twenty minutes, he sits down to the table with his wife Anita, also 40, and three children, Tom, age 12, Alice, age 9, and Joe, age 4. George takes a man-sized bite of the roast beef before him and says "What terrible roast beef!"*

I invite you to think with me about the various ways these same five people might be thinking, feeling, and acting at 9 P.M., the same day, three hours later. Let me illustrate by six possibilities:

> *Possibility I (9:00 P.M.).* George is outside the couple's locked bedroom door loudly pounding, demanding to be let in; and Anita is equally loudly

and emphatically stating that such will not be the case. Tom, age 12, is busy trying to herald a frightened Alice and a crying Joe to bed.

Possibility II (9:00 P.M.). George is at the local bar getting soused, and Anita is at her mother's home mustering support to divorce her "no good" husband. Alice and Joe are a model of speechlessness. Tom has disappeared.

Possibility III (9:00 P.M.). Anita is hysterically weeping and threatening suicide with George alternately mollifying and pleading, then demanding that she stop. Tom is loudly playing a record player in his room. Alice is strangely quiet, looking into space, and Joe is clinging to Tom.

Possibility IV (9:00 P.M.). Anita and George are frantically trying to reach a doctor as Tom is having an asthmatic attack. Alice and Joe are "peacefully" asleep.

Possibility V (9:00 P.M.). Anita and George are at a romantically lighted local bistro, dining on spaghetti and chianti wine. Tom is finishing his homework at home. Alice is reading a story to Joe who is already in bed. The nice elderly lady from next door is getting some bedtime snacks ready for the children.

Possibility VI (9:00 P.M.). Anita and George are sitting together in the living room amiably and playfully discussing how they can find a new butcher so George will have a better chance to enjoy roast beef the way he likes it. Tom is just finishing his homework and earnestly contributes that his best friend's mother gets her meat at Max's butcher shop. Alice and Joe are fast asleep.

Many more possibilities could be postulated. The same happening can have different outcomes. What accounts for the difference? I should like to offer the explanation that the different family systems will account for the difference.

It takes very little further thought to imagine how in all but the last two possibilities, any one of the five characters could be a potential visitor to a clinician's private office, an outpatient clinic, the local jail, the mental hospital, a general hospital, or maybe become a recipient of the local relief program.

The happening that was described could occur in any family in the United States. In fact, it may even be considered par for the course. So the happening itself is not the chief determinant; it must be the way it is perceived, interpreted, and then used.

Happenings much as the above, frequently as they may be in human experience, can be a potential threat to any of the persons present. If it is perceived as such by any one person, naturally it will activate the ways each individual has of handling threat. Since family members are in a situation of commitment to one another because of legal and blood ties, a series of reactions and reactions to reactions will occur, and thus the family system will be set in motion.

Human beings seem to use external happenings as a way of validating self-worth and lovability and competence, which I include in my concept of self esteem. Self esteem appears to be basic to any human being's way of handling reality. If this is true, then observing anyone's handling of a reality situation will give reliable clues to his conclusions about self esteem. Listening to and watching the communication will yield the clues to how the self attempts to maintain, protect, and enhance self esteem. This is the data from which the family therapist derives his notions of family functioning and dysfunctioning.

I doubt now whether there is such a thing as a universal traumatic event because any happening can be used in different ways, only one of which may be traumatic. The big question for the therapist is to find out how a happening was used by that self, whether for assault and distortion or enhancement and clarity. This is obviously a process.

For me to understand the meaning of any behavior, including that which is labelled symptomatic, I need to find out what that behavior means in terms of a person's self esteem, his evaluation of reality, his means of manifesting himself, and how this conforms to the family system of which he is a part. I can get clues to all of this by listening to and watching communication among family members. The communication tells me about the family system; the system tells me about the family "rules" for its members. The "rules" tell me about the chances each person has of surviving without too much pain, growing in terms of his own uniqueness, getting close to others directly and openly, and producing appropriately, creatively, and abundantly. Deviation from this can be reflected in clinically labelled symptomatology.

Man remains essentially related to another throughout life. Three factors make this so. *First*, the nature of our origins is such that it still requires a two-person negotiation (male and female); *second*, the nature of the new human is such that he would die if there were not other older humans to insure his life. This must go on for a protracted period; *third*, the nature of that which continues to make life possible requires the resources and the means of cooperation in their use.

How the self-other relationship is developed is crucial to all persons in determining their behavior. Therefore, the beginnings of life, *survival*, preparation for life, *development of self esteem and self image*, and the means of implementing the things in the world that make life possible (productivity) are fundamentally based in self-other operations and negotiations. It follows then, that whatever is labelled as the behavior of one person is inextricably bound up with another.

Therefore, to understand any person's behavior at any point in time, one must understand his perceptions and experiences about his beginnings, his preparation, and his productivity over time within the system in which it developed. All of these represent his experience with others. As I see it, all human beings have to have and do have self esteem, evidences of their productivity, and a means of giving and receiving and checking out information (which I call communication). It is not a question of "if", but a question of the kind (description), the manifestation, and the utility (use).

The family is the "little black box" through which all humans are begun, grow, and learn how to implement the work of the world. The biological family from which the person wearing a symptom emerged, would offer the maximum and primary data on which to base an understanding of any current behavior.

If the identified patient is an adult, who is labelled a husband, wife, father or mother in a family unit, it would make sense to extend the treatment unit, to include the biological family from which the "now" adult initially emerged. This is not always possible, but desirable when possible. I think that there is plenty of evidence in research in sociology, psychology, and psychiatry to conclude that there is a mandatory and essential relationship between one's *family of origin*, his *mate selection*, and his *curriculum for child rearing*.

This could be one obvious explanation of reappearance of similar behavior over generations. It merely means that there is a continuation and perpetuation of the same family system—just new bodies come in to function in the same part.

To take our hypothetical couple, George and Anita, and their children, Tom, Alice, and Joe, as an example, if I knew about the children's behavior, I know something quite definitive about George and Anita's curriculum for child rearing. I should also know something definitive about how they selected each other. I should also know something definitive about how George and Anita were themselves brought up. Further, if I know something about how George and Anita were brought up, I should be able to have some fairly accurate predictions to make about how they will get on as a marital pair and something equally accurate about how their children will fare. If these connections are valid, which I believe they are, analysis of human ills becomes more simplified, diagnosis more accurate, and treatment procedures more clear.

I see therapy as a means by which one person officially labelled a helper assists another or a group of others to find different ways to find answers, not to find answers, to achieve survival, growth, getting close to others, and productivity. The seeking of help by any person, regardless of the circumstances, signals that he is seeking ways that he has not been able to find, or is currently using ways which do not come out fittingly for him in his eyes or in the eyes of others.

The signals may come via the physical, emotional, intellectual or social operations of the individual. That is, the behavior which signals attention to unfitting ways of coping may be labelled psychosomatic, psychotic, neurotic, delinquent, or mentally retarded. Whatever way the behavior is labelled, it is a shorthand for saying that the person is not functioning—that his ways of coping do not "fit" and the system he is a part of is also in trouble.

One criteria for labelling, either by a self or some other, a piece of behavior as a symptom, something bad, sick, stupid, or crazy, is that the behavior does not fit either the expectation of self, some other, or the time and situation in which the person lives. The labelling of the symptom could depend upon *who* sees it, and *where* that person is when he sees it.

Every person who gets a label seems to have defects in his ways of manifesting authority, autonomy, and sexuality, and in reacting to other's authority (power), autonomy (independence), and sexuality (maleness and femaleness). All of us know that our ways of perceiving, manifesting, utilizing and reacting to authority, autonomy and sexuality are learned through the adults who were survival figures over time and through experience.

How does a child learn this? I would offer that it comes through how the child is touched, and spoken to, and what he sees and hears, what he is told and what he is permitted to do. The majority of us have had at least two adults, one male and one female (our parents), operating with and around us, but many humans have many more, like grandparents, foster and adoptive parents, step parents, aunts, uncles, unrelated but very significant adults from the outside, houseparents, teachers, therapists. From all these adults, the child must make some kind of single sense for the development of identity and an integration of self concept. If he can't make single sense, then he has to make double or triple or no sense, which means he must become dichotomized. This will obviously retard and distort his integration, rather than to implement, assist, and insure it. Symptoms are one outcome of this dichotomizing process.

How does any one of us know about another person, or for that matter how does one know about himself. It is by how one looks, how one sounds, what one says, and what one does. The self, unfortunately, can know more about what he says and does than how he looks and sounds. The other usually knows more about how any self looks and sounds than the self does. Fortunately for all of us, each of us knows more about what the self feels and thinks than any other. There is not always a matching relationship between what a self thinks and feels and how he looks, sounds, and what he says and does.

Since self and other are essential to each other, this situation becomes of paramount importance in any joint outcome attempted by two or more people.

One could say, as I do, that if how one looks, sounds, what one says and does do not match, that this is a reflection of being unable to make single sense out of all the observations, directions, and opportunities to perform that one was exposed to during his period of development. To me, it further reflects that there were rules in his family system which directly or indirectly forbade his commenting on inconsistencies, or asking the questions that would clear up the discrepancy. I find that such rules are taken over by the child because the commenting or asking questions about inconsistencies seemed to him to raise serious questions of self esteem of the adults. These were manifested in terms of attack, anger, blame, withdrawal, hurt, isolation. All of these are present in symptomatic conditions. The child served his survival needs best by not making his puzzles explicit and drawing his conclusions internally and privately. Each time this occurs, another reinforcement of self esteem and expectation of others is made. If the conclusion is dysfunctional, he can become symptomatic. The sad part is that when the above situation applies, what the child concluded had relatively little to do with direct recommendations for him, but rather reflected the low esteem, personal pain, self doubt, and trouble of the adults who were committed to him and in his presence.

A large part of the treatment technique by the family therapist consists of making things explicit, direct, and clear by asking the appropriate question at an appropriate time in an appropriate sequence. Most all dysfunctional families have areas of "dangerous information." Almost all turn out to be in some degree victims of the comedy of errors because they have operated in a context where it is dangerous to directly comment or question that which is not clear.

The therapist needs to demonstrate that he can directly comment on and question anything and he can continue to the point of complete clarity without anyone dropping dead, which is what everyone is literally or figuratively afraid of. The therapist through his interventions gives a demonstration that dysfunction rules can be broken. The outcome is relief and growth rather than death.

The human family system has to continually accommodate to change. This is mandatory because of inevitable growth that takes place from the time of birth to physiological maturity, the time at the end of puberty. Dysfunctional families have failed to make these changes.

If we treat each person that belongs to a family system in terms of absence and presence in time, places, and other persons, and each person in terms of his growth at a particular time as a separate variable, the family system is continually having to readapt. If the system fails to do this—distortion of growth, confusion of direction, and lack of achievement of hoped for outcomes, and sometimes death results. Casualties, which we call symptoms, result.

Perhaps no other system in the world is required to carry so heavy a load as the family system without elaborate equipment, years of research prior to the setting up of the system, and ongoing predictability and performance checks. Sometimes I wonder how we humans survive as well as we do.

The years of prior research necessary to set up an automation system corresponds to the years a human being spent learning how to survive, grow, get close to others, produce, and communicate with others. If the research scientist treated his data which he would use to set up his automation in the same way that human beings treat learning how to survive, grow, get close to others, produce and communicate with others, it is doubtful that science and technology would have gone anywhere.

I have often wondered why human beings have not done more to bring in an organized way all we know about *how* human beings survive, grow, get close to others, produce, and communicate with others. Perhaps the quest for the single answer and the effort at maintaining individual uniqueness have stood in the way.

What are the implications for a therapist when he views individual behaviors as a reflection of the system in which he is both a contributing and receiving part?

1. First, diagnostically all persons wearing labels should be seen literally with all the members of their systems in order to understand the meaning of their behavior which means a different way to understand, analyze and diagnose behavior.

2. Secondly, diagnostically every other member can be looked at in terms of what dysfunction he is currently experiencing or will in all likelihood experience (prevention).

3. Thirdly, the therapist will behave more as a camera, a model of communication, and a resource person, rather than as a direct transference object.

4. Fourthly, the emphasis for change is heavy on perception, interaction, transaction, and communication instead of being limited to intra-psychic phenomena. This requires further learning on the part of most therapists and suggests a much broader and more faceted context in which to understand, analyze, and diagnose human behavior.

5. Fifth, there are implications for economy and efficiency of treatment time.
6. Sixth, there seems to be a greater possibility for development of hope on the part of both therapist and patients.
7. Finally, there are suggestions for a more comprehensive theory of human behavior.

Bibliography

1. Ackerman, N. W. "Behavior trends and disturbances of the contemporary family." In I. Galdston (Ed.), *The Family in Contemporary Society*, New York: Int. Univ. Press, 1958.
2. Ackerman, N. W., Beatman, F. L., Sanford, S. (Eds.), *Exploring the Base for Family Therapy*. New York: Family Service Assoc., 1961.
3. Bateson, G., Jackson, D. D., Haley, Jr., and Weakland, J. H. "Toward a theory of schizophrenia." *Behav. Sci.*, 1:251–264, 1956.
4. Haley, J., *Strategies of Psychotherapy*. New York: Grune & Stratton, 1963.
5. Jackson, D. D. "The question of family homeostasis." *Psychiat. Quart. Suppl.*, 31:79–90, 1957; first presented at APA, St. Louis, 1954.
6. Satir, V. M. *Conjoint Family Therapy*, Science and Behavior Books, Inc., 1964.
7. Satir, V. M. "Schizophrenia and family therapy." In *Social Work Practice*, 1963, published for the National Conference on Social Welfare, Columbus, Ohio. New York: Columbia Univ. Press, 1963.

31. TRAINING PARENTS AND TEACHERS IN NEW WAYS OF TALKING TO KIDS

Thomas Gordon

Nine out of ten adults talk to children an youth in ways that are destructive to both the kids and the relationships.

This is the conclusion reached by instructors of Parent Effectiveness Training and Teacher Effectiveness Training, two courses being taught throughout the country under the aegis of the organization to which I belong, Effectiveness Training Associates. The 20,000 parents and teachers who have enrolled in these courses, have led us to this evaluation about the quality of communication in the parent-child relationship.

Source.   Thomas Gordon, "Training Parents and Teachers in New Ways of Talking to Kids." *Edvance,* 1969, Vol. 1–4.

Each of these enrollees reveals his habits of communication as a parent with his own children, or as a teacher with his students. Each parent or teacher is asked to demonstrate how he talks with kids in three critical but entirely different kinds of interpersonal situations:

1. When the *child* is troubled, needful, disturbed, bothered, upset, unhappy, frustrated, and so on, because he is having some problem with his own behavior (WHEN THE *CHILD* OWNS THE PROBLEM).
2. When the *parent or teacher* is troubled, needful, disturbed, bothered, frustrated, upset, or unhappy because the behavior of the child is causing the adult a problem (WHEN THE *ADULT* OWNS THE PROBLEM).
3. When the adult and the child find themselves in a disagreement or in a conflict, involving a clash between the needs of each (WHEN THE *RELATIONSHIP* OWNS THE PROBLEM).

WHEN THE CHILD OWNS THE PROBLEM

How does the typical parent talk to a child after hearing a message from him that the child is experiencing a problem in his own life, separate from the parent?

"Mother, I don't know why boys don't ask me for dates."
"I'm so fat—I hate myself."
"I hate school—it's a bore."
"These problems are too hard."
"I don't have anyone to play with."
"I'm afraid to go swimming in the ocean."

Conservatively, 9 out of 10 adults respond to such feelings by jumping right in, to send messages that have a high probability of shutting off further communication from the child, making him defensive and resistive, making him feel resentful or angry, reducing his self-esteem, making him feel inadequate or not trusted, making him feel guilty, making him feel unaccepted as a person. Specifically, adult messages fall into the following categories with very few exceptions:

1. Ordering, directing, commanding
2. Warning, admonishing, threatening
3. Exhorting, moralizing, preaching
4. Advising, giving solutions or suggestions
5. Lecturing, teaching, giving logical arguments
6. Judging, criticizing, disagreeing, blaming
7. Praising, agreeing
8. Name-calling, ridiculing, shaming

9. Interpreting, analyzing, diagnosing
10. Reassuring, sympathizing, consoling, supporting
11. Probing, questioning, interrogating
12. Withdrawing, distracting, humoring, diverting

Anyone trained as a professional counselor will undoubtedly recognize that this is a list of those types of communication that he was taught during his training, types to avoid when counseling another person with *his* problems. These "Twelve Roadblocks to Communication" are definitely not appropriate tools for an effective counselor, for they so frequently impede further communication, deteriorate the counselor-client relationship, or inflict psychological damage on the client's self-esteem or his feeling of self-worth.

In short, the Twelve Roadblocks are antithetical to the role of an effective counselor whose primary function is to communicate understanding, warmth, empathy, acceptance, and a deep trust in the client's capacity *to solve his own problem*.

Thus, many American parents and teachers are often ineffective as counselors for their children or their students. Their habits of communication—the essential tools—are often "non-therapeutic," non-facilitative, non-accepting. They may be destructive to the child, and to the relationship itself. Hence, most children learn early in life that "you can't talk to adults," "adults don't really understand kids," "they just don't listen," "adults really turn you off," or "it's better not to share your problems with parents or teachers."

The new model of counseling may be described briefly as one in which (1) the adult responds to feelings rather than content, (2) listens passively (silence), (3) listens actively (feeding-back or reflecting the essential meaning of the child's message), (4) uses door-openers or open-ended invitations for the child to share his problem, (5) conveys warmth and empathy, and (6) leaves the locus of responsibility for the problem-solving process with the child.

Most parents can acquire a reasonable level of competence in using the new model of counseling, and many parents report improved communication in the home. Some parents have reported dramatic descriptions of helping a child constructively resolve some serious problem—such as fear of the dark, refusing to go to school, conflict with a teacher, panic when parent leaves, afraid to go to sleep, and the like. Probably the most frequently reported outcome for parents is relief—an attitude of being relieved of the terrible responsibility or obligation for their coming up with solutions to all the problems their children encounter. Instead, they express greater faith in the child's problem-solving potential.

Teachers find application for the new listening skills in facilitating effective classroom discussions, in counseling individual students and in conducting more effective parent conferences.

WHEN THE ADULT OWNS THE PROBLEM

How does the typical parent or teacher talk to a child when the behavior of that child is tangibly and concretely interfering with some need of the adult—when the child's behavior is *a problem to the adult* by virtue of threatening the adult's right to enjoy life or satisfy legitimate needs?

Child has his feet on rungs of new chair
Child interrupts your conversation with a friend
Child leaves toys and clothes in living room
Child won't feed his pet
Child not carrying his load of work at home
Child playing guitar so loud you cannot think
Child disrupting others in classroom

When encountering such behavior, most parents and teachers send messages to children that have a high probability of putting them down (reducing their self-esteem), making them feel guilty or bad, making them *resist* changing their behavior rather than *wanting* to change their behavior, or making them feel their needs are not at all important.

Specifically, with few exceptions the messages most adults send fall into the following categories:

1. Blaming, judging, name-calling, or impugning the child's character ("You-are" messages) "You are thoughtless,"—"You are acting like a baby,"—"You are a brat,"—"You are stupid,"—"You are driving me crazy,"—"You'll be the death of me yet."
2. Telling the child exactly what solution is expected to solve the adult's problem ("You" messages that convey "You must,"—"You should,"—"You'd better,"—"You'll have to,"—"You need to.").

Both of these categories of "You-messages" can be non-therapeutic for the child or detrimental to the relationship. Put-down or "You-are" messages reduce the child's self-esteem, provoke resistance or rebellion, or generate counter "You-are" messages ("You're not so neat yourself" or "You don't always pick up your clothes" or "You're too fussy.").

Solution-messages provoke negativism and resistance to being told what to do, foster resentment and hostility, and make the child feel his needs are of secondary importance to the adult's. Of greatest importance, however, is that the adult never gives the child a chance to independently initiate corrective behavior out of consideration for the adult's needs. To be told what to do denies one the opportunity to act independently or responsibly. Parents and teachers, by daily "telling kids what they must or should do," impedes the development of self-responsibility.

In Effectiveness Training programs, parents and teachers are shown a new model for dealing with behavior of children that interferes with the adult's rights. Most professionals familiar with the concept of "congruency," "transparency," "authenticity," "realness" or "being open, honest and direct," will recognize the origins of this new model. We use a more descriptive term—namely, "I-messages" (in contrast to the destructive "You-messages").

These "I-messages" contain neither put-downs nor implied solutions:

"I cannot think when the guitar is so loud."
"I would hate to see the new chairs ruined."
"I want to talk to my friend but I can't when I'm interrupted."
"I get upset when I clean up the living room and then find it has been messed up."
"I don't feel it is fair for me to do most of the work around the house when others in the family might help."

Learning this new way of confrontation is not easy, for parents and teachers have strongly ingrained habits of confronting kids with "You-messages." Both parents and teachers report greater effectiveness in getting kids to modify their behavior and less defensiveness and counter-aggression. Many parents report an increase in children's courage to both respect and communicate their own needs and feelings.

WHEN THE RELATIONSHIP OWNS THE PROBLEM

The "moment-of-truth" in adult-child relationships is when a disagreement or conflict-of-needs occurs.

Johnny wants to keep playing, but the family has to leave right away.
Sue won't wear her raincoat to school but mother doesn't want cleaning or doctor bills.
Frankie wants to play with pots and pans on kitchen floor, but this slows down Mother's dinner preparation for guests.
Tim wants to go into the toy store but Mother doesn't have time.
Billy pesters Dad to play ball at night, but Dad is too tired when he first gets home.
Fred often comes in late to class; teacher is interrupted by this.

How do most adults handle such conflicts? Almost all parents and teachers are by habit firmly locked-into only two methods of conflict resolution, both of which result in someone winning and someone losing. Both of these two "win-lose" methods invariably result in resentment, an escalating power-struggle, and a deterioration of the adult-child relationship. In both methods one or both of the contestants has the attitude of "I want my way and I'm going to use my power to get it—I want to win, even at the expense of the other losing."

Method I, where the adult wins and the child loses, is a conflict-resolution method familiar to all, adults and children alike. It has many different names: parental authority, setting and enforcing limits, unilateral decision-making, autocratic management, being strict, parent-centered discipline. The kind of parental talk involved in Method I is power-oriented.

"Do as I say."
"Father knows best."
"We can't let you."
"This is our limit."
"If you do, you'll be punished."
"Obey."
"I'm the boss."
"That's the way it will be, no argument."

Method II, where the child wins and the parent loses, is employed by some adults, far fewer in number than those who use Method I. In Method II, the adult "gives in" to the child, for reasons that are quite varied. The adult may be afraid of conflict, the adult may be embarrassed by the child's use of his power (i.e., temper tantrum, loud crying, whining, etc.), the adult may have been taught it is not wise to frustrate the needs of children. Whatever the reason, the adult permits the child to get his way at the expense of the adult not getting his needs met.

In both Method I and Method II there is resulting resentment—from the loser to the winner. Often in both methods, guilt is experienced by the winner.

Method I provokes rebellion, resistance, lying, counter-agression, forming alliances with other kids, getting back at the adult, and other "fighting" coping mechanisms. Or, Method I may produce such coping mechanisms as submission, conformity, apple-polishing, buttering-up, tattling.

Method II is more apt to produce children who become selfish, inconsiderate, unmanageable and uncooperative (the spoiled child syndrome). The formula for such children seems to be, "If I put up enough fuss (use my power), I can get my own way."

A new model for conflict-resolution—called the "No-Lose Method III," is a method enabling adult and child to join together in a mutual search for a solution that is acceptable to both—no one loses, or both win.

Method III is a *problem-solving* approach—"We have a problem in our relationship, so let's find a solution acceptable to both that will enable each of us to get our needs met."

The language of Method III is the language of non-power:

"I respect your needs, but I respect my own, too."
"How can we work this out so we both win?"
"What is a good solution for both of us?"
"Let's put our heads together on this."
"I don't want to get my way at your expense, but I don't want you to get your way at my expense."

Students of decision-making or conflict resolutions will immediately recognize Method III as another term for:

Democratic problem-solving
Mutual decision-making
Group-centered decision-making
Participative problem-solving
Negotiating a contract
Mutual agreement

In Method III, there is far less chance (if any) for resentment, for both agree on the solution. Furthermore, children are much more motivated to implement (or stick to) the solution, having participated in making the decision (the Principle of Participation). Using Method III, parents have no need to use their power, and likewise children have no need to use theirs.

The most significant benefits of Method III derive from the effects of this type of continuous conflict-resolution in the home. Parents who learn the skills of Method III report that their children are no longer rebellious (kids don't rebel against parents, they rebel against parental power and authority). Punishment becomes unnecessary. Problems get out in the open. One Mother reported that her formerly rebellious adolescent son now "calls his parents two of his favorite people." A parent wrote me the following:

"The changes in our family relationships have been subtle but real. The older children especially appreciate these changes. At one time, our home had "emotional smog"—critical, resentful, hostile feelings that were held in check until something would trigger an explosion. Since sharing our new skills with all the children, the "emotional smog" is gone. The air is clear and stays clear. We have no tension in our home except that necessary for coping with everyday schedules. We deal with problems as they arise, and all tune in to the feelings of others as well as ourselves. My eighteen-year old son says he can feel tension in the homes of his friends, and he expresses appreciation for the lack of tension in our home. We have closed the 'generation gap'. And since we can communicate freely, my children are open to the teaching of my own value system and my perspective on life. But their views are enriching to me."

No longer can our society treat children and youth as they were treated two thousand years ago. We need a new philosophy for adult-child relationships.

32. MULTIPLE-FAMILY GROUP COUNSELING

S. Richard Sauber

Even though the community mental health movement has expanded considerably during the past decade, the local psychological and child guidance clinics that have been established are not sufficient to meet the growing demand for the services required. In response to the rise in the number of children and families needing help, the helping professions must develop new types of treatment facilities and innovative practices. The growing knowledge of communication theory, family interaction, and group counseling within the setting of the public school seems to offer the greatest possibilities for reaching the young student and treating his family.

It is proposed that the public school system provide the services for short-term, multiple-family group counseling which appears to be an effective treatment for family problems of which the student is the "identified client." Since the current philosophy in the school does not give sanction to a long-term therapeutic approach, nor can it afford the financial and time investments of individual family counseling, an appropriate plan of action would be to implement a multiple-family group approach. The concept of multiple-family group counseling (MFGC) is based on the premise that the world of the home and school are inseparable; and with the family being the primary influence, school personnel are often powerless unless

Source. S. Richard Sauber, "Multiple Family Group Counseling." *Personnel and Guidance Journal*, 1971, Vol. 49–6, 459–465. Copyright 1971 by the American Personnel and Guidance Association and reproduced by permission.

communication has been established with the parents. Furthermore, it is postulated that the place to attack the problem is with the people whom it involves and the setting where it occurs. Working with the problem student in a school situation would offer students and parents the unique benefit of "sharing responsibility" in an atmosphere of mutuality in which the concerns of the school and family could be integrated, discussed, and dealt with in a more efficacious manner.

MFGC is a relatively new form of family treatment in which several families are brought together in weekly group sessions. This approach offers the advantage of family wholeness rather than fragmentation; at the same time, cross-influences and cross-interactions from family to family are often more effective than counseling with individuals or with single-family units in which there is a rigid structure. The purpose of MFGC may be defined as assisting the families in developing a shared view of the student's difficulty and in evaluating a collaborative plan of changing the maladaptive behaviors. In Osberg's (1962) words, MFGC is designed

". . . to facilitate communication within the family, help family members to become more aware of their difficulties so that they themselves may find more adequate solutions to their problems, and to offer a brief type of service."

In recent years, the importance of the family as a unit of therapeutic focus has been supported by thearapists such as Ackerman (1958), Jackson (1959), and Bell (1961). These and other writers have contributed extensively by way of theoretical formulations and empirical studies to an understanding of the family process. This increased interest in the family of the identified client has led to the emergence of conjoint therapy, which has in turn given rise to short-term procedures in which groups of families participate. The treatment settings for the multiple-family group approach have included hospitalized patients in mental institutions (e.g., Levin, 1966), out-patients in community mental health clinics (e.g., Kimbro, Tashman, Wylie, & MacLennan, 1967), and problem students in secondary schools (e.g., Durell, 1969). A general overview of family therapy is discussed by Sager (1968).

MFGC combines the advantages of both group therapy and family counseling plus its own unique expression. Kimbro et al. (1967) find that the advantages of group therapy include the sharing and mutual exploration of common concerns with the opportunity to view such problems in a manner more objective because they are discussed and resolved by others confronted with similar situations. All family members can share in the helping role as well as have other people from the community—seen as one's peers—available to challenge, support, desensitize, and educate them. In family group counseling, the specific advantage is that the parents and student are seen together. All of these assets are retained in MFGC in addition to allowing for the development of extrafamilial adolescent-adult relationships. The presence and support of peers help in this development.

The junior and senior high school present the adolescent with a new and often difficult adjustment problem. The student must develop a greater degree of autonomy than he required in his elementary school experiences. In spite of the intervention of the guidance counselor, some students begin a downhill course in their studies which results in a severe disruption of their secondary school education. Some students sit in class and daydream, withdrawn and preoccupied; others misbehave and fall further behind in their work. Of all the students who begin high school, 30 to 40 percent fail to complete it (Schreiber, 1964).

The source and solution of many such problems can often be traced beyond the confines of the school to the internal strife taking place within the family. Several common family–school problems with which the counselor is likely to be confronted include difficulties encountered in home–family, boy–girl, or student–teacher relationships; student and parent apathy and dissatisfaction with school experiences, concerns about school success, and pressures of vocational choice; and problems simply related to responsibility, dependency, and morality.

STRUCTURE OF THE COUNSELING

In most cases, multiple-family group leaders report a preference, based upon experience, for working with three or four families per counselor, and meeting together once a week for about six consecutive sessions (e.g., Durell, 1969; Kimbro et al., 1967; Levin, 1966). The structure within the group varies according to the counselor's orientation. Most groups with one counselor remain together for two hours, while other groups offering multiple counseling meet together in one large group for one hour, and then the adult family members and the youngsters meet separately for the other hour with a counselor present in each group. At the end of each session, time is allotted to review what has taken place, to determine the counseling objectives for certain individuals, and to discuss areas for further elaboration. Individual counseling is available for anyone needing additional help in handling their emotional problems.

Multiple-family groups, in contrast to other types of family therapy, do not include the younger children. For the most part, children under nine years of age are not mature enough verbally and intellectually to undertake the communication demanded in this group method. Furthermore, there are often struggles between the older child and his parents that only involve the other children in the family in a fringe way.

It is recommended that the counselor have some training in working with groups and families. For assistance, he should consult or work with a family therapist. Since the counselor assumes the responsibility for planning and managing the group, and it may very well be his first attempt in using this approach, one-hour staff conferences held weekly are recommended for the purpose of evaluating the group needs, the counselor's activity, and the structure for the following meeting.

The first task of the counselor is to compile a list of students with academic difficulties and disciplinary problems that may be associated with tensions within the home or may be improved with the cooperation of the parents. The counselor's function as leader of the family group activity, as suggested by Kimbro et al. (1967), is as follows: He (a) establishes, reviews and enforces ground rules for the group; (b) encourages individual participation and group interaction; (c) supports group members' shared human concerns and feelings; (d) directs or redirects group discussion of issues; (e) conceptualizes and summarizes themes and interactions; (f) challenges the reality or universality of personal attitudes; (g) responds with information and direct guidance.

WHAT THE COUNSELING INVOLVES

Schreiber (1966) has outlined the criteria for assessing defects in the family interactional process. The following concepts of a functional family are defined in relation to which dysfunction processes could be evaluated:

1. *Communication.* Each family member is able to speak for himself, to express his thoughts and needs appropriately in relation to his role in the family, whether positively or negatively. No conflicting double-level messages should be communicated in nonverbal ways in this process.
2. *Role functions.* Each family member accepts his own and other people's roles in the family, properly related to age, sex, physical and mental factors, and subject to growth, changing needs, and capacities. No one attempts to control or dominate others.
3. *Integration of differences.* Each family member understands, integrates, and can accommodate to differences within the family group. No one is singled out as the scapegoat or problem bearer for the whole family, and there are no implied or explicit coalitions among its members.
4. *Individual responsibility.* Each family member is able to make decisions and take responsibility for himself, appropriate to the circumstances, which will lead to maximum use of capacities and maturation.

5. *Unity and cohesion.* The family is able to function as a unit with mutual support and cooperation in the achievement of realistic and socially valued goals.

Some observations of the changes in the pattern of group interaction might best illustrate how the counselor attempts (a) to foster the group process toward clarity and intimacy within the communication network, and (b) to develop stronger family cohesion and mutually satisfying goals. To offer family members a relatively nonthreatening experience, the protection and enhancement of self-esteem becomes essential; and the group moves away from a defensive position toward one of providing its members with a sense of participation in an equal but separate problem-solving process. For example, a "son" describes his feelings of being a failure at the time when he presented his report card to his parents:

MRS. A. *(to Gary)*:	"Well, what happened when your parents saw your grades?"
GARY'S MOTHER:	"He silently and sullenly stalked out of the room."
GARY:	"She asked me, Mom, not you!"
MRS. M.:	"Well, why were you so nasty?"
GARY:	"I guess I was afraid of you, Dad."
BETH:	"The only time my parents ever show any interest in what I am doing in school is when I get into trouble or have bad grades."
GARY'S FATHER:	"Gary is always up to something; he has recently been caught lying to his teacher.
MRS. A.:	"Let me stop you for a minute, Mr. P. *(to Gary)* It seems to me your father is as much to blame as you are, Gary. Because you lied . . ."
GARY *(simultaneously)*:	"I don't know *(sighing).* But, Dad, you make me feel like a failure, like I'm just no good at anything. This is the same way I feel in school. My teachers get on my back. I just don't like school. And you and Mom just yell at each other about me; and it makes me so angry, I just have to get away."

In order to facilitate the group process between the members and help them deal directly with the problem at hand, the counselor might inter-

280 Parent and Family Group Counseling and Consultation

vene, for example, and instruct the son to explore how he feels about his poor grades; what he might do to "succeed"; ask the parents for suggestions of how they could be more constructive and less punitive in their transactions; comment on the son's anger and his need to lie in school; and point out how the son might resist the temptation to play "Let-Mom-and-Dad-Fight." A role-played family discussion would be helpful in this case.

Coughlin and Wimberger (1968) have identified three growth stages through which the parents and students progress. Stage one, the first few meetings, is marked by dependence, isolation, and low self-esteem. Most often students choose to sit next to their own parents who carry the burden of the interaction. The group focus is directed toward the problem student: How can we straighten him out? The parents are reluctant to question their part in the problem as they are threatened by admitting fallibility. For example, they are anxious to offer the boys as scapegoats even though they (the parents) convey underlying feelings of guilt, failure, and helplessness. The boys and girls are perceived as rebellious with sullen hostility, and the parents are fearful of losing their tenuous authority. Some role-playing is demonstrated in order to bring out the interaction component of family problems by dealing with such feelings as rejection and inadequacy as well as the fear of losing control and being dependent.

By the third session, separate groups are usually introduced for parents and students, and this stage is characterized by peer identification, support, and sympathy. This seems to be a necessary prerequisite before exploring the parent–child relationship. The two subgroups then rejoin for the second hour of the session, and two distinct warring camps often develop —the adolescent peer group against the united front of the mothers and fathers. Both students and parents seem fearful of testing out their new communications skills in the larger group. The parents become annoyed at the anger expressed by the students and perceive them as "unfeeling," "uncaring," and "unappreciative." They accuse the students of not trying to improve themselves and of expecting them (the parents) to make all the changes. The counselor's task is to reinterpret the influence the peer group has in meeting a basic need of adolescents, and to instruct the parents on how to help the boys and girls gradually move away from their parents toward a more appropriate, adjustive identification with their peers.

Parents and students may use the technique of role-playing to bridge the separate meetings and to move into the third stage—group interaction. This "awareness technique" initiates an exchange of comments between and within the families as well as offering behavioral alternatives. The parents begin to voice their dissatisfaction with each other as spouse and parent and to examine their different and conflicting expectancies regarding the behavior patterns of their children. However, this exploration is usually the result of the counselor's repeated interruptions to interpret the feelings, attitudes, and behaviors being expressed. By the final session, the groups meet for the full time as one unit. Both parents and students find themselves beginning to improve their ability to solve problems with greater communication, increased insight, and more realistic expectations of each other. They also have an enhanced sense of belonging to the community and understanding of the school's role and the teacher's task.

MULTIPLE-FAMILY GROUP SENSITIVITY

Clarke (1969) has developed a set of group procedures to stimulate awareness and communication of positive feelings between parents and adolescents. His criterion for student selection is directed at the typical, normal family in which the "generation gap" has broken down communication lines between the members. This approach is only briefly mentioned since it is oriented toward sensitivity rather than counseling, although its implementation is equally as justified.

As many as six families are used by one leader, involving a total of 12 parents and 9 adolescents. In getting parents and students to talk to each other, six different group formations are utilized during the five, two-hour sessions. For example, the "simulated family group" consists of an unrelated father, mother, and one or two students; the "role group in a concentric circle" may consist of all the mothers talking among themselves in the inner circle while the fathers and students sit in the outer circle observing. A number of topics are discussed in the various groupings within the context of all possible relationships. An illustration within the father-son relationship from the son's perspective would include the following: (a) the father's and son's positive behavior which makes the son feel loved, appreciated, valued, and understood; (b) the positive characteristics which his father likes, admires, and respects; (c) the commitment behavior and wished-for behaviors; and (d) the feedback from all participants revealing their feelings about the session, themselves, or other members.

According to the findings of Clarke's follow-up (1969), the participants —students as well as parents—exhibited and reported a new spontaneity, trust, and openness of feeling, and a strong sense of group membership. For example, the students comfortably shared their feelings with their peers, their parents, and the other parents. This increase in sensitivity was also reflected in the students' general attitude toward school and particularly in their improved academic performance.

RESEARCH FINDINGS

Several schools have attempted to elicit parental understanding and co-operation through systematic, small-group meetings with parents and counselors (e.g., Buehmueller, Porter, & Gildea, 1954; Keppers & Caplan, 1962). More recent investigations of assisting junior and senior high school students with short-term MFGC have been performed by Clarke (1969), Durell (1969), and McWhirter (1966). It should be noted that when the original plans were formulated, a number of the school staff expressed considerable doubt about the feasibility of such a group; they questioned whether the parents and students would be willing to communicate freely and openly with each other in a group session. However, the consensus among studies supports McWhirter's (1966) findings that the families felt that (a) MFGC should definitely be continued as part of the guidance program at their school; (b) their particular family unit difficulties have been more clearly defined, and movements have taken place toward solving these problems; and (c) there has been an increase in communication within the family as a direct consequence of the multiple-family group experience, Moreover, there has been substantial change in the participating students' school work (e.g., higher grade point averages, fewer disciplinary problems, better attendance records, etc.).

Although these findings are encouraging, caution should be exercised in using this approach. First, its novelty requires answers to questions still being formulated. Ongoing process research is needed in addition to out-come evaluation. Second, MFGC is characterized as "time-limited," thereby restricting, to some extent, the intensity and extensity of the therapeutic experience. Periodic referrals to community agencies may be necessary depending on the nature and severity of the adolescent–family–school difficulty.

CONCLUSION

Family counseling is largely community- and public health-oriented. In a search for effective time-limited approaches, MFGC has been shown to be a useful, short-term technique for working with the problem student and his family in community service agencies as well as in public schools. Since school adjustment is the immediate concern, treatment should be arranged so that the interaction between the family members and the school culture can be easily influenced and kept under constant scrutiny. This can be achieved by counseling with several family units within the school's milieu. This new modality for a group approach offers the counselor at least a partial solution to increasing both his effectiveness and the size of the population he reaches.

References

Ackerman, N. *The psychodynamics of family life.* New York: Basic Books, 1958.

Bell, J. *Family group therapy, Public Health Monograph No. 64.* Washington, D.C.: Department of Health, Education and Welfare, 1961.

Buehmueller, A., Porter, F., & Gildea, M. A group therapy project with parents of behavior problem children in public schools. *Nervous Child,* 1954, *10,* 415–424.

Clarke, C. Group procedures for stimulating awareness and communication of positive feelings between parents and young adults. Paper read at the meeting of Family Life Council, Goldsboro, North Carolina, October 1969.

Coughlin, B., & Wimberger, L. Group family therapy. *Family Process,* 1968, *7,* 37–50.

Durell, V. Adolescents in multiple family group therapy in a school setting. *International Journal of Group Psychotherapy,* 1969, *19,* 44–52.

Jackson, D. D. Family interaction, family homeostasis, and some implications for conjoint family psychotherapy. In J. H. Masserman (Ed.), *Individual and familiar dynamics.* New York: Grune & Stratton, 1959.

Keppers, G., & Caplan, S. Group counseling with academically able underachieving students. *New Mexico Social Studies Education Research Bulletin,* 1962, *12,* 17–28.

Kimbro, E., Tashman, H., Wylie, H., & MacLennan, B. Multiple family group approach to some problems of adolescents. *International Journal of Group Psychotherapy,* 1967, *17,* 18–24.

Levin, E. Therapeutic multiple family groups. *International Journal of Group Psychotherapy,* 1966, *16,* 203–208.

McWhirter, J. Family group consultation and the secondary schools. *Family Coordinator,* 1966, *15,* 183–185.

Osberg, J. Initial impressions of the use of short-term family group conferences in a community mental health clinic. *Family Process,* 1962, *1,* 37–50.

Sager, C. An overview of family therapy. *International Journal of Group Psychotherapy,* 1968, *18,* 302–312.

Schreiber, D. (Ed.) *Guidance and the school dropout.* Washington, D.C.: National Education Association and American Personnel and Guidance Association, 1964.

Schreiber, L. Evaluation of family group treatment in a family agency. *Family Process,* 1966, *5,* 21–29.

Index